iters: **MARC BERNARDIN**
& ADAM FREEMAN

ist: **LEE GARBETT**

lorist: **JONNY RENCH**

terer: **ROB LEIGH**

llected Edition and Original Series Covers by

RIAN STELFREEZE

n Lee, Editorial Director
n Nee, Senior VP—Business Development
ott Peterson, Editor
sty Quinn, Assistant Editor
Roeder, Art Director
l Levitz, President & Publisher
rg Brewer, VP—Design & DC Direct Creative
hard Bruning, Senior VP—Creative Director
rick Caldon, Executive VP—Finance & Operations
is Caramalis, VP—Finance
n Cunningham, VP—Marketing
ri Cunningham, VP—Managing Editor
on Gill, VP—Manufacturing
vid Hyde, VP—Publicity
nk Kanalz, VP—General Manager, WildStorm
la Lowitt, Senior VP—Business & Legal Affairs
ryEllen McLaughlin, VP—Advertising & Custom
lishing
gory Noveck, Senior VP—Creative Affairs
e Pohja, VP—Book Trade Sales
ve Rotterdam, Senior VP—Sales & Marketing
ryl Rubin, Senior VP—Brand Management
f Trojan, VP—Business Development, DC Direct
Wayne, VP—Sales

D0117681

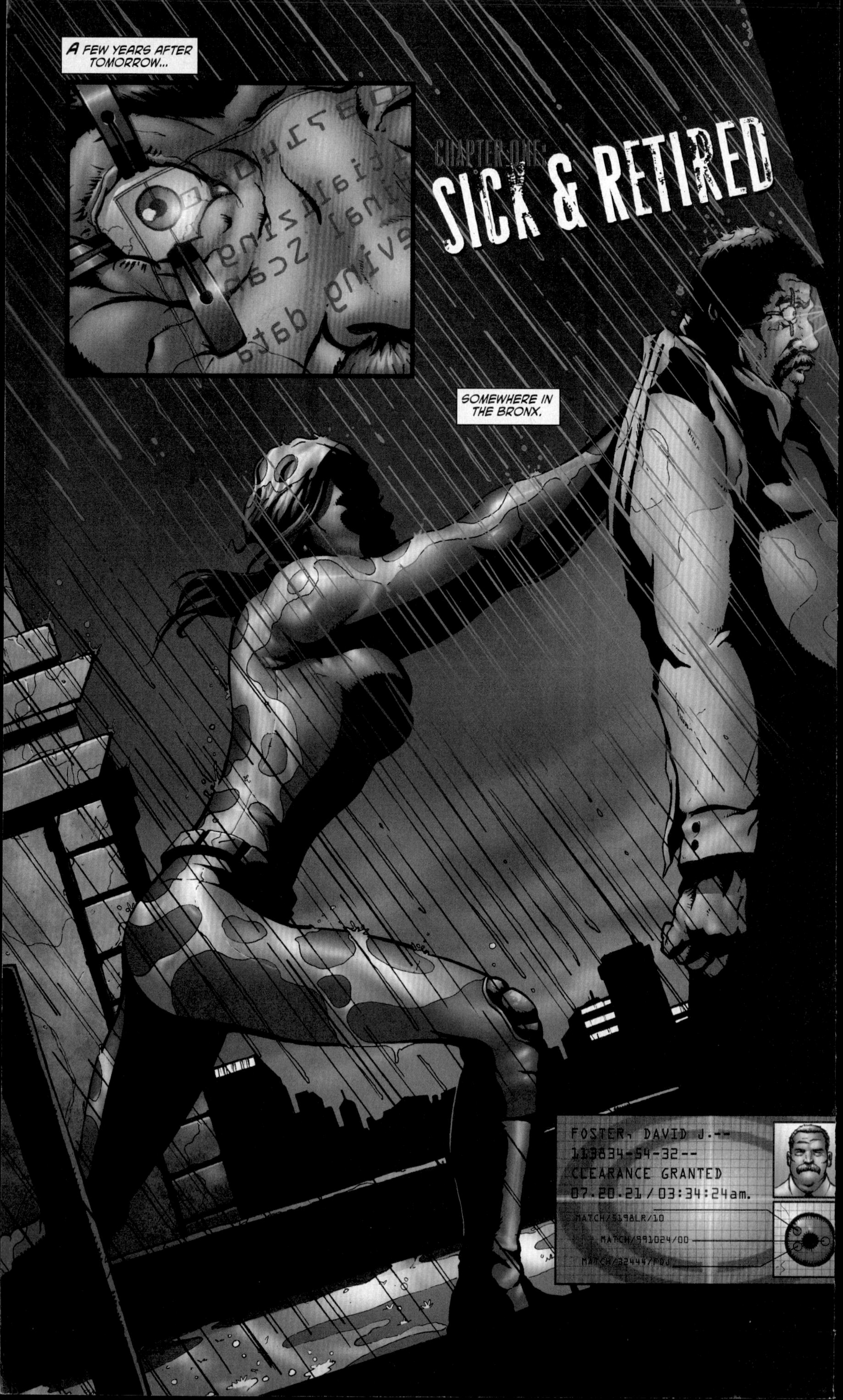
A FEW YEARS AFTER TOMORROW...
CHAPTER ONE:
SICK & RETIRED
SOMEWHERE IN THE BRONX.
FOSTER, DAVID J.--
113834-54-32--
CLEARANCE GRANTED
07.20.21 / 03:34:24am.
MATCH/5198LR/10
MATCH/991024/00
MATCH/32444/FDJ

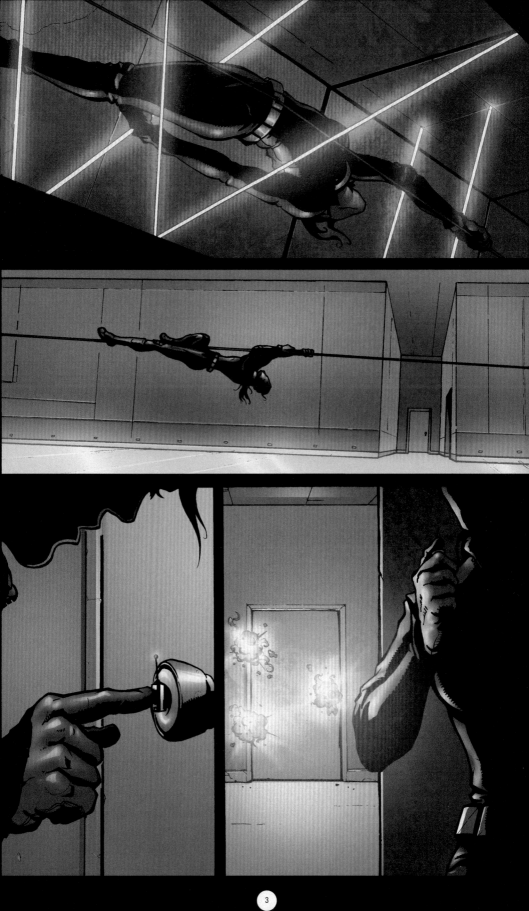

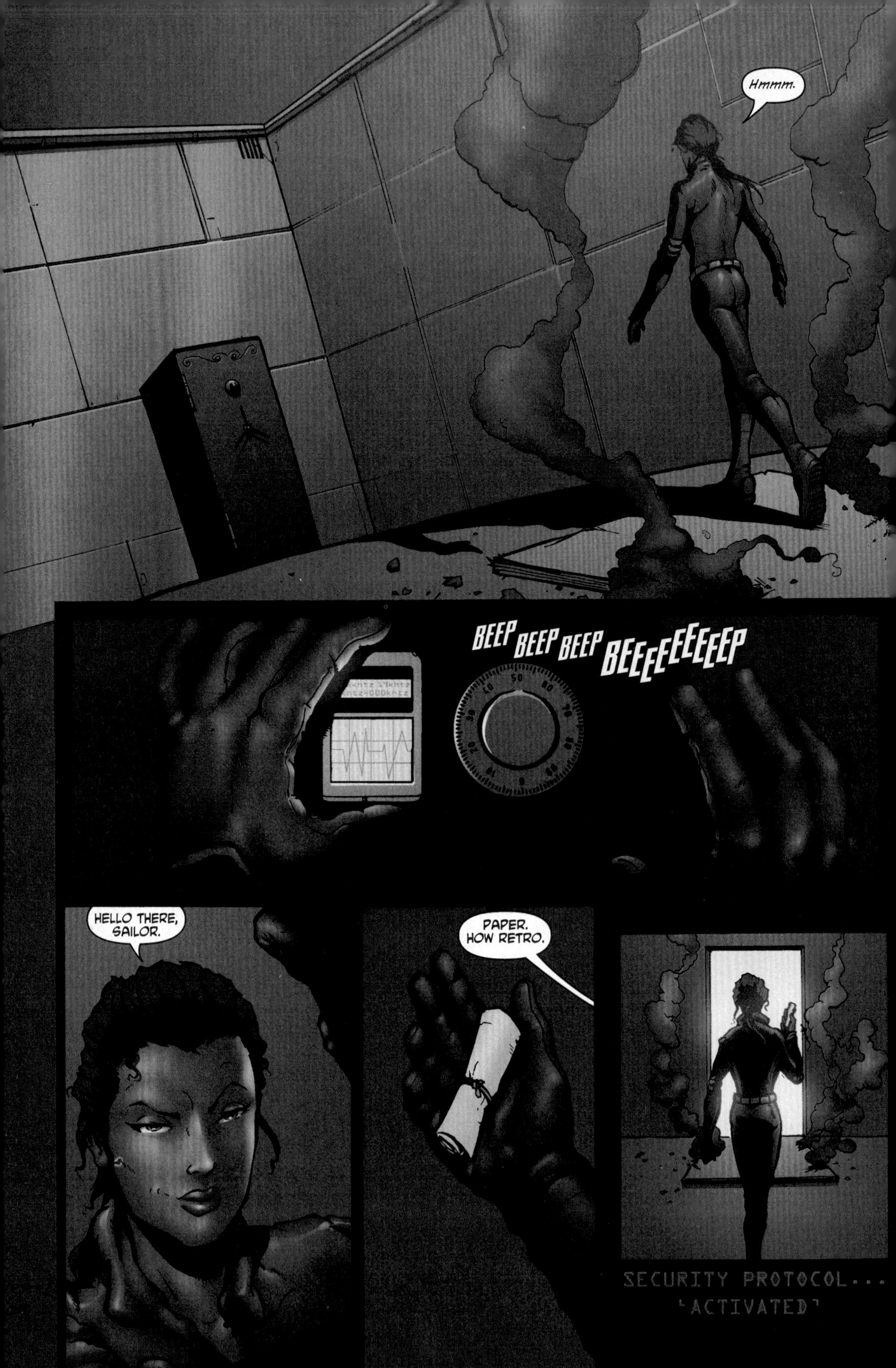
Hmmm.
BEEP BEEP BEEP BEEEEEEEEEP
HELLO THERE, SAILOR.
PAPER. HOW RETRO.
SECURITY PROTOCOL...
'ACTIVATED'

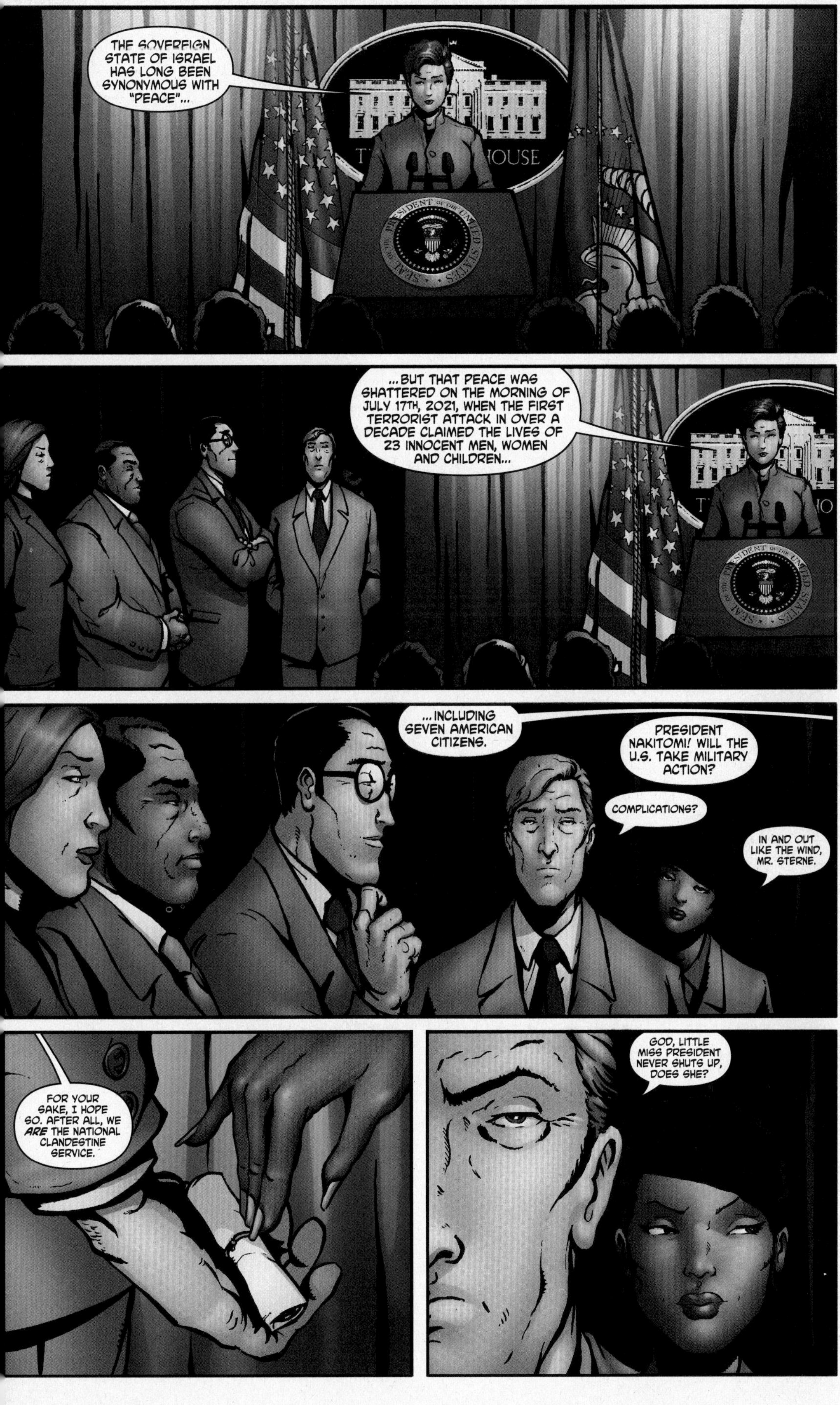
THE SOVEREIGN STATE OF ISRAEL HAS LONG BEEN SYNONYMOUS WITH "PEACE"...
...BUT THAT PEACE WAS SHATTERED ON THE MORNING OF JULY 17TH, 2021, WHEN THE FIRST TERRORIST ATTACK IN OVER A DECADE CLAIMED THE LIVES OF 23 INNOCENT MEN, WOMEN AND CHILDREN...
...INCLUDING SEVEN AMERICAN CITIZENS.
PRESIDENT NAKITOMI! WILL THE U.S. TAKE MILITARY ACTION?
COMPLICATIONS?
IN AND OUT LIKE THE WIND, MR. STERNE.
FOR YOUR SAKE, I HOPE SO. AFTER ALL, WE *ARE* THE NATIONAL CLANDESTINE SERVICE.
GOD, LITTLE MISS PRESIDENT NEVER SHUTS UP, DOES SHE?

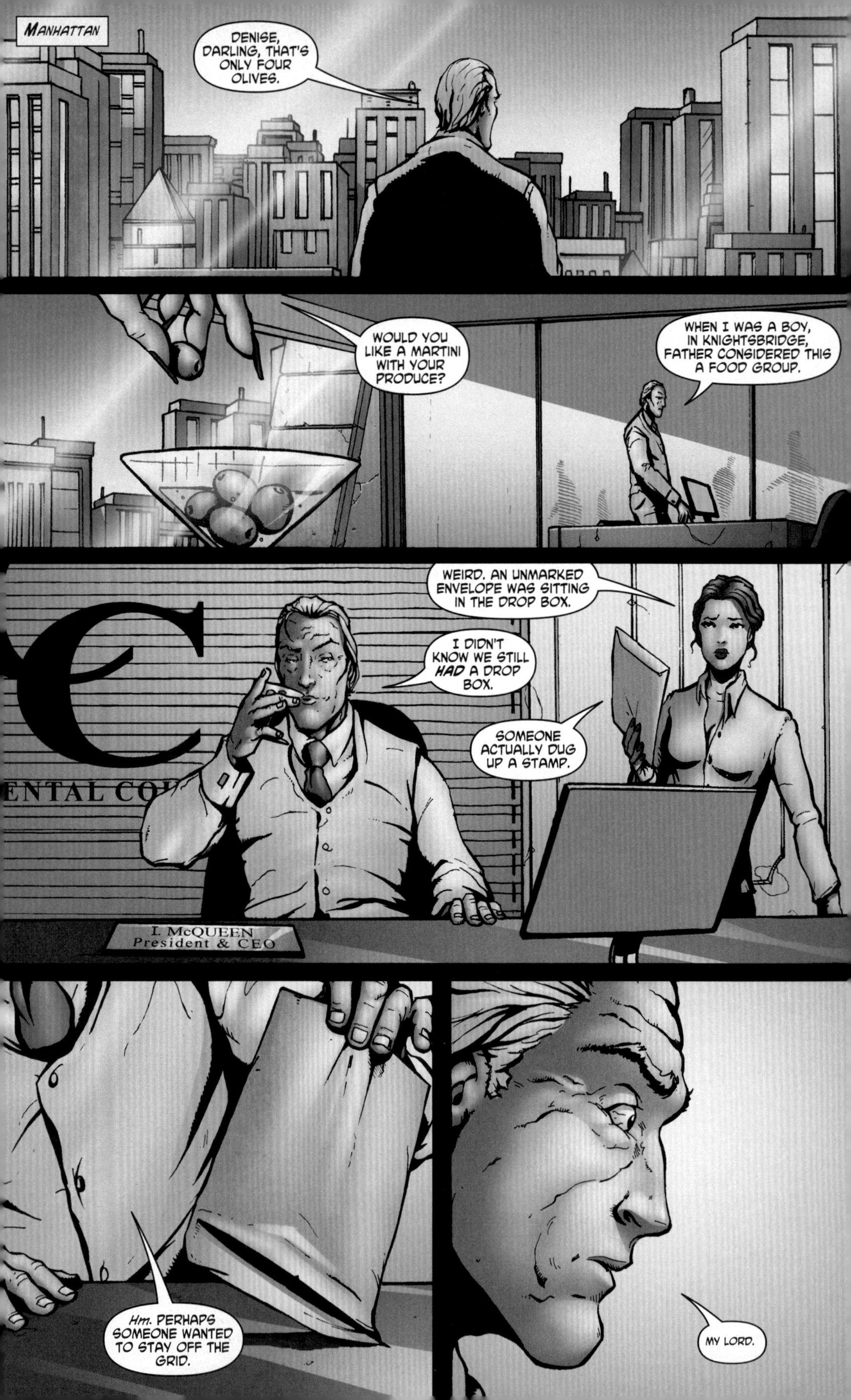
MANHATTAN
DENISE, DARLING, THAT'S ONLY FOUR OLIVES.
WOULD YOU LIKE A MARTINI WITH YOUR PRODUCE?
WHEN I WAS A BOY, IN KNIGHTSBRIDGE, FATHER CONSIDERED THIS A FOOD GROUP.
WEIRD. AN UNMARKED ENVELOPE WAS SITTING IN THE DROP BOX.
I DIDN'T KNOW WE STILL *HAD* A DROP BOX.
SOMEONE ACTUALLY DUG UP A STAMP.
ENTAL CO
I. McQUEEN
President & CEO
Hm. PERHAPS SOMEONE WANTED TO STAY OFF THE GRID.
MY LORD.

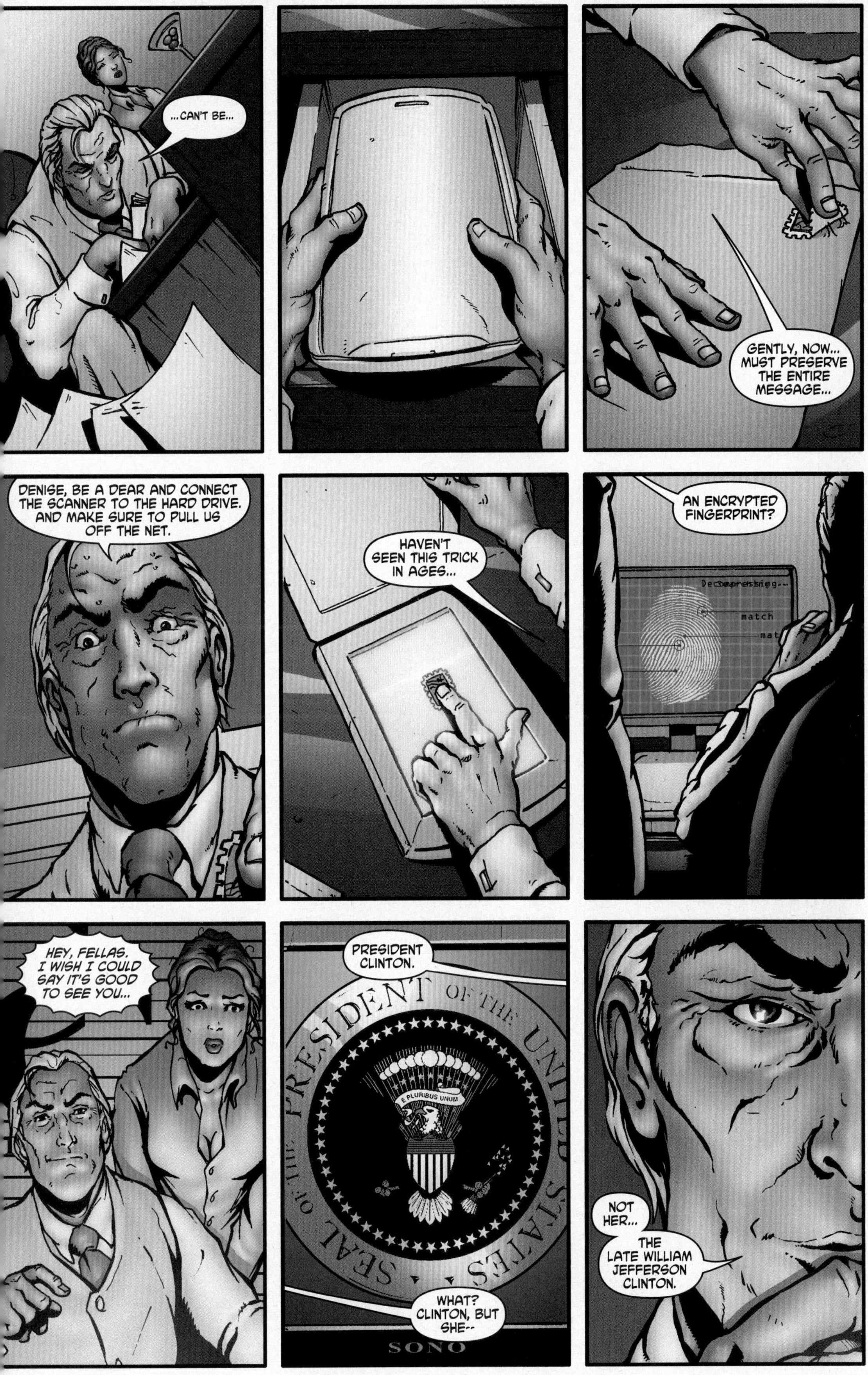
...CAN'T BE...
GENTLY, NOW... MUST PRESERVE THE ENTIRE MESSAGE...
DENISE, BE A DEAR AND CONNECT THE SCANNER TO THE HARD DRIVE. AND MAKE SURE TO PULL US OFF THE NET.
HAVEN'T SEEN THIS TRICK IN AGES...
AN ENCRYPTED FINGERPRINT?
match
HEY, FELLAS. I WISH I COULD SAY IT'S GOOD TO SEE YOU...
PRESIDENT CLINTON.
SEAL OF THE PRESIDENT OF THE UNITED STATES
E PLURIBUS UNUM
WHAT? CLINTON, BUT SHE--
SONO
NOT HER...
THE LATE WILLIAM JEFFERSON CLINTON.

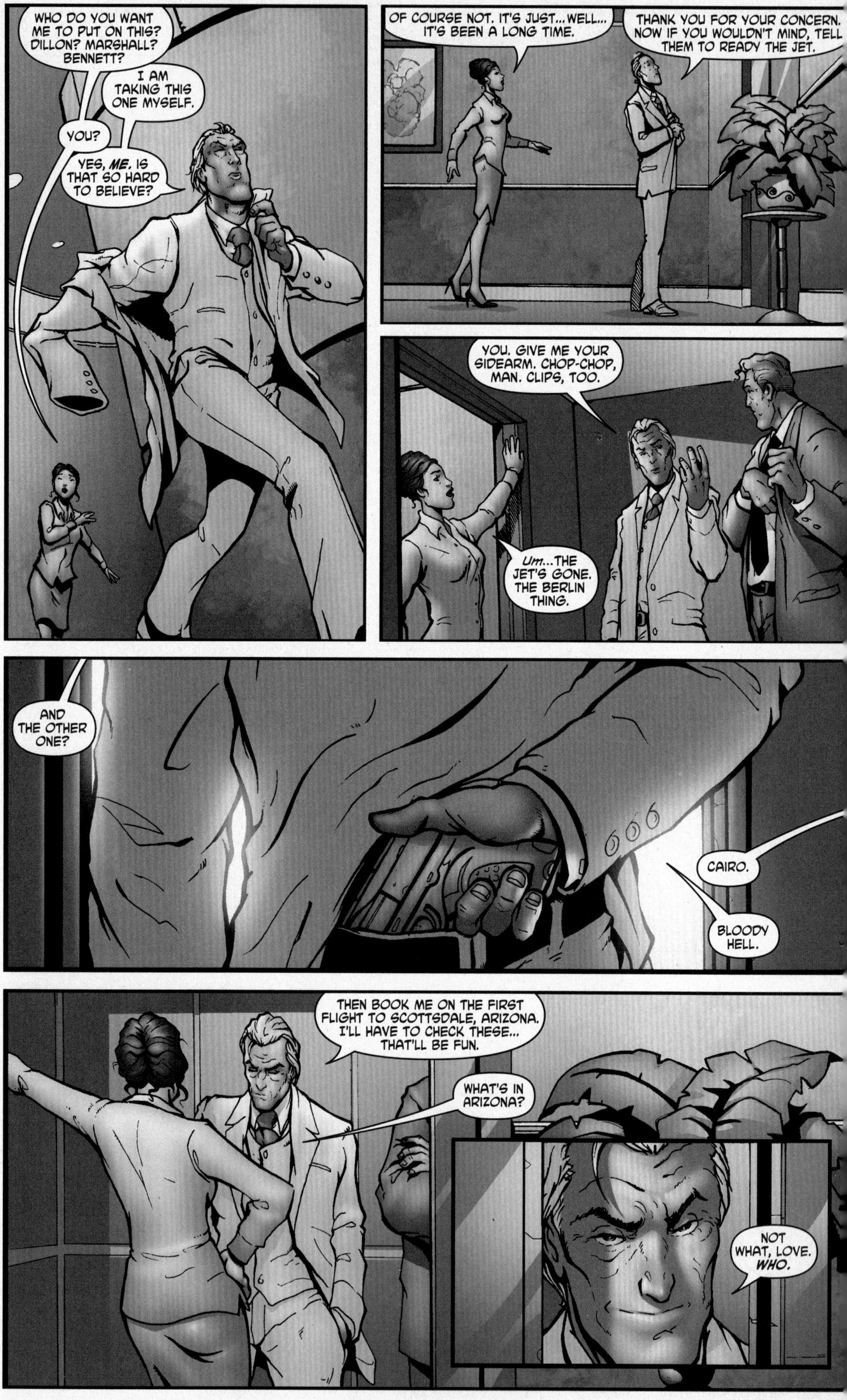
WHO DO YOU WANT ME TO PUT ON THIS? DILLON? MARSHALL? BENNETT?
I AM TAKING THIS ONE MYSELF.
YOU?
YES, *ME.* IS THAT SO HARD TO BELIEVE?
OF COURSE NOT. IT'S JUST...WELL... IT'S BEEN A LONG TIME.
THANK YOU FOR YOUR CONCERN. NOW IF YOU WOULDN'T MIND, TELL THEM TO READY THE JET.
YOU. GIVE ME YOUR SIDEARM. CHOP-CHOP, MAN. CLIPS, TOO.
Um...THE JET'S GONE. THE BERLIN THING.
AND THE OTHER ONE?
CAIRO.
BLOODY HELL.
THEN BOOK ME ON THE FIRST FLIGHT TO SCOTTSDALE, ARIZONA. I'LL HAVE TO CHECK THESE... THAT'LL BE FUN.
WHAT'S IN ARIZONA?
NOT WHAT, LOVE. *WHO.*

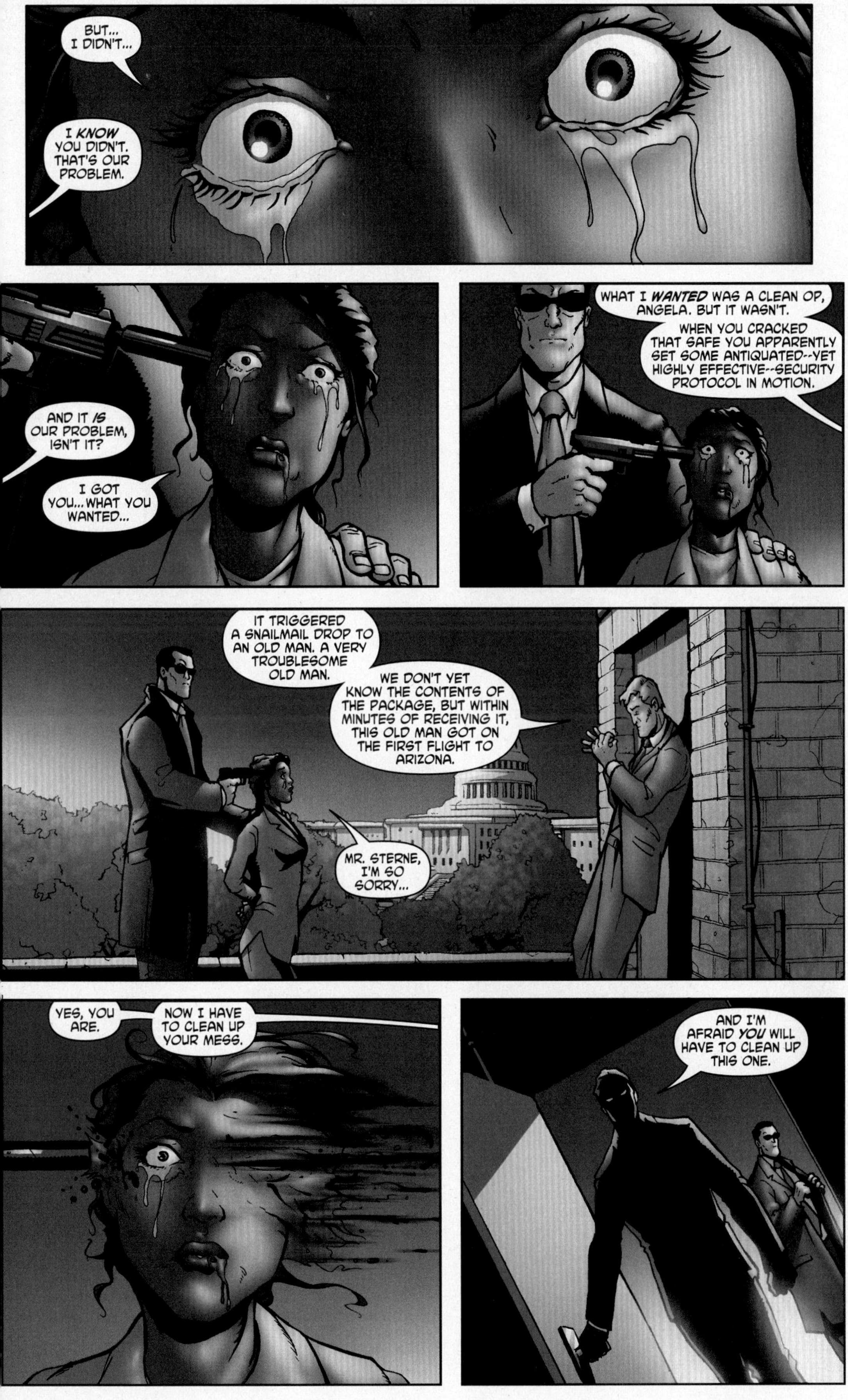
BUT... I DIDN'T...
I KNOW YOU DIDN'T. THAT'S OUR PROBLEM.
AND IT IS OUR PROBLEM, ISN'T IT?
I GOT YOU...WHAT YOU WANTED...
WHAT I WANTED WAS A CLEAN OP, ANGELA. BUT IT WASN'T.
WHEN YOU CRACKED THAT SAFE YOU APPARENTLY SET SOME ANTIQUATED--YET HIGHLY EFFECTIVE--SECURITY PROTOCOL IN MOTION.
IT TRIGGERED A SNAILMAIL DROP TO AN OLD MAN. A VERY TROUBLESOME OLD MAN.
WE DON'T YET KNOW THE CONTENTS OF THE PACKAGE, BUT WITHIN MINUTES OF RECEIVING IT, THIS OLD MAN GOT ON THE FIRST FLIGHT TO ARIZONA.
MR. STERNE, I'M SO SORRY...
YES, YOU ARE.
NOW I HAVE TO CLEAN UP YOUR MESS.
AND I'M AFRAID YOU WILL HAVE TO CLEAN UP THIS ONE.

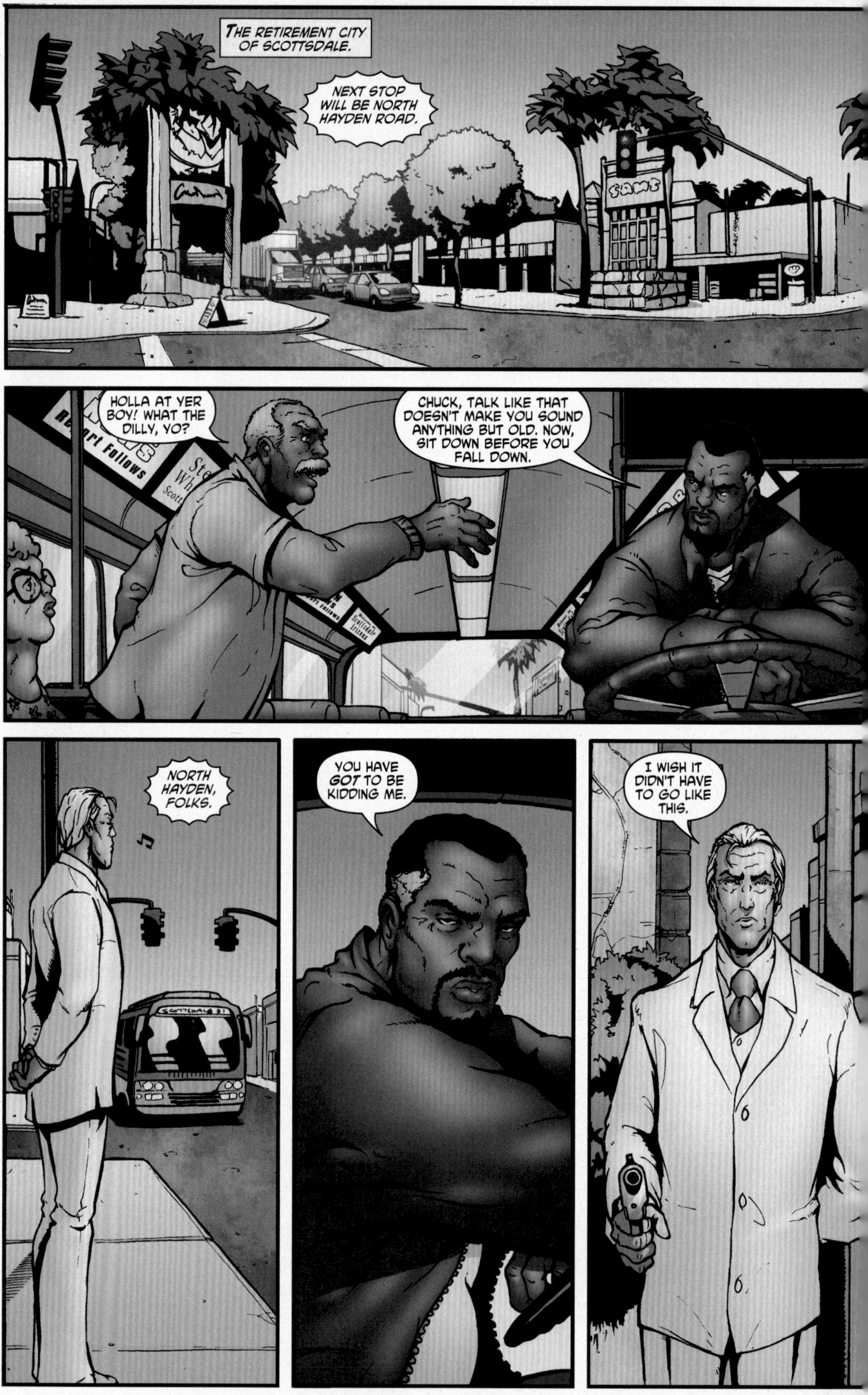
THE RETIREMENT CITY OF SCOTTSDALE.
NEXT STOP WILL BE NORTH HAYDEN ROAD.
HOLLA AT YER BOY! WHAT THE DILLY, YO?
CHUCK, TALK LIKE THAT DOESN'T MAKE YOU SOUND ANYTHING BUT OLD. NOW, SIT DOWN BEFORE YOU FALL DOWN.
NORTH HAYDEN, FOLKS.
YOU HAVE *GOT* TO BE KIDDING ME.
I WISH IT DIDN'T HAVE TO GO LIKE THIS.

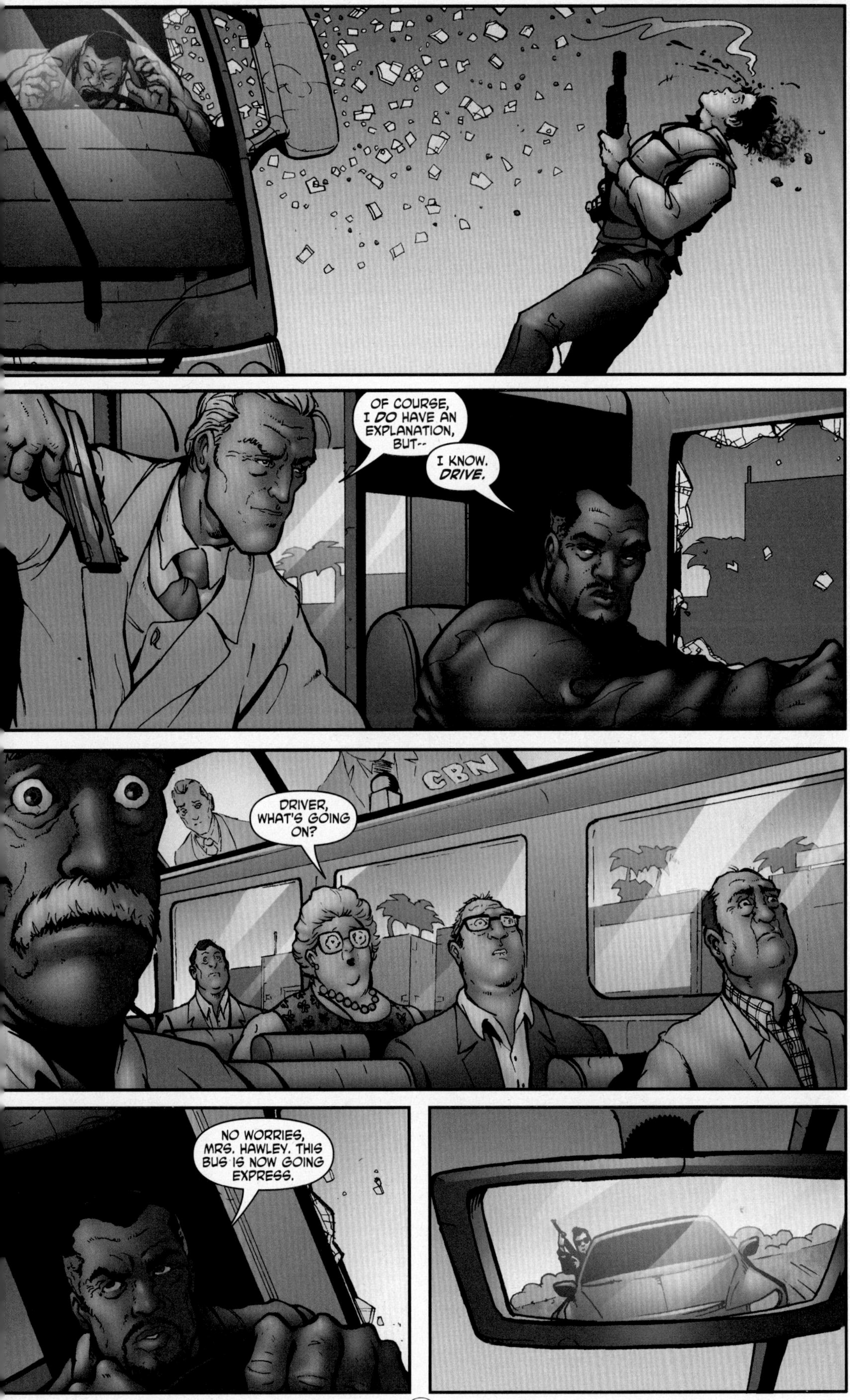
OF COURSE, I DO HAVE AN EXPLANATION, BUT--
I KNOW. DRIVE.
CBN
DRIVER, WHAT'S GOING ON?
NO WORRIES, MRS. HAWLEY. THIS BUS IS NOW GOING EXPRESS.

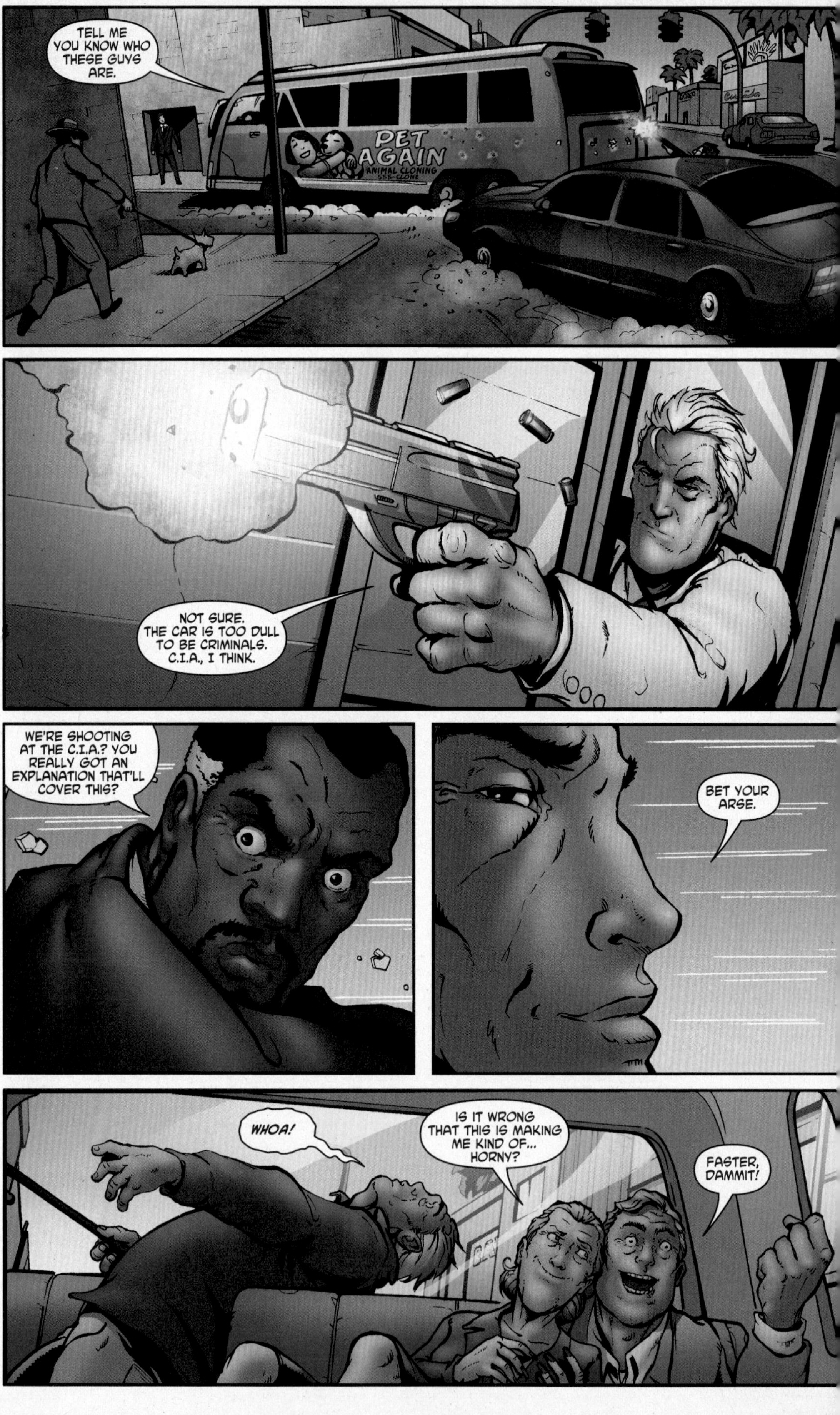
TELL ME YOU KNOW WHO THESE GUYS ARE.
PET AGAIN
ANIMAL CLONING
555-CLONE
NOT SURE. THE CAR IS TOO DULL TO BE CRIMINALS. C.I.A., I THINK.
WE'RE SHOOTING AT THE C.I.A.? YOU REALLY GOT AN EXPLANATION THAT'LL COVER THIS?
BET YOUR ARSE.
WHOA!
IS IT WRONG THAT THIS IS MAKING ME KIND OF... HORNY?
FASTER, DAMMIT!

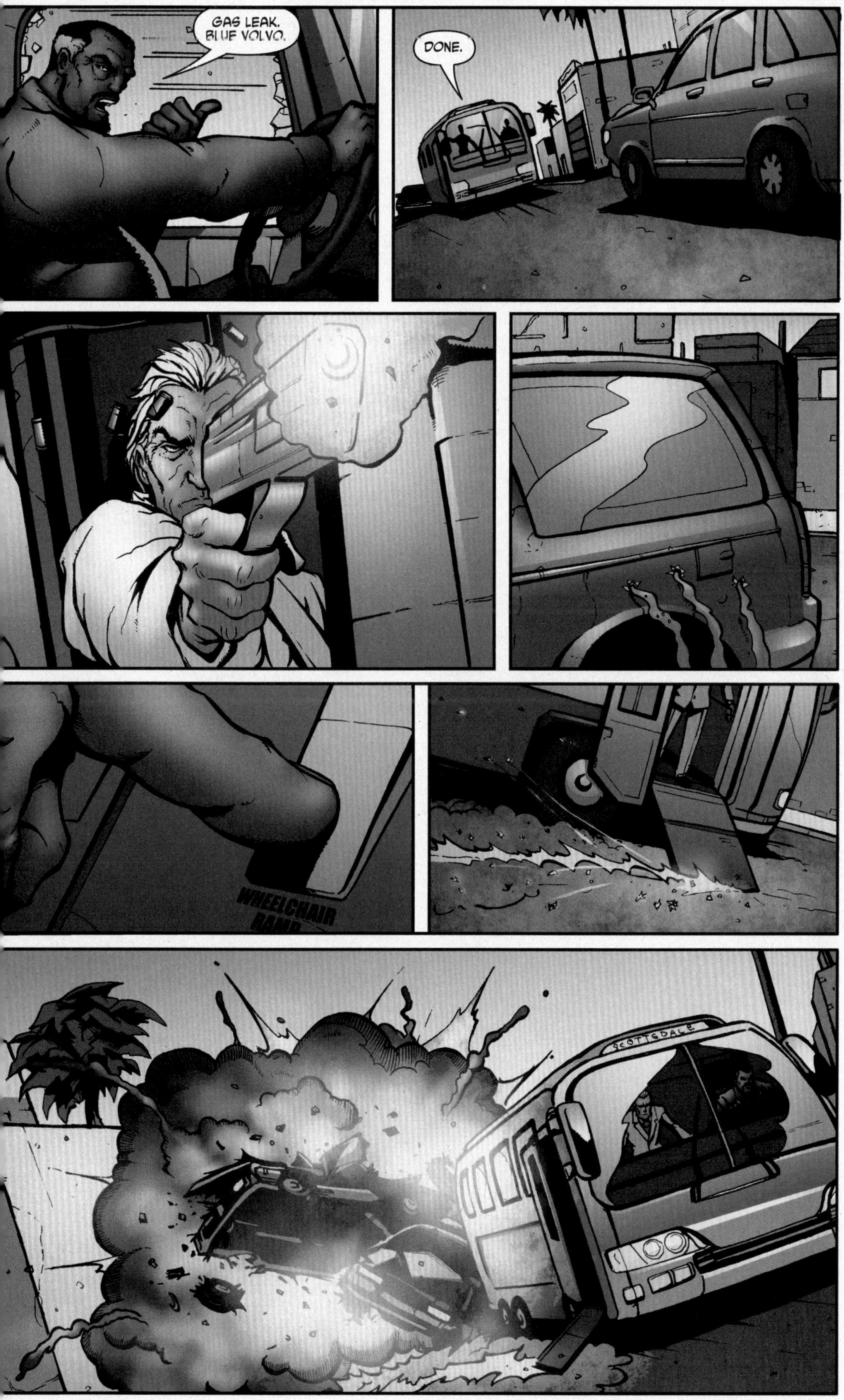
GAS LEAK. BLUE VOLVO.
DONE.
WHEELCHAIR RAMP
SCOTTSDALE

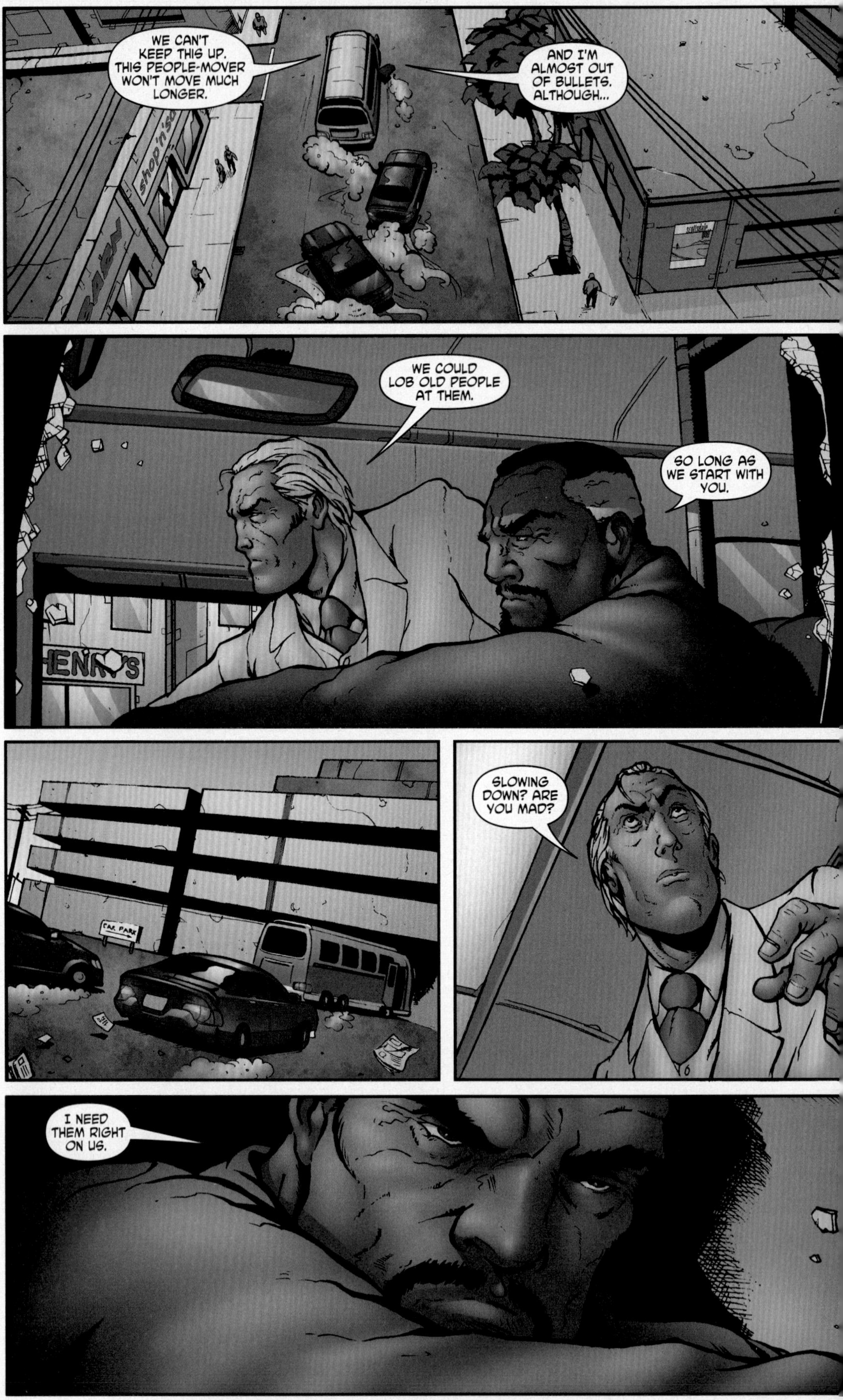
WE CAN'T KEEP THIS UP. THIS PEOPLE-MOVER WON'T MOVE MUCH LONGER.
AND I'M ALMOST OUT OF BULLETS. ALTHOUGH...
WE COULD LOB OLD PEOPLE AT THEM.
SO LONG AS WE START WITH YOU.
CAR PARK
SLOWING DOWN? ARE YOU MAD?
I NEED THEM RIGHT ON US.

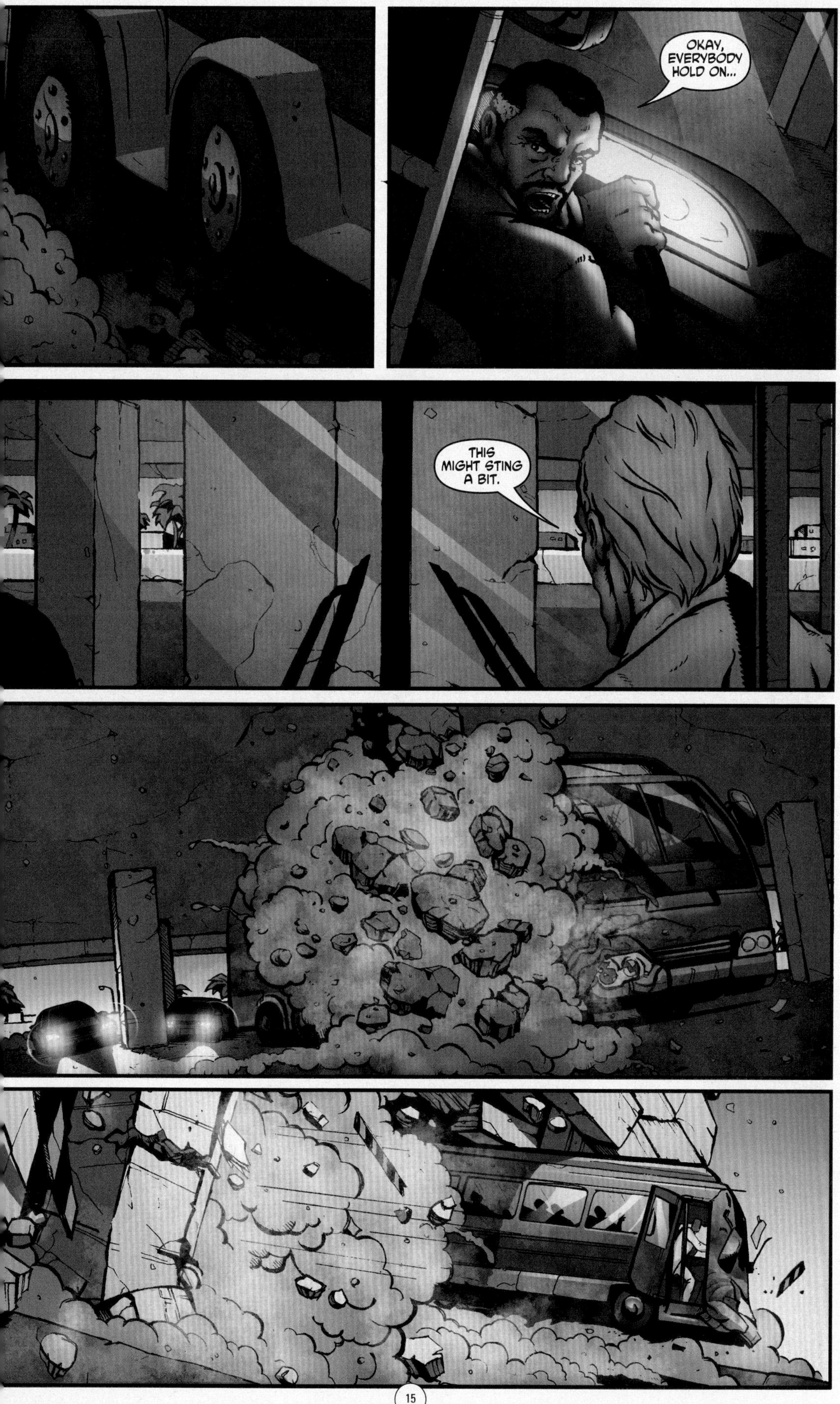
OKAY, EVERYBODY HOLD ON...
THIS MIGHT STING A BIT.

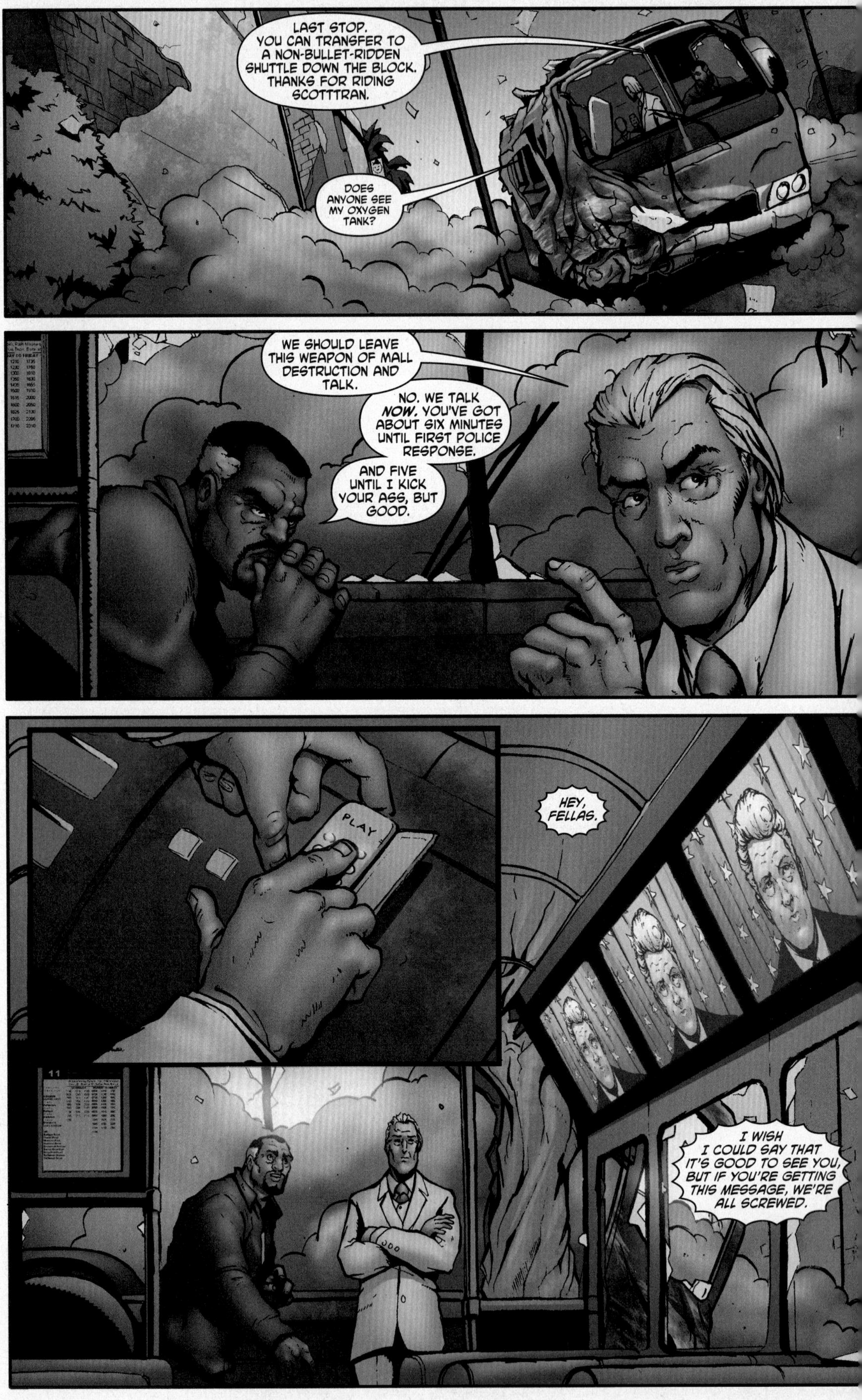

LAST STOP. YOU CAN TRANSFER TO A NON-BULLET-RIDDEN SHUTTLE DOWN THE BLOCK. THANKS FOR RIDING SCOTTTRAN.
DOES ANYONE SEE MY OXYGEN TANK?
WE SHOULD LEAVE THIS WEAPON OF MALL DESTRUCTION AND TALK.
NO. WE TALK *NOW.* YOU'VE GOT ABOUT SIX MINUTES UNTIL FIRST POLICE RESPONSE.
AND FIVE UNTIL I KICK YOUR ASS, BUT GOOD.
PLAY
HEY, FELLAS.
I WISH I COULD SAY THAT IT'S GOOD TO SEE YOU, BUT IF YOU'RE GETTING THIS MESSAGE, WE'RE ALL SCREWED.

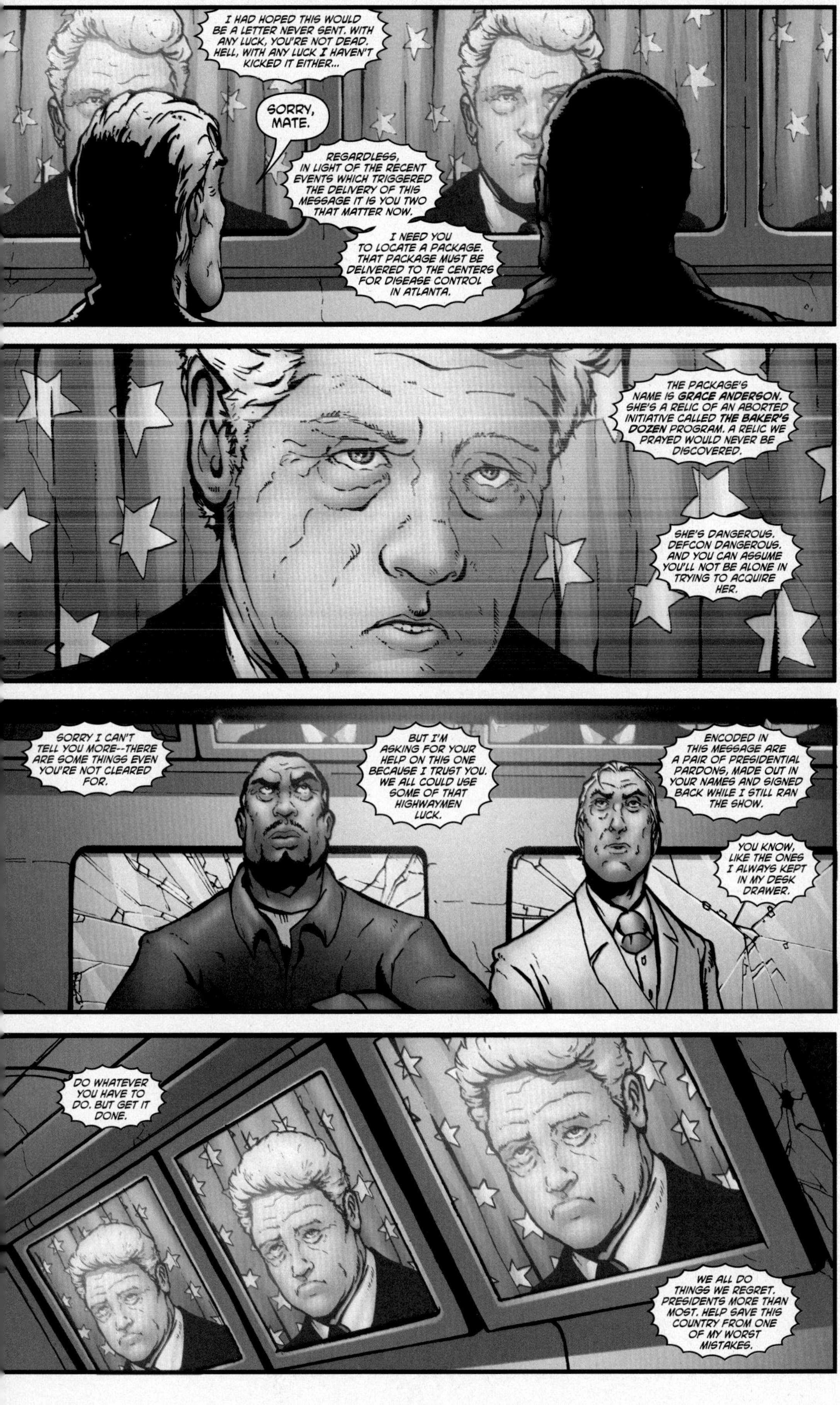
I HAD HOPED THIS WOULD BE A LETTER NEVER SENT. WITH ANY LUCK, YOU'RE NOT DEAD. HELL, WITH ANY LUCK I HAVEN'T KICKED IT EITHER...
SORRY, MATE.
REGARDLESS, IN LIGHT OF THE RECENT EVENTS WHICH TRIGGERED THE DELIVERY OF THIS MESSAGE IT IS YOU TWO THAT MATTER NOW.
I NEED YOU TO LOCATE A PACKAGE. THAT PACKAGE MUST BE DELIVERED TO THE CENTERS FOR DISEASE CONTROL IN ATLANTA.
THE PACKAGE'S NAME IS GRACE ANDERSON. SHE'S A RELIC OF AN ABORTED INITIATIVE CALLED THE BAKER'S DOZEN PROGRAM. A RELIC WE PRAYED WOULD NEVER BE DISCOVERED.
SHE'S DANGEROUS. DEFCON DANGEROUS. AND YOU CAN ASSUME YOU'LL NOT BE ALONE IN TRYING TO ACQUIRE HER.
SORRY I CAN'T TELL YOU MORE--THERE ARE SOME THINGS EVEN YOU'RE NOT CLEARED FOR.
BUT I'M ASKING FOR YOUR HELP ON THIS ONE BECAUSE I TRUST YOU. WE ALL COULD USE SOME OF THAT HIGHWAYMEN LUCK.
ENCODED IN THIS MESSAGE ARE A PAIR OF PRESIDENTIAL PARDONS, MADE OUT IN YOUR NAMES AND SIGNED BACK WHILE I STILL RAN THE SHOW.
YOU KNOW, LIKE THE ONES I ALWAYS KEPT IN MY DESK DRAWER.
DO WHATEVER YOU HAVE TO DO. BUT GET IT DONE.
WE ALL DO THINGS WE REGRET. PRESIDENTS MORE THAN MOST. HELP SAVE THIS COUNTRY FROM ONE OF MY WORST MISTAKES.

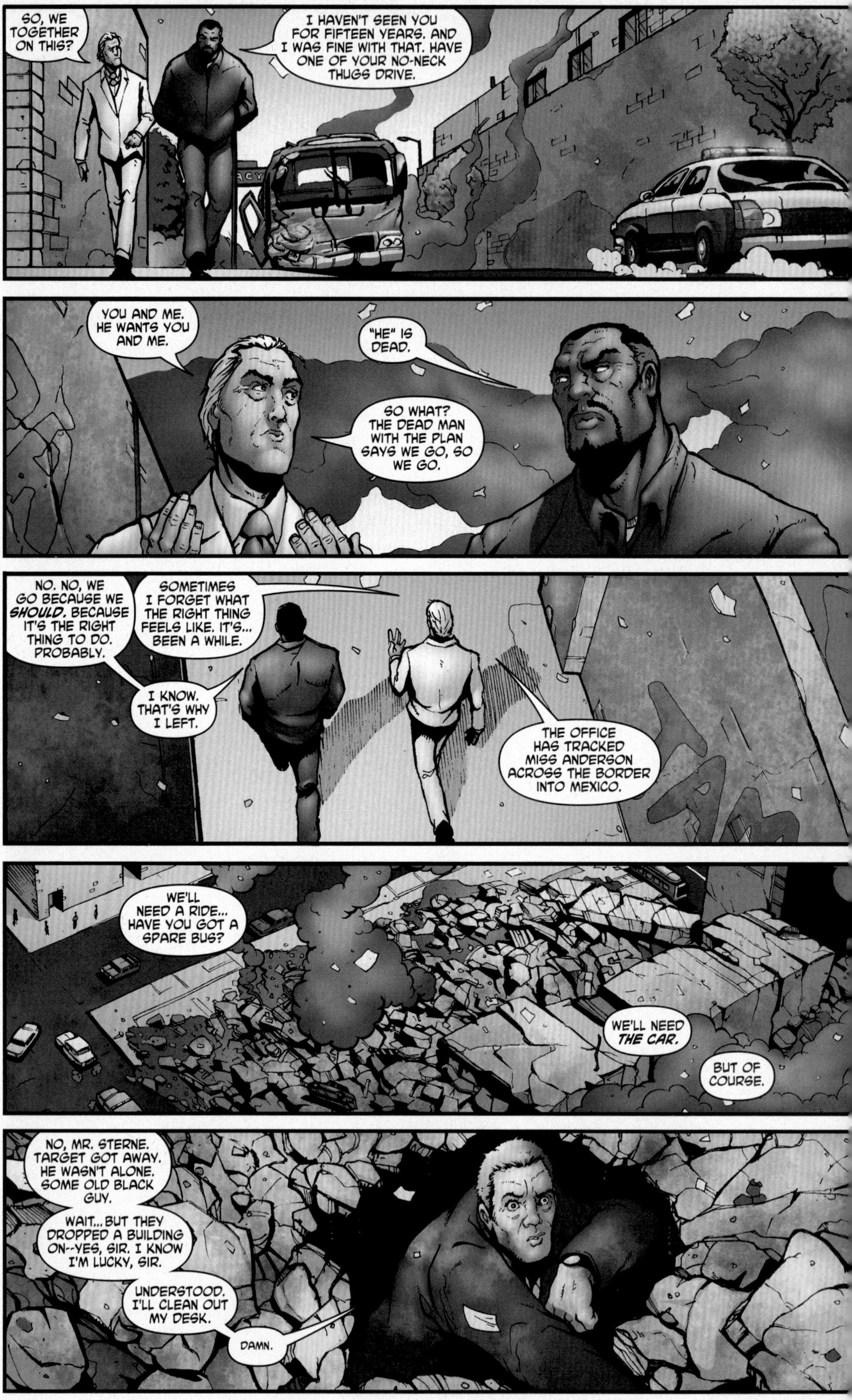
SO, WE TOGETHER ON THIS?
I HAVEN'T SEEN YOU FOR FIFTEEN YEARS. AND I WAS FINE WITH THAT. HAVE ONE OF YOUR NO-NECK THUGS DRIVE.
YOU AND ME. HE WANTS YOU AND ME.
"HE" IS DEAD.
SO WHAT? THE DEAD MAN WITH THE PLAN SAYS WE GO, SO WE GO.
NO. NO, WE GO BECAUSE WE *SHOULD.* BECAUSE IT'S THE RIGHT THING TO DO. PROBABLY.
SOMETIMES I FORGET WHAT THE RIGHT THING FEELS LIKE. IT'S... BEEN A WHILE.
I KNOW. THAT'S WHY I LEFT.
THE OFFICE HAS TRACKED MISS ANDERSON ACROSS THE BORDER INTO MEXICO.
WE'LL NEED A RIDE... HAVE YOU GOT A SPARE BUS?
WE'LL NEED *THE CAR.*
BUT OF COURSE.
NO, MR. STERNE. TARGET GOT AWAY. HE WASN'T ALONE. SOME OLD BLACK GUY.
WAIT... BUT THEY DROPPED A BUILDING ON--YES, SIR. I KNOW I'M LUCKY, SIR.
UNDERSTOOD. I'LL CLEAN OUT MY DESK.
DAMN.

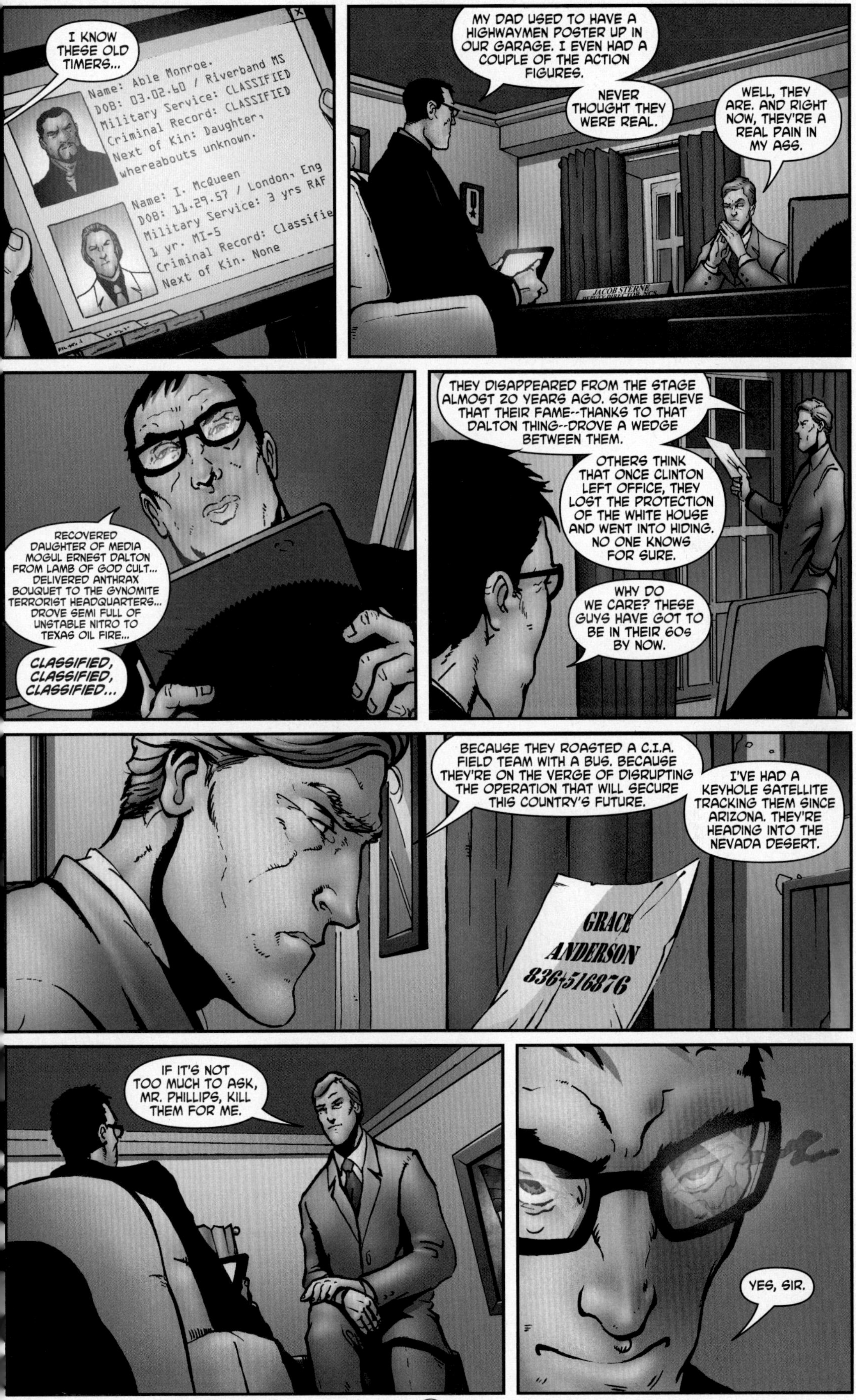

I KNOW THESE OLD TIMERS...
Name: Able Monroe.
DOB: 03.02.60 / Riverband MS
Military Service: CLASSIFIED
Criminal Record: CLASSIFIED
Next of Kin: Daughter, whereabouts unknown.
Name: I. McQueen
DOB: 11.29.57 / London, Eng
Military Service: 3 yrs RAF
1 yr. MI-5
Criminal Record: Classifie
Next of Kin. None
MY DAD USED TO HAVE A HIGHWAYMEN POSTER UP IN OUR GARAGE. I EVEN HAD A COUPLE OF THE ACTION FIGURES.
NEVER THOUGHT THEY WERE REAL.
WELL, THEY ARE. AND RIGHT NOW, THEY'RE A REAL PAIN IN MY ASS.
JACOB STERNE
RECOVERED DAUGHTER OF MEDIA MOGUL ERNEST DALTON FROM LAMB OF GOD CULT... DELIVERED ANTHRAX BOUQUET TO THE GYNOMITE TERRORIST HEADQUARTERS... DROVE SEMI FULL OF UNSTABLE NITRO TO TEXAS OIL FIRE...
CLASSIFIED, CLASSIFIED, CLASSIFIED...
THEY DISAPPEARED FROM THE STAGE ALMOST 20 YEARS AGO. SOME BELIEVE THAT THEIR FAME--THANKS TO THAT DALTON THING--DROVE A WEDGE BETWEEN THEM.
OTHERS THINK THAT ONCE CLINTON LEFT OFFICE, THEY LOST THE PROTECTION OF THE WHITE HOUSE AND WENT INTO HIDING. NO ONE KNOWS FOR SURE.
WHY DO WE CARE? THESE GUYS HAVE GOT TO BE IN THEIR 60s BY NOW.
BECAUSE THEY ROASTED A C.I.A. FIELD TEAM WITH A BUS. BECAUSE THEY'RE ON THE VERGE OF DISRUPTING THE OPERATION THAT WILL SECURE THIS COUNTRY'S FUTURE.
I'VE HAD A KEYHOLE SATELLITE TRACKING THEM SINCE ARIZONA. THEY'RE HEADING INTO THE NEVADA DESERT.
GRACE ANDERSON 836-516876
IF IT'S NOT TOO MUCH TO ASK, MR. PHILLIPS, KILL THEM FOR ME.
YES, SIR.

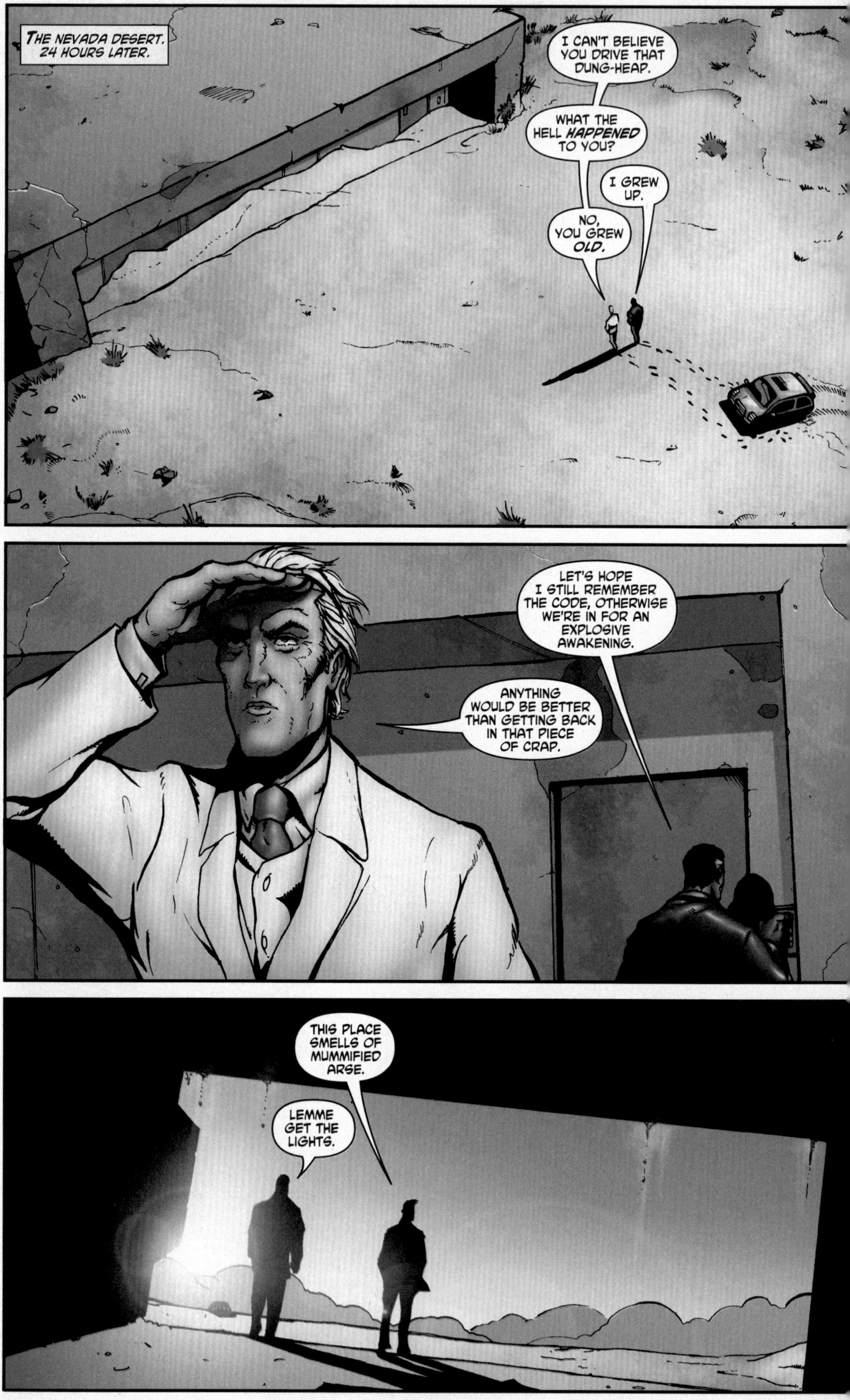
THE NEVADA DESERT. 24 HOURS LATER.
I CAN'T BELIEVE YOU DRIVE THAT DUNG-HEAP.
WHAT THE HELL *HAPPENED* TO YOU?
I GREW UP.
NO, YOU GREW *OLD.*
LET'S HOPE I STILL REMEMBER THE CODE, OTHERWISE WE'RE IN FOR AN EXPLOSIVE AWAKENING.
ANYTHING WOULD BE BETTER THAN GETTING BACK IN THAT PIECE OF CRAP.
THIS PLACE SMELLS OF MUMMIFIED ARSE.
LEMME GET THE LIGHTS.

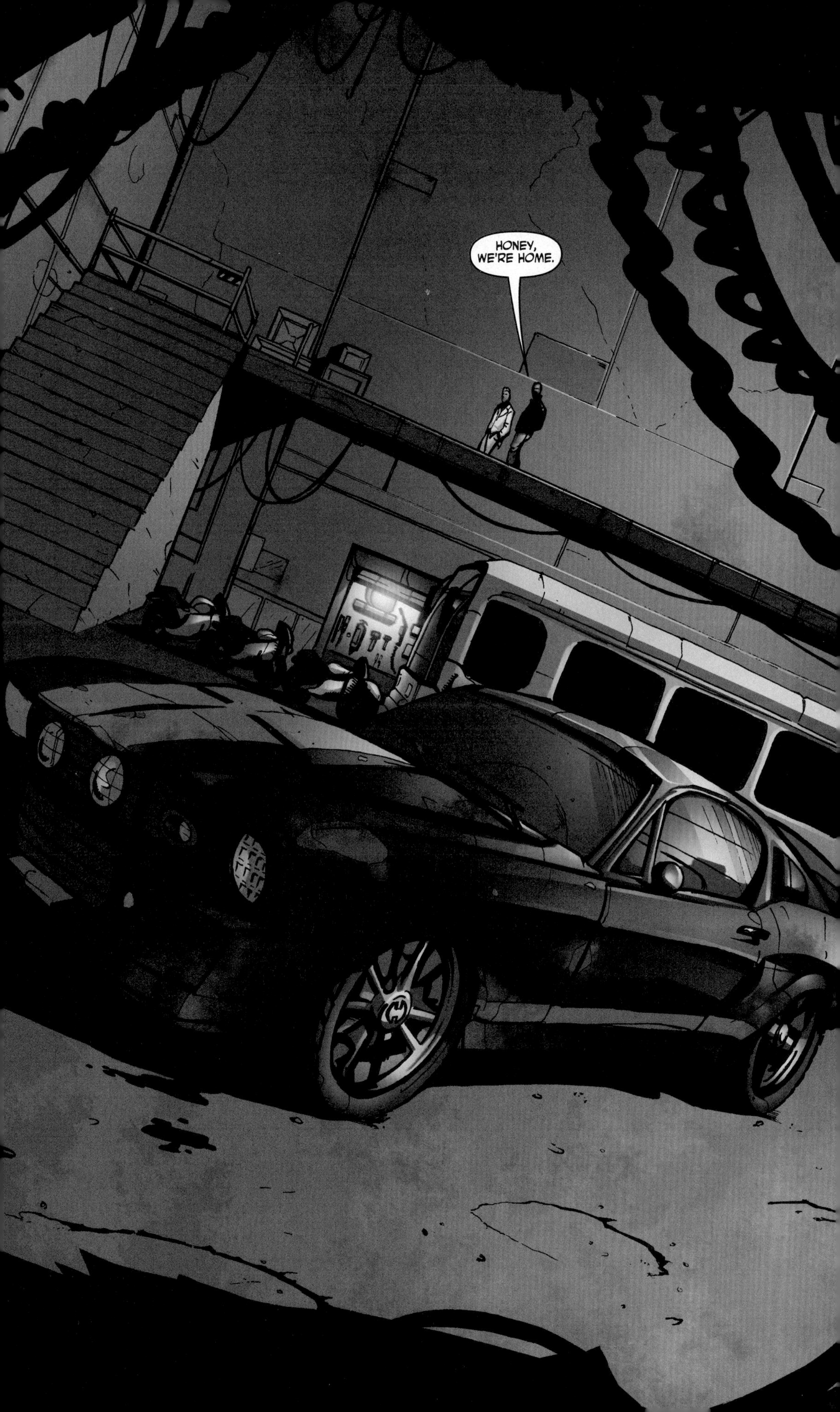
HONEY, WE'RE HOME.

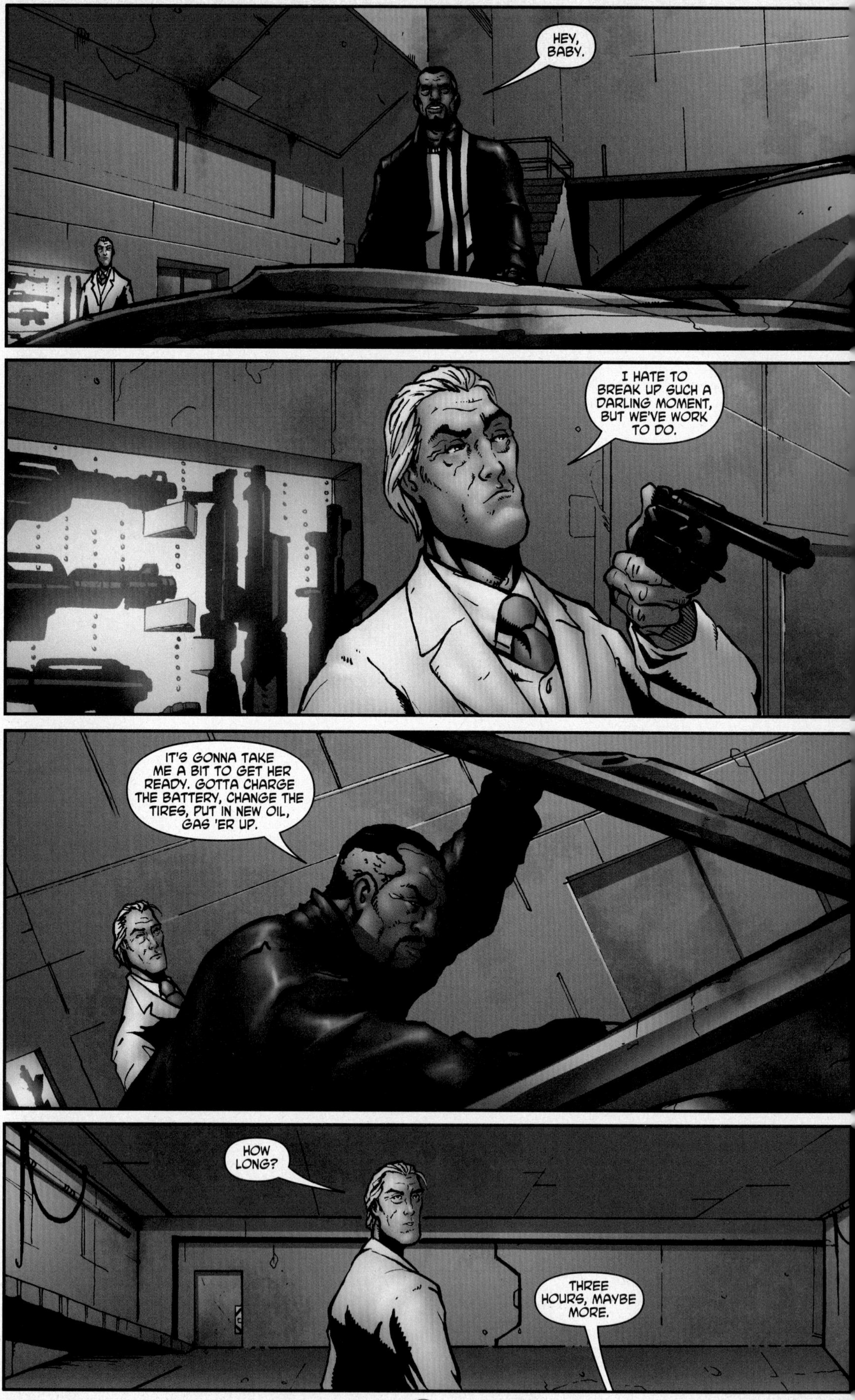
HEY, BABY.
I HATE TO BREAK UP SUCH A DARLING MOMENT, BUT WE'VE WORK TO DO.
IT'S GONNA TAKE ME A BIT TO GET HER READY. GOTTA CHARGE THE BATTERY, CHANGE THE TIRES, PUT IN NEW OIL, GAS 'ER UP.
HOW LONG?
THREE HOURS, MAYBE MORE.

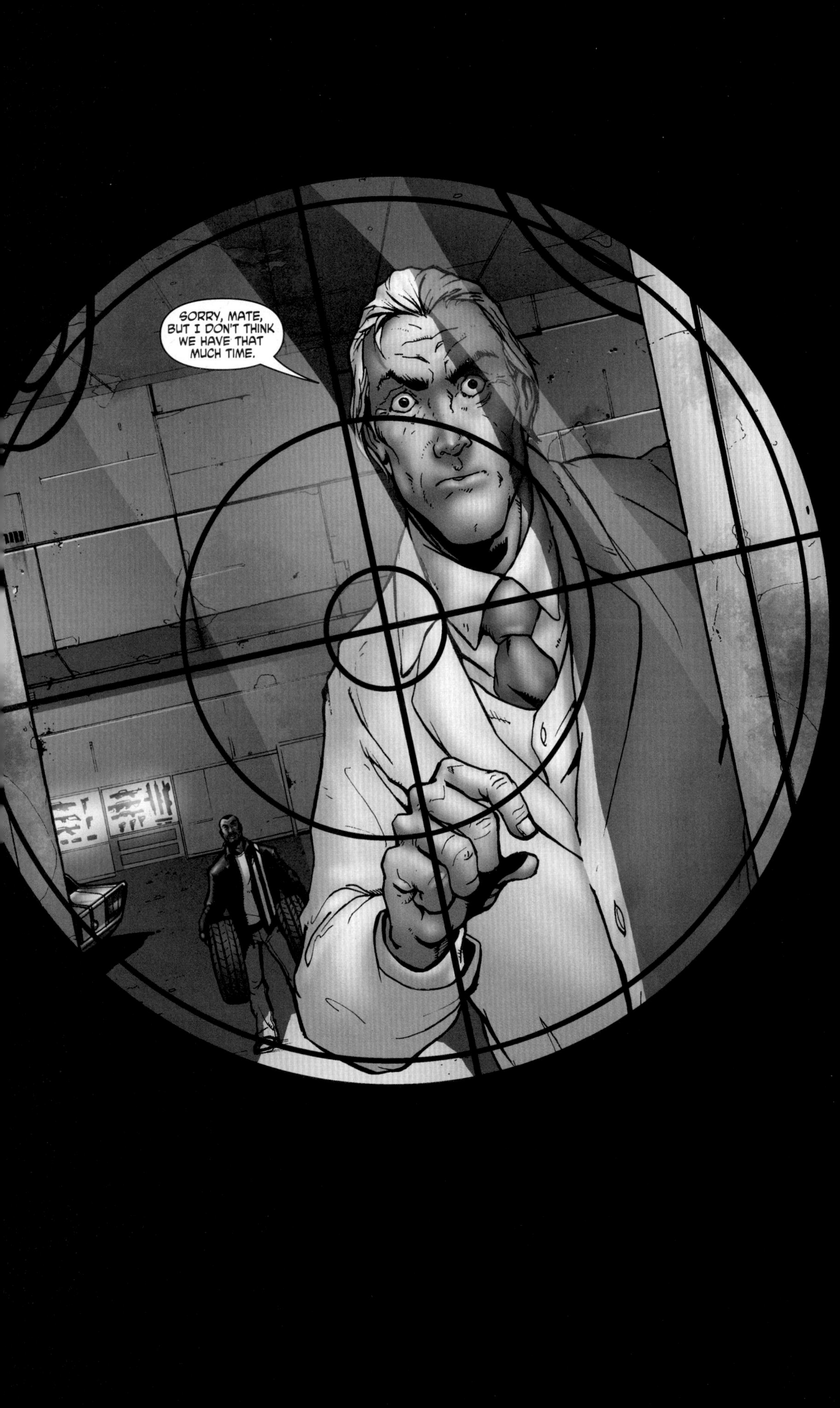
SORRY, MATE, BUT I DON'T THINK WE HAVE THAT MUCH TIME.

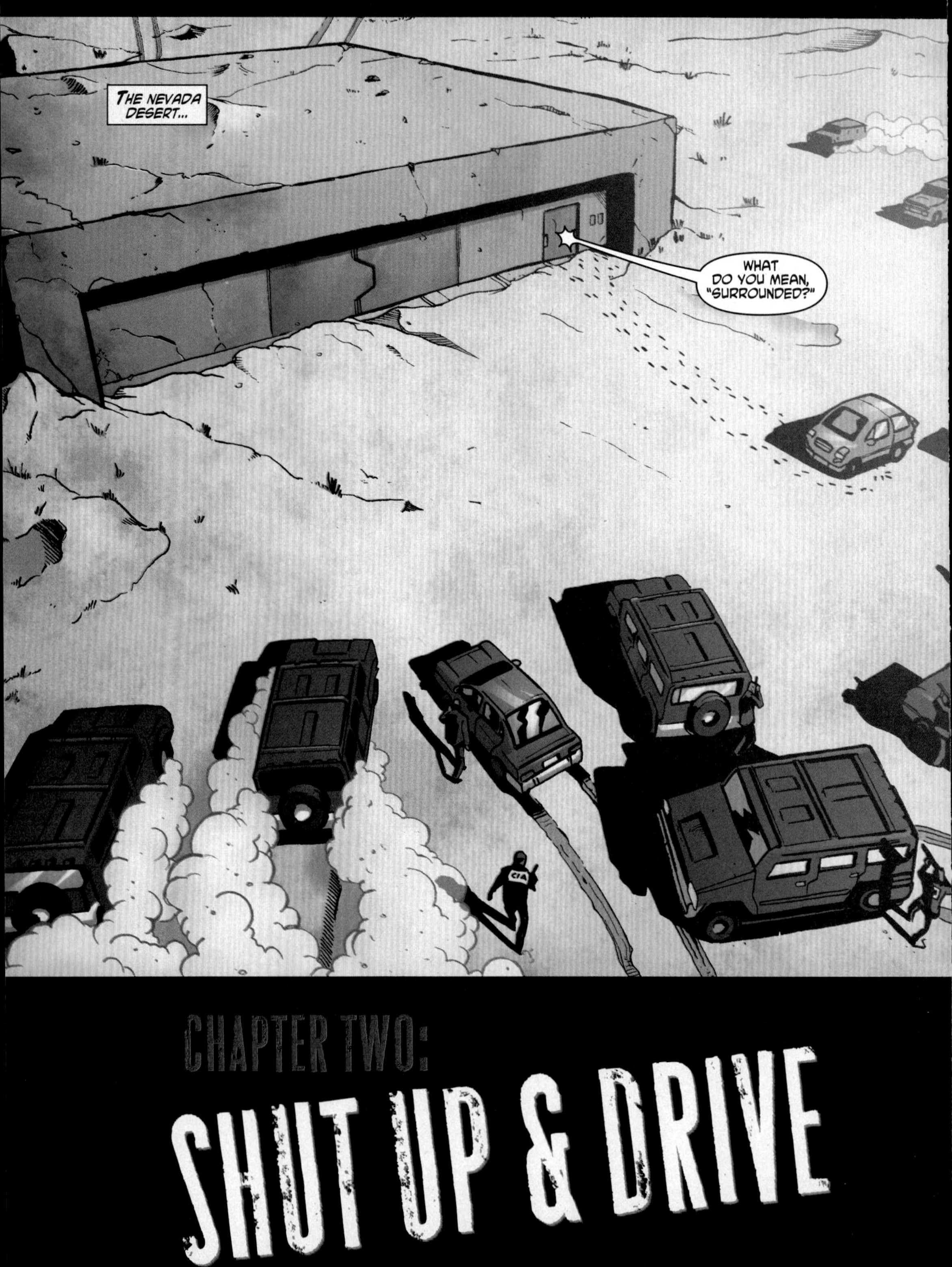
THE NEVADA DESERT...
WHAT DO YOU MEAN, "SURROUNDED?"
CIA

CHAPTER TWO: SHUT UP & DRIVE

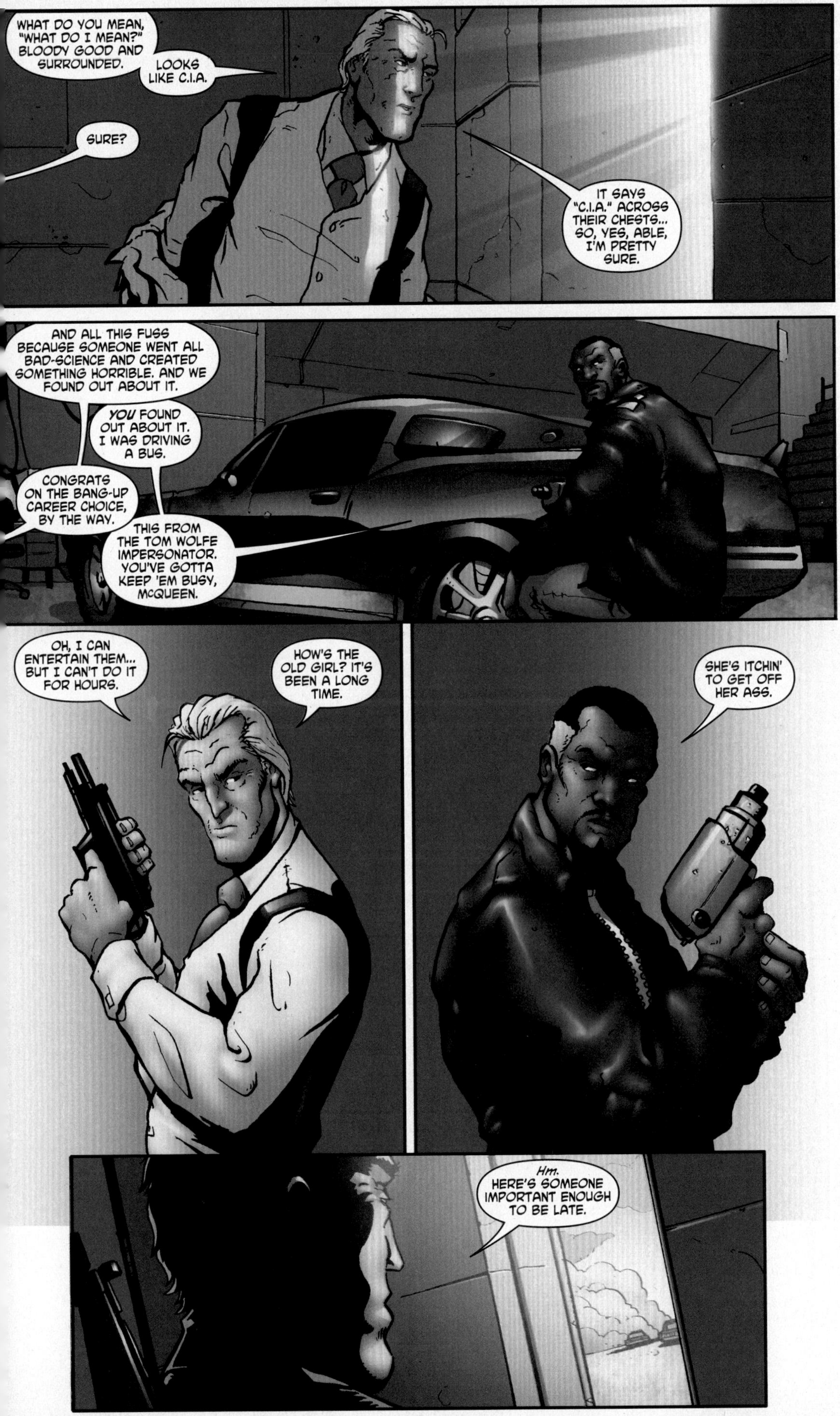
WHAT DO YOU MEAN, "WHAT DO I MEAN?" BLOODY GOOD AND SURROUNDED.
LOOKS LIKE C.I.A.
SURE?
IT SAYS "C.I.A." ACROSS THEIR CHESTS... SO, YES, ABLE, I'M PRETTY SURE.
AND ALL THIS FUSS BECAUSE SOMEONE WENT ALL BAD-SCIENCE AND CREATED SOMETHING HORRIBLE. AND WE FOUND OUT ABOUT IT.
YOU FOUND OUT ABOUT IT. I WAS DRIVING A BUS.
CONGRATS ON THE BANG-UP CAREER CHOICE, BY THE WAY.
THIS FROM THE TOM WOLFE IMPERSONATOR. YOU'VE GOTTA KEEP 'EM BUSY, McQUEEN.
OH, I CAN ENTERTAIN THEM... BUT I CAN'T DO IT FOR HOURS.
HOW'S THE OLD GIRL? IT'S BEEN A LONG TIME.
SHE'S ITCHIN' TO GET OFF HER ASS.
Hm. HERE'S SOMEONE IMPORTANT ENOUGH TO BE LATE.

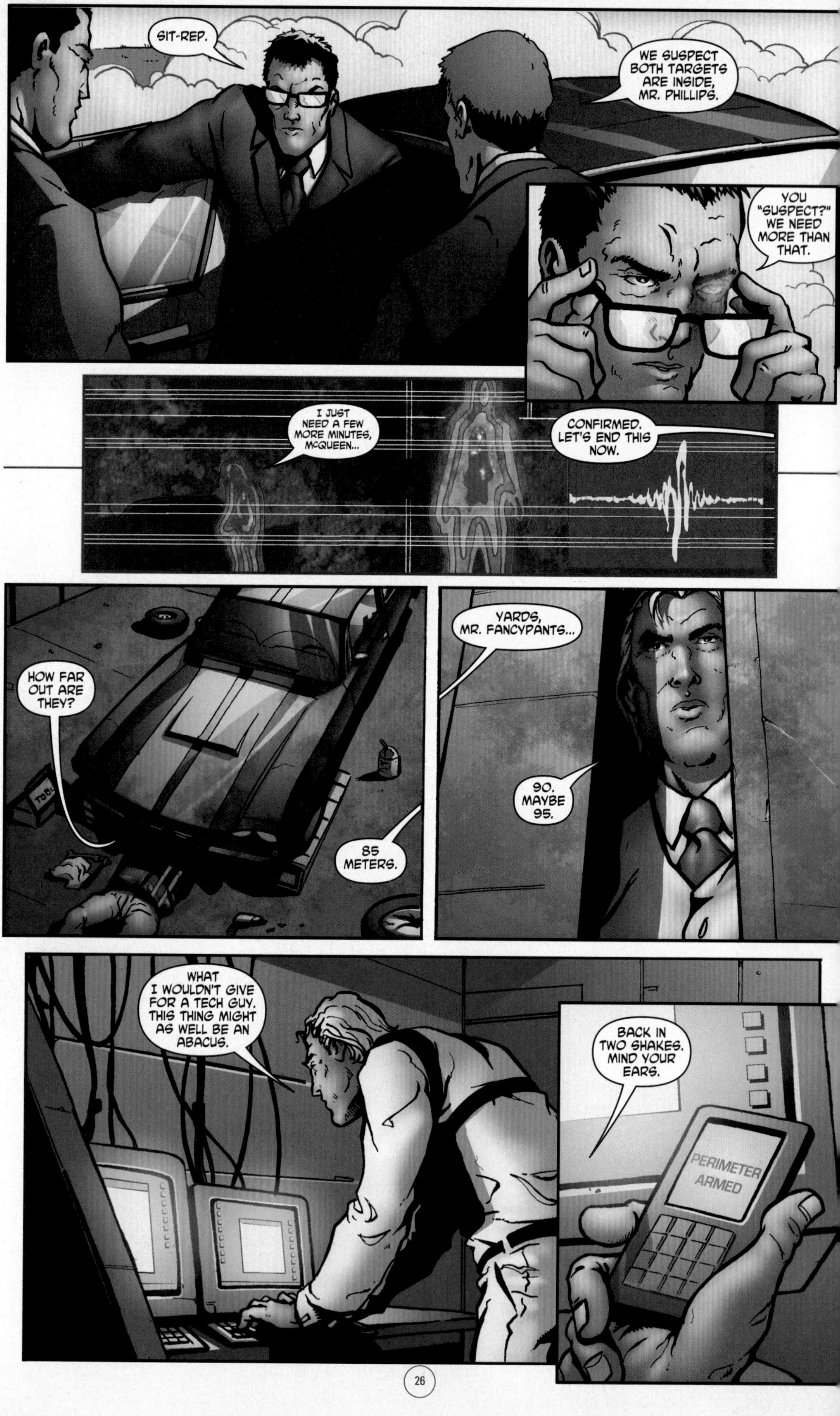
SIT-REP.
WE SUSPECT BOTH TARGETS ARE INSIDE, MR. PHILLIPS.
YOU "SUSPECT?" WE NEED MORE THAN THAT.
I JUST NEED A FEW MORE MINUTES, McQUEEN...
CONFIRMED. LET'S END THIS NOW.
HOW FAR OUT ARE THEY?
85 METERS.
YARDS, MR. FANCYPANTS...
90. MAYBE 95.
WHAT I WOULDN'T GIVE FOR A TECH GUY. THIS THING MIGHT AS WELL BE AN ABACUS.
BACK IN TWO SHAKES. MIND YOUR EARS.
PERIMETER ARMED

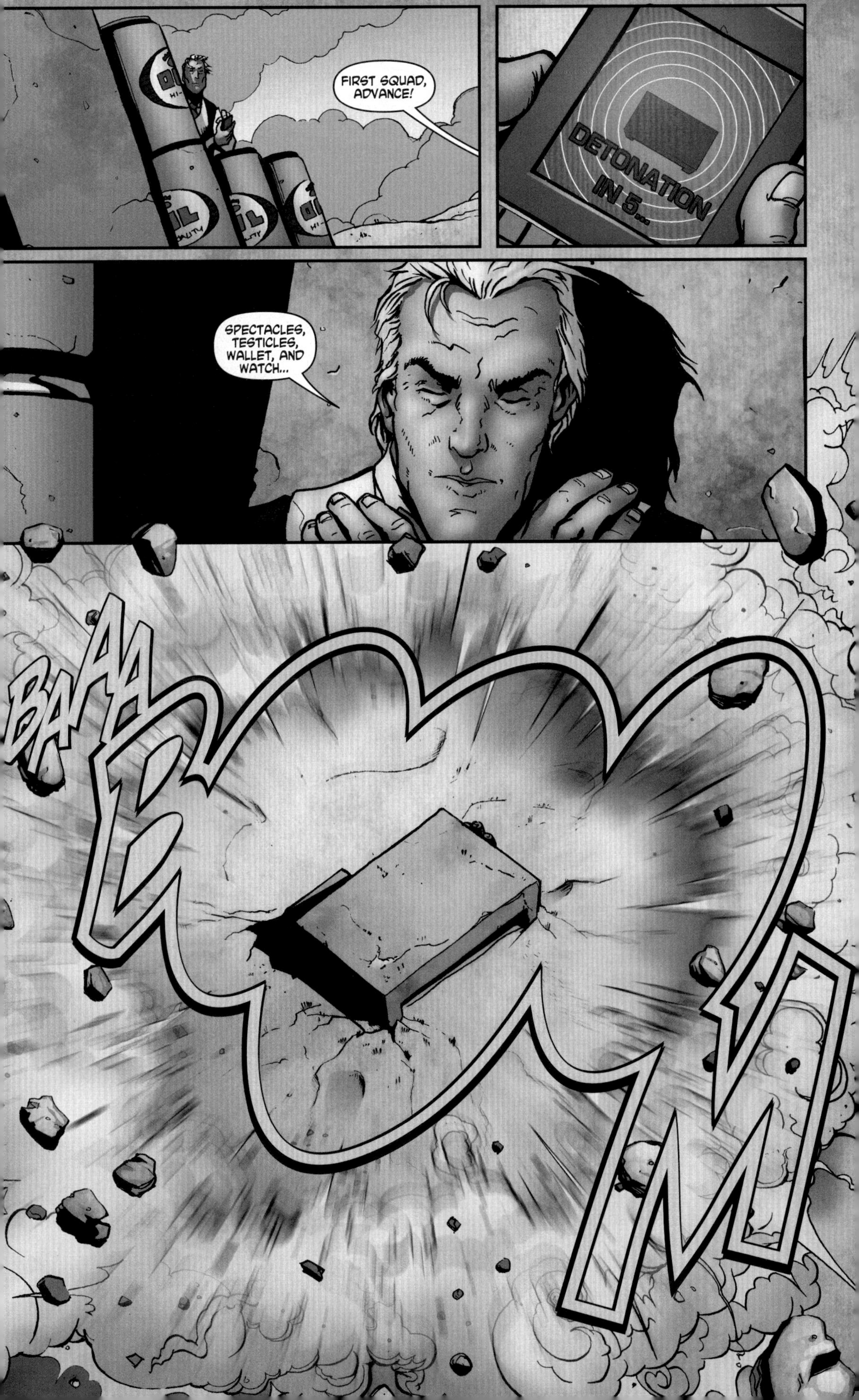
FIRST SQUAD, ADVANCE!
DETONATION IN 5...
SPECTACLES, TESTICLES, WALLET, AND WATCH...
BAAADOOM

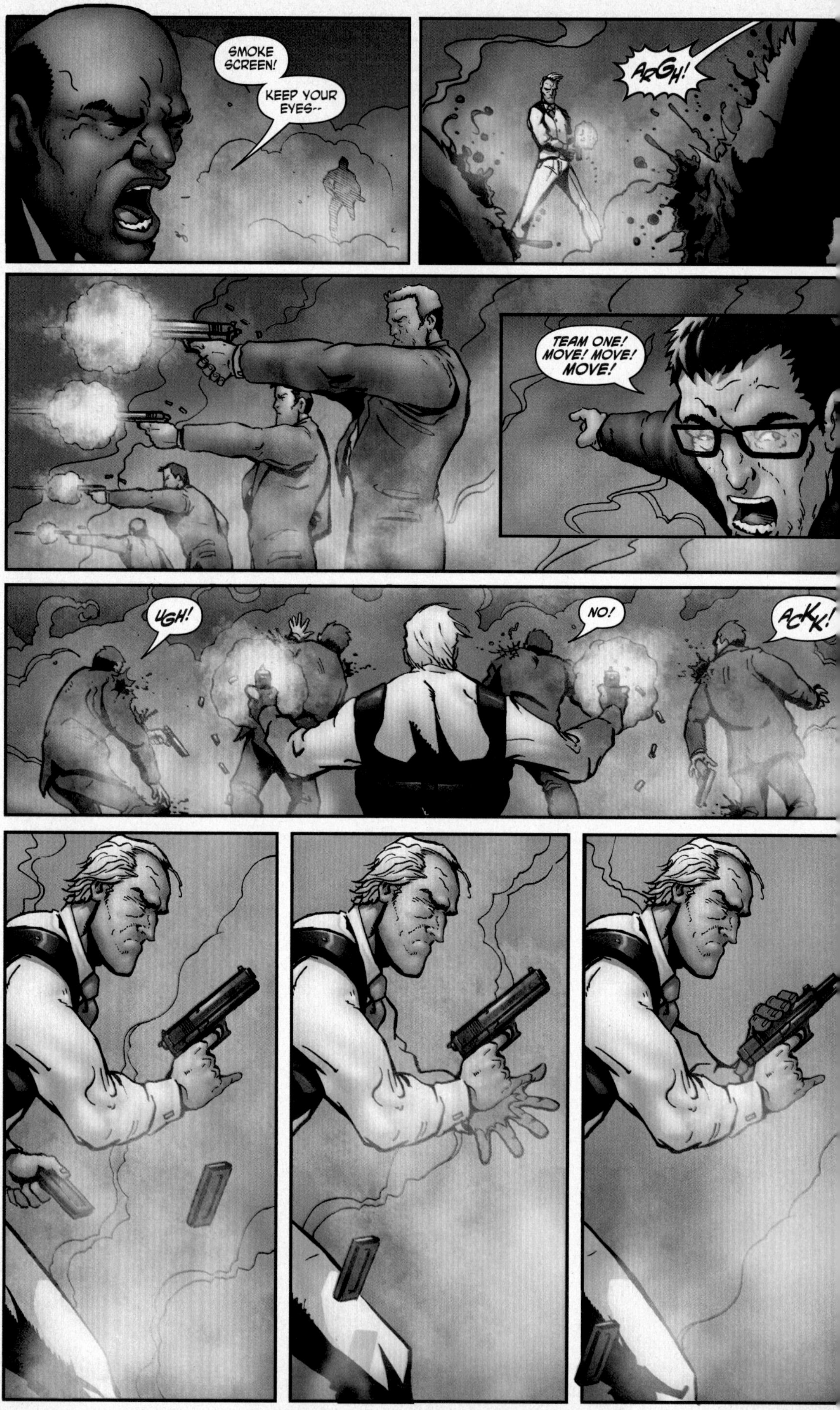
SMOKE SCREEN!
KEEP YOUR EYES--
ARGH!
TEAM ONE! MOVE! MOVE! MOVE!
UGH!
NO!
ACKK!

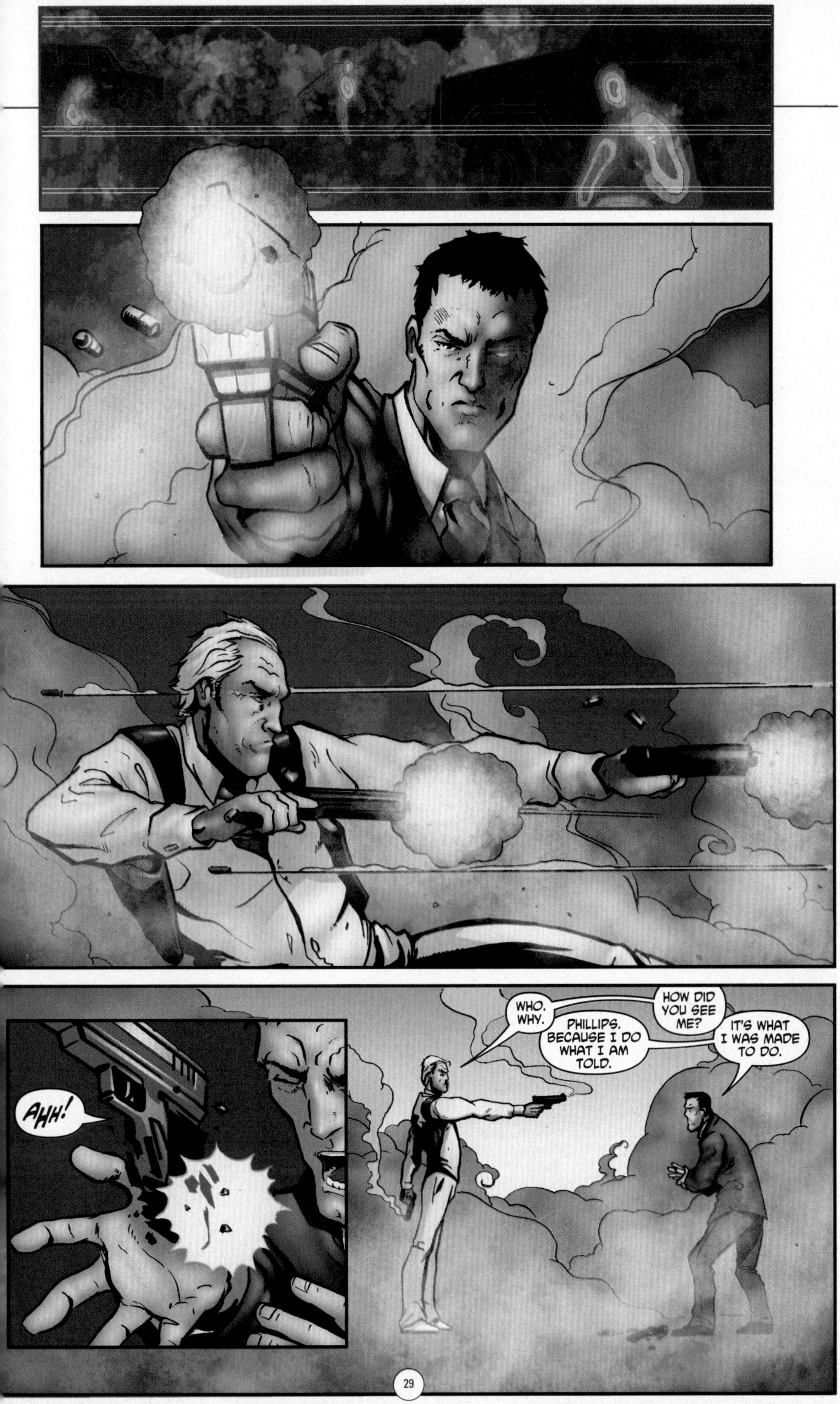
AHH!
WHO. WHY.
PHILLIPS. BECAUSE I DO WHAT I AM TOLD.
HOW DID YOU SEE ME?
IT'S WHAT I WAS MADE TO DO.

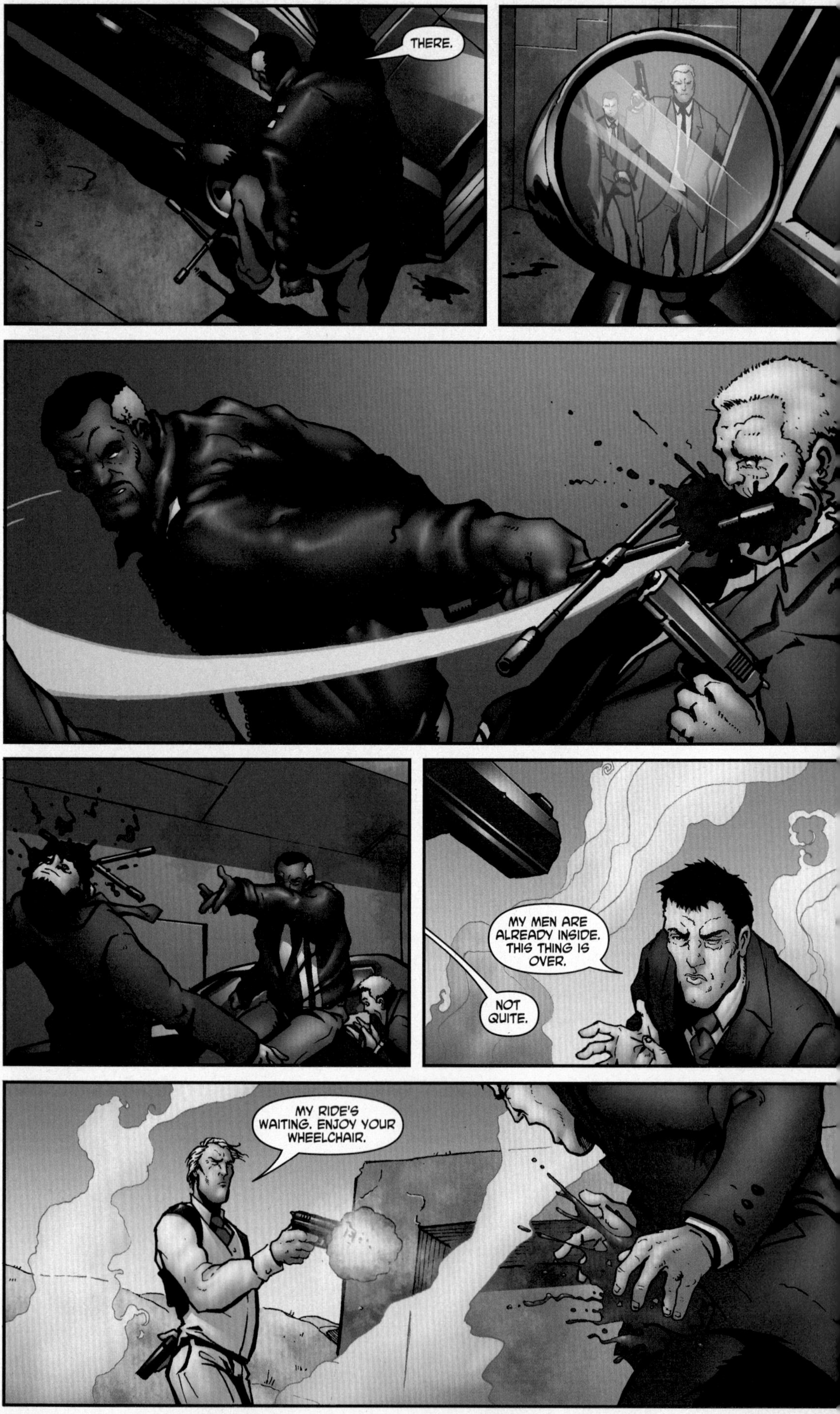
THERE.
MY MEN ARE ALREADY INSIDE. THIS THING IS OVER.
NOT QUITE.
MY RIDE'S WAITING. ENJOY YOUR WHEELCHAIR.

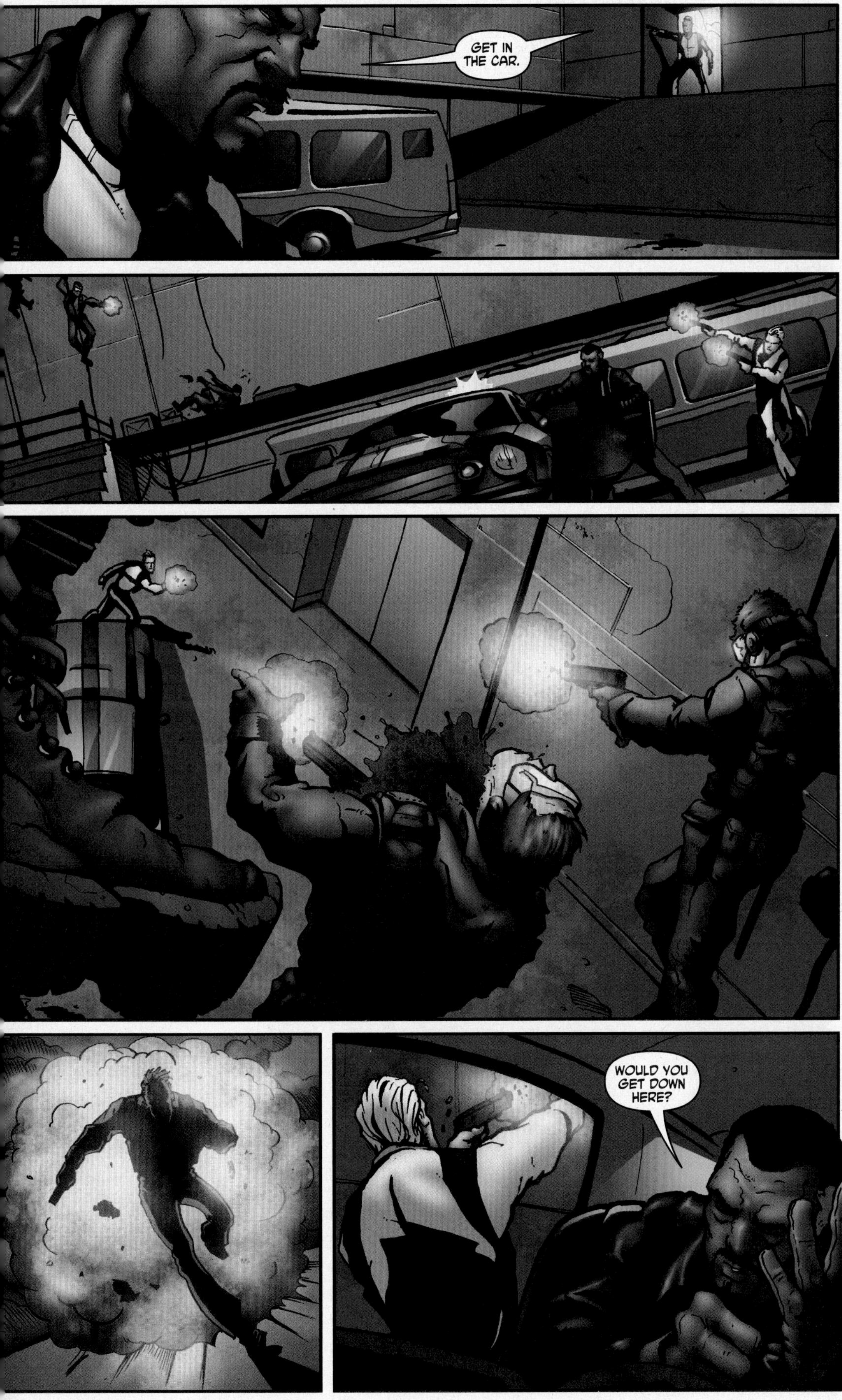
GET IN THE CAR.
WOULD YOU GET DOWN HERE?

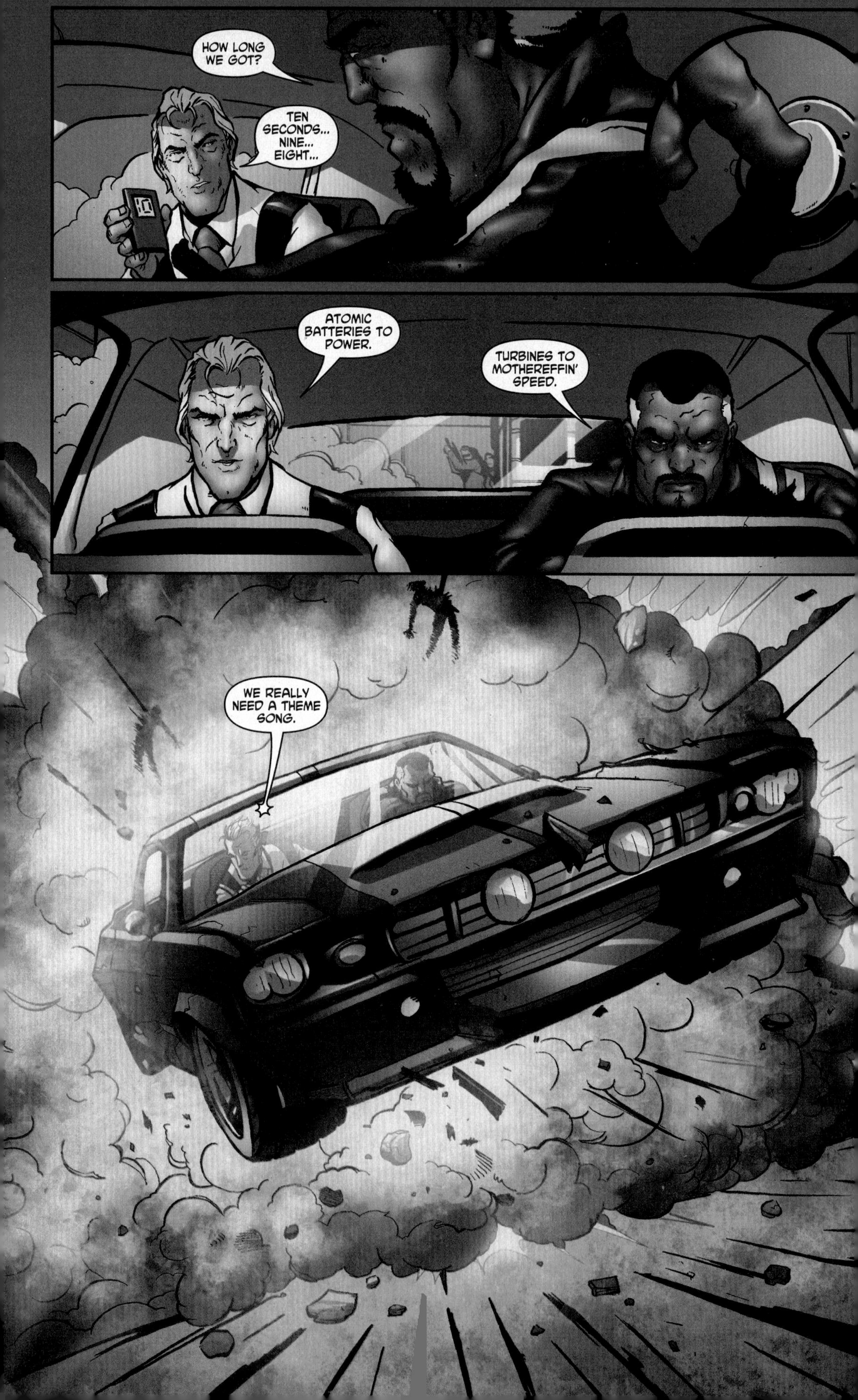
HOW LONG WE GOT?
TEN SECONDS... NINE... EIGHT...
ATOMIC BATTERIES TO POWER.
TURBINES TO MOTHEREFFIN' SPEED.
WE REALLY NEED A THEME SONG.

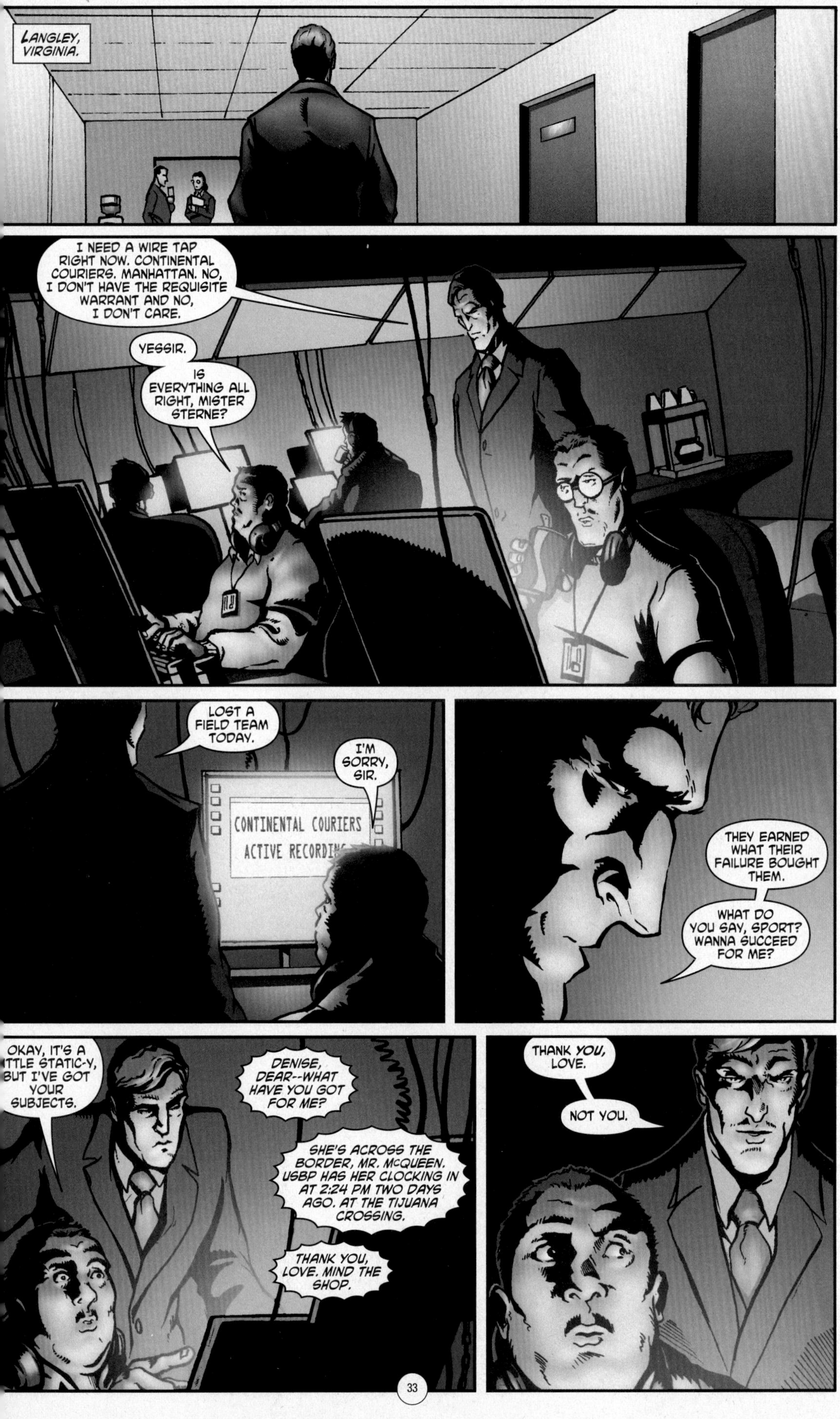
LANGLEY, VIRGINIA.
I NEED A WIRE TAP RIGHT NOW. CONTINENTAL COURIERS. MANHATTAN. NO, I DON'T HAVE THE REQUISITE WARRANT AND NO, I DON'T CARE.
YESSIR.
IS EVERYTHING ALL RIGHT, MISTER STERNE?
LOST A FIELD TEAM TODAY.
I'M SORRY, SIR.
CONTINENTAL COURIERS
ACTIVE RECORDING
THEY EARNED WHAT THEIR FAILURE BOUGHT THEM.
WHAT DO YOU SAY, SPORT? WANNA SUCCEED FOR ME?
OKAY, IT'S A LITTLE STATIC-Y, BUT I'VE GOT YOUR SUBJECTS.
DENISE, DEAR--WHAT HAVE YOU GOT FOR ME?
SHE'S ACROSS THE BORDER, MR. McQUEEN. USBP HAS HER CLOCKING IN AT 2:24 PM TWO DAYS AGO. AT THE TIJUANA CROSSING.
THANK YOU, LOVE. MIND THE SHOP.
THANK YOU, LOVE.
NOT YOU.

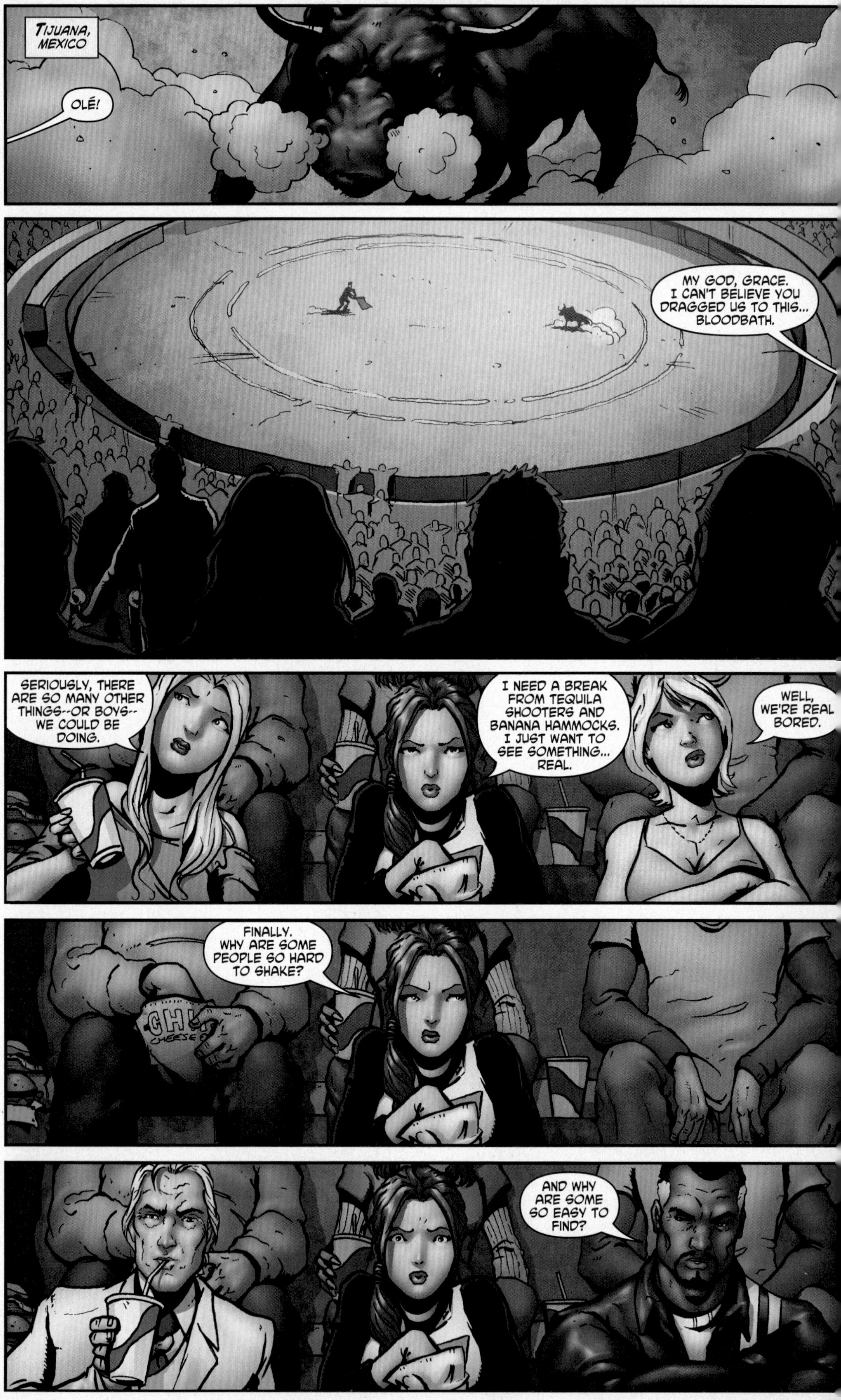
TIJUANA, MEXICO
OLÉ!
MY GOD, GRACE. I CAN'T BELIEVE YOU DRAGGED US TO THIS... BLOODBATH.
SERIOUSLY, THERE ARE SO MANY OTHER THINGS--OR BOYS--WE COULD BE DOING.
I NEED A BREAK FROM TEQUILA SHOOTERS AND BANANA HAMMOCKS. I JUST WANT TO SEE SOMETHING... REAL.
WELL, WE'RE REAL BORED.
FINALLY. WHY ARE SOME PEOPLE SO HARD TO SHAKE?
AND WHY ARE SOME SO EASY TO FIND?

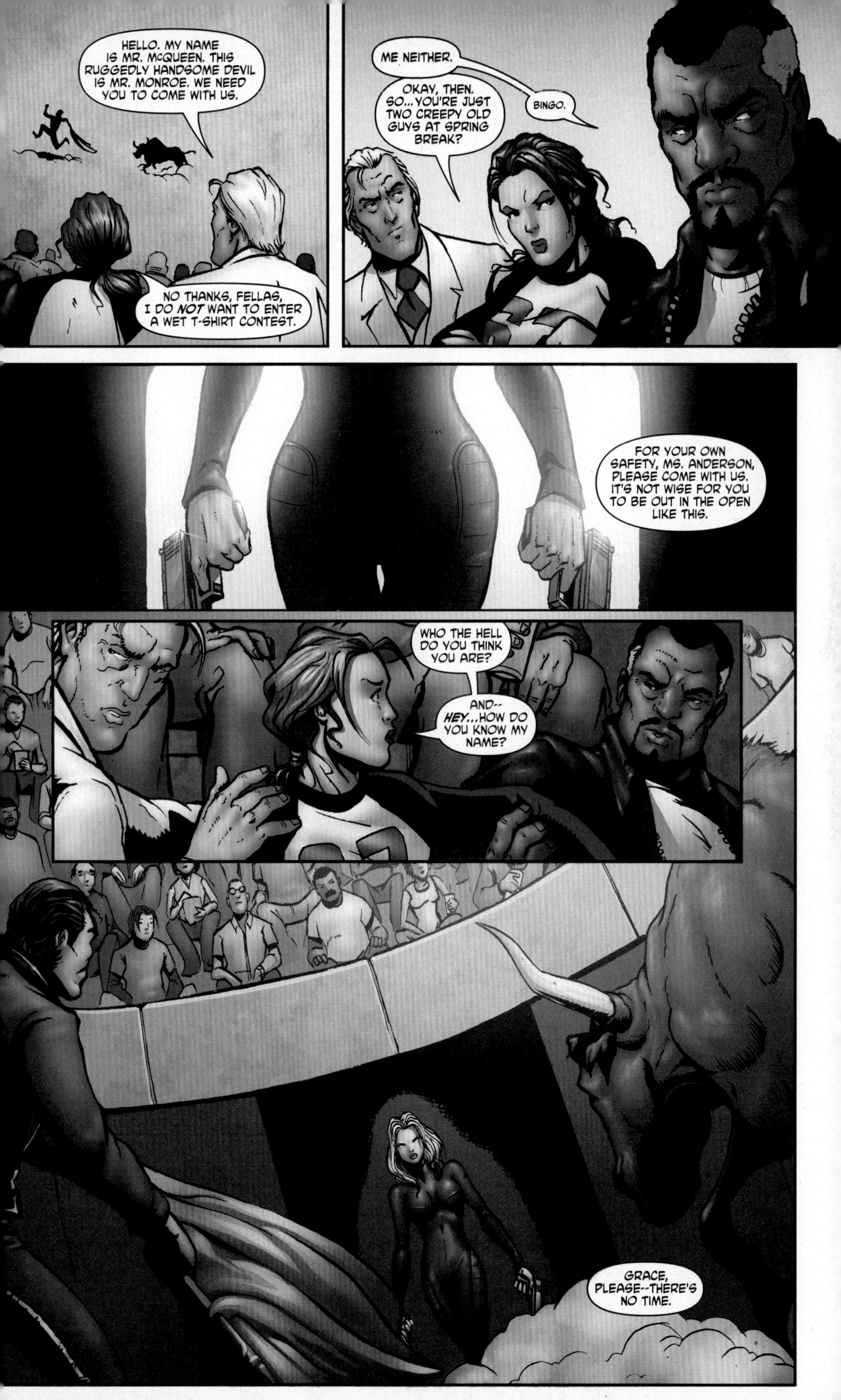
HELLO. MY NAME IS MR. McQUEEN. THIS RUGGEDLY HANDSOME DEVIL IS MR. MONROE. WE NEED YOU TO COME WITH US.
NO THANKS, FELLAS, I DO *NOT* WANT TO ENTER A WET T-SHIRT CONTEST.
ME NEITHER.
OKAY, THEN. SO... YOU'RE JUST TWO CREEPY OLD GUYS AT SPRING BREAK?
BINGO.
FOR YOUR OWN SAFETY, MS. ANDERSON, PLEASE COME WITH US. IT'S NOT WISE FOR YOU TO BE OUT IN THE OPEN LIKE THIS.
WHO THE HELL DO YOU THINK YOU ARE?
AND-- *HEY*... HOW DO YOU KNOW MY NAME?
GRACE, PLEASE--THERE'S NO TIME.

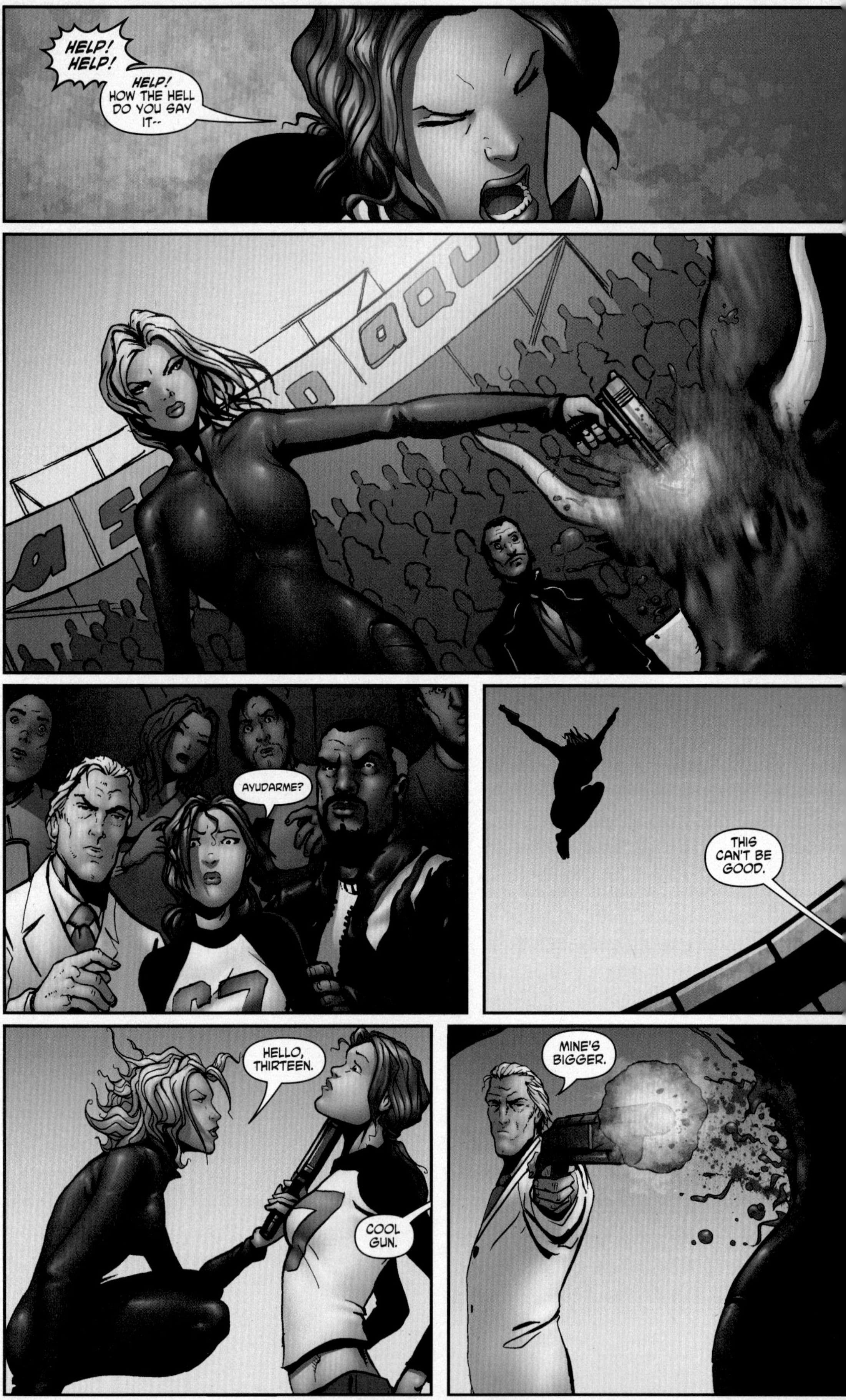
HELP! HELP!
HELP! HOW THE HELL DO YOU SAY IT--
AYUDARME?
THIS CAN'T BE GOOD.
HELLO, THIRTEEN.
COOL GUN.
MINE'S BIGGER.

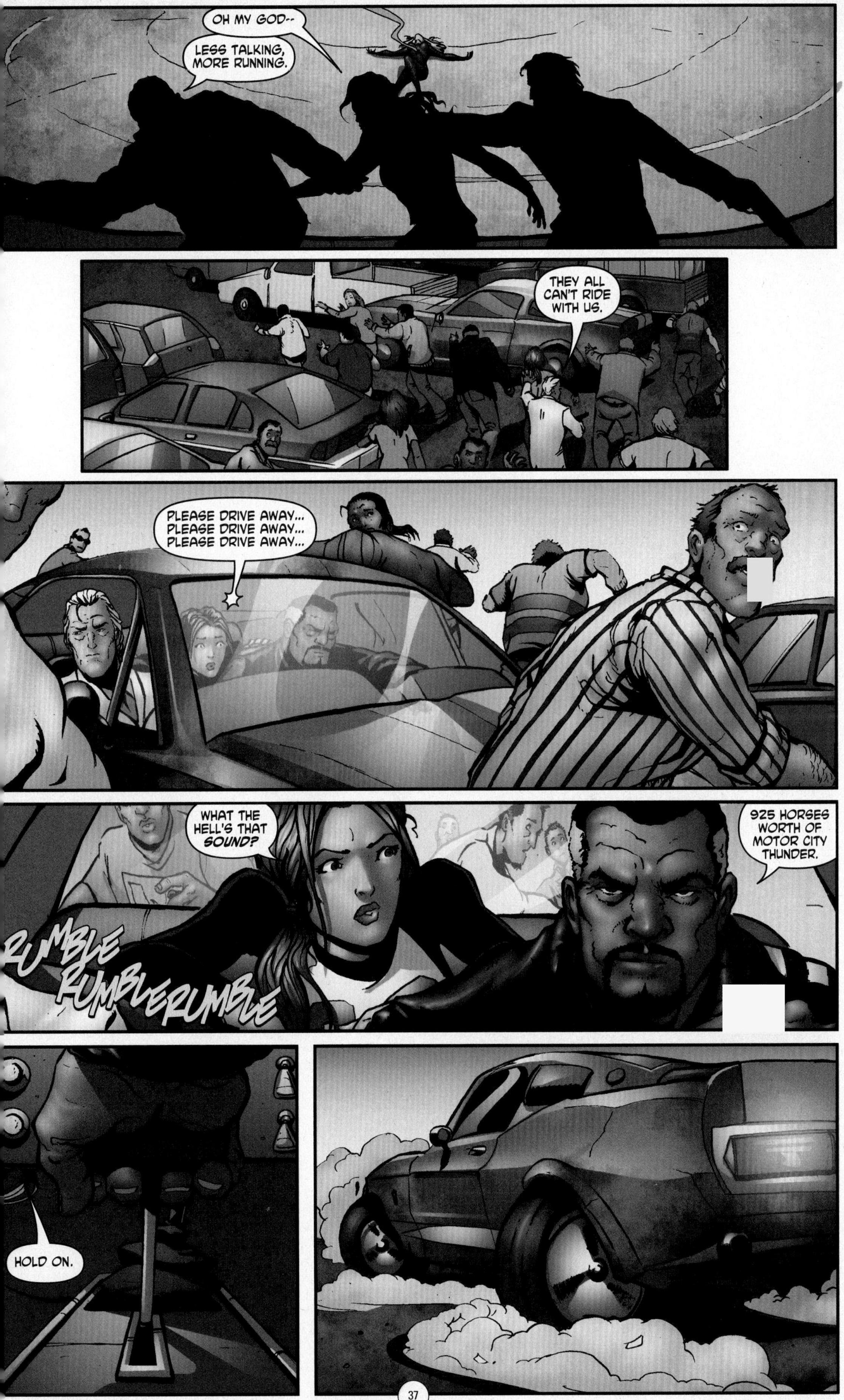
OH MY GOD--
LESS TALKING, MORE RUNNING.
THEY ALL CAN'T RIDE WITH US.
PLEASE DRIVE AWAY... PLEASE DRIVE AWAY... PLEASE DRIVE AWAY...
WHAT THE HELL'S THAT SOUND?
925 HORSES WORTH OF MOTOR CITY THUNDER.
RUMBLE RUMBLERUMBLE
HOLD ON.

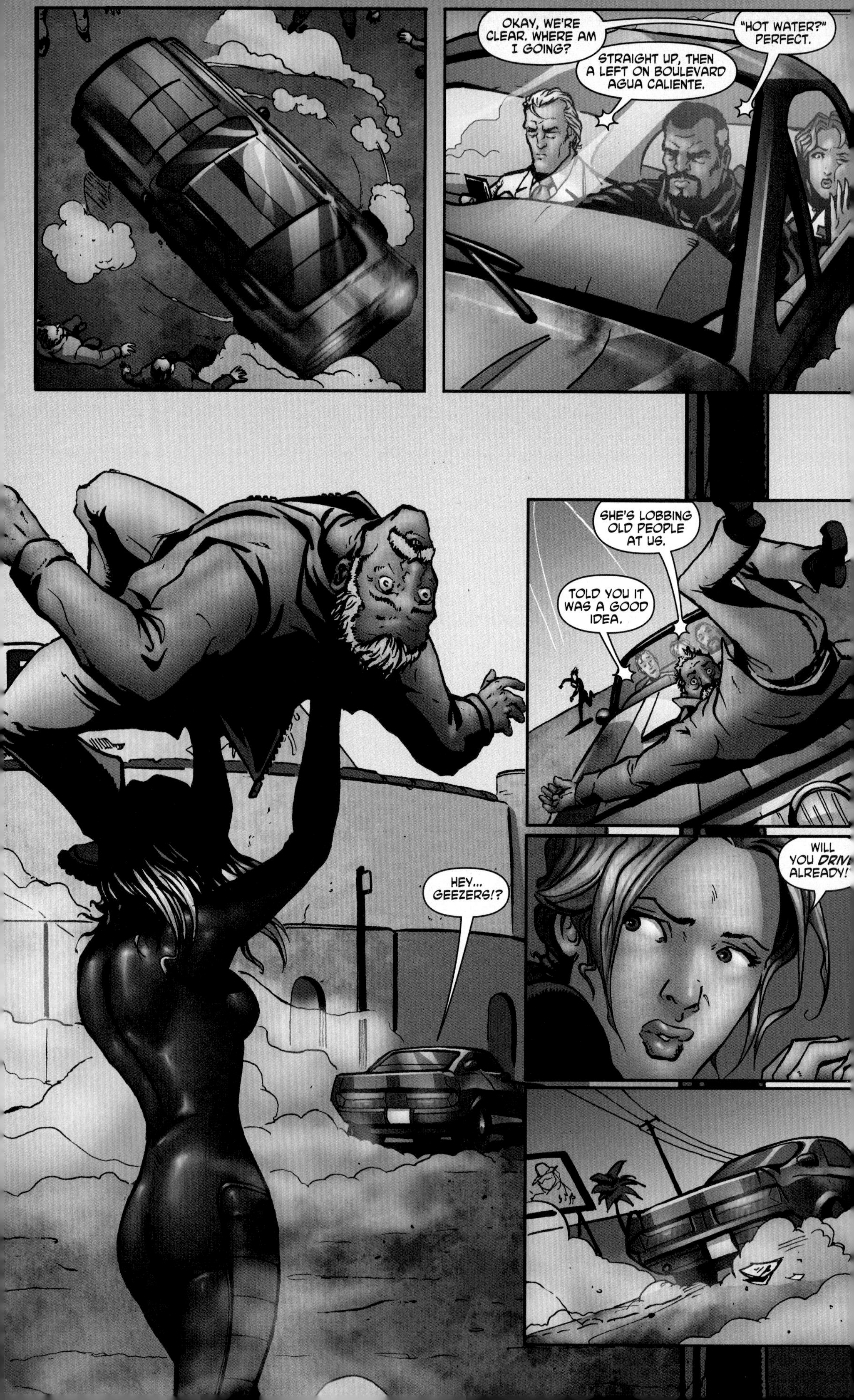
OKAY, WE'RE CLEAR. WHERE AM I GOING?
STRAIGHT UP, THEN A LEFT ON BOULEVARD AGUA CALIENTE.
"HOT WATER?" PERFECT.
SHE'S LOBBING OLD PEOPLE AT US.
TOLD YOU IT WAS A GOOD IDEA.
HEY... GEEZERS!?
WILL YOU *DRIV* ALREADY!

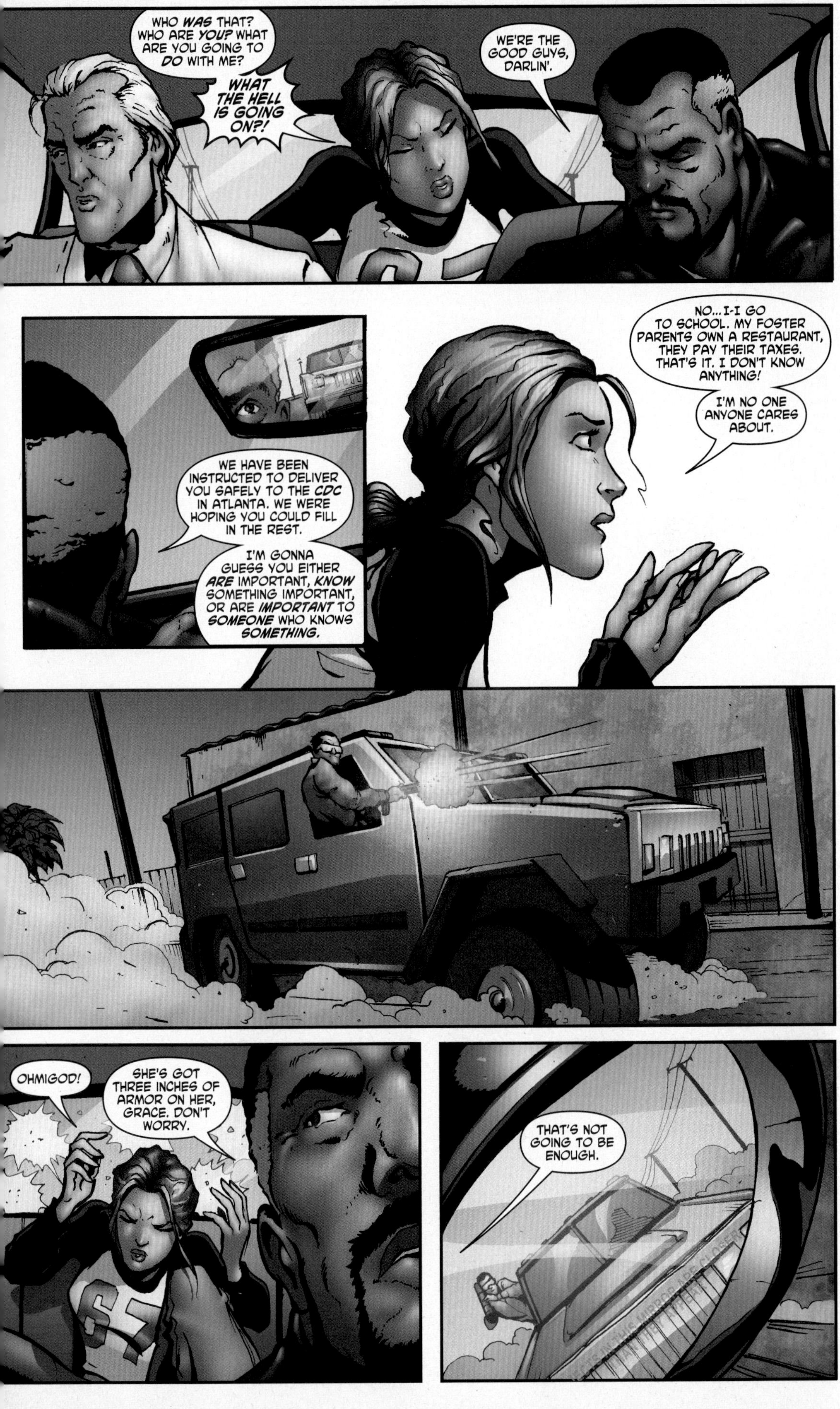
WHO *WAS* THAT? WHO ARE *YOU?* WHAT ARE YOU GOING TO *DO* WITH ME?
WHAT THE HELL IS GOING ON?!
WE'RE THE GOOD GUYS, DARLIN'.
WE HAVE BEEN INSTRUCTED TO DELIVER YOU SAFELY TO THE *CDC* IN ATLANTA. WE WERE HOPING YOU COULD FILL IN THE REST.
I'M GONNA GUESS YOU EITHER *ARE* IMPORTANT, *KNOW* SOMETHING IMPORTANT, OR ARE *IMPORTANT* TO *SOMEONE* WHO KNOWS *SOMETHING.*
NO... I-I GO TO SCHOOL. MY FOSTER PARENTS OWN A RESTAURANT, THEY PAY THEIR TAXES. THAT'S IT. I DON'T KNOW ANYTHING!
I'M NO ONE ANYONE CARES ABOUT.
OHMIGOD!
SHE'S GOT THREE INCHES OF ARMOR ON HER, GRACE. DON'T WORRY.
THAT'S NOT GOING TO BE ENOUGH.

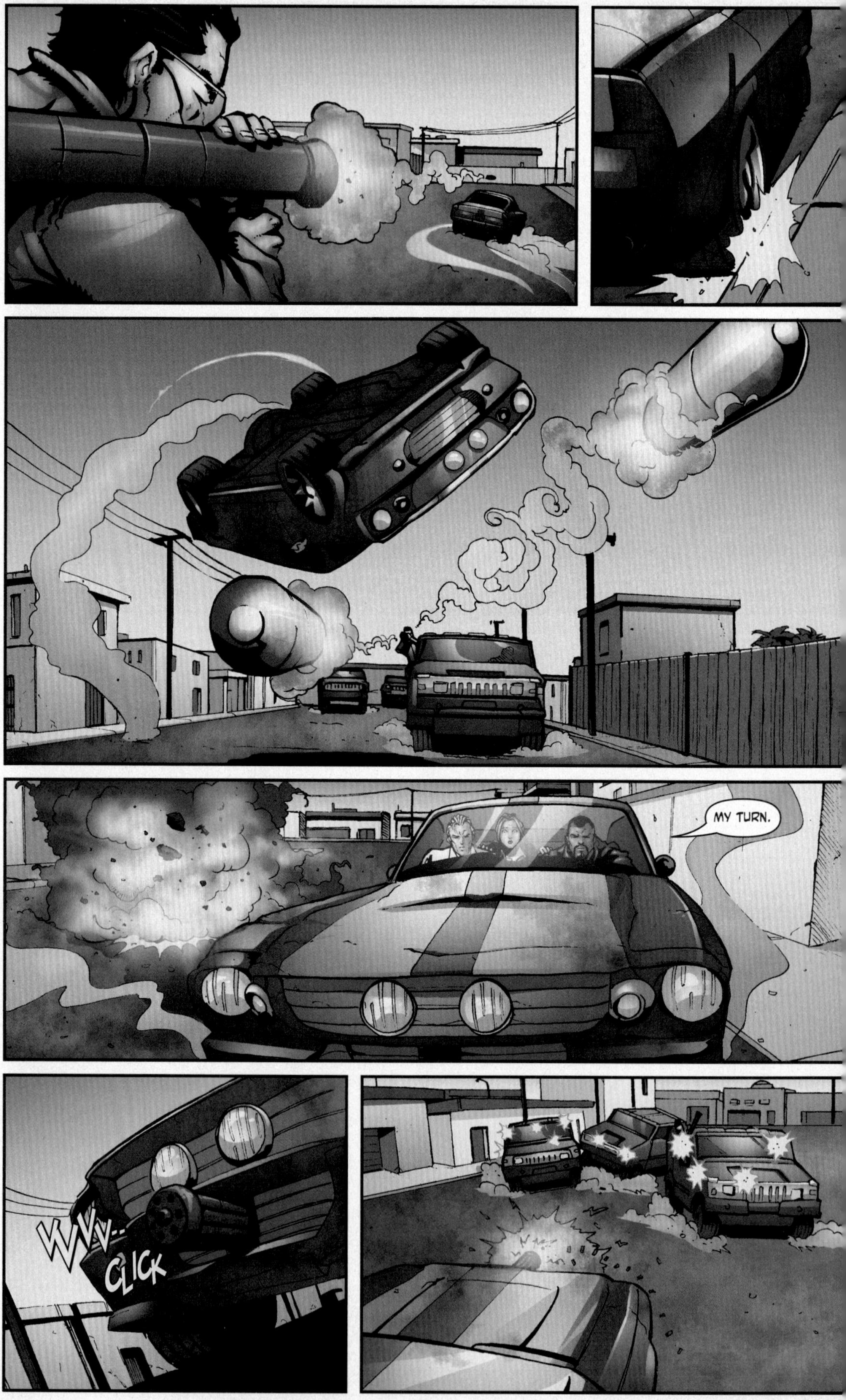
MY TURN.
WVVV...
CLICK

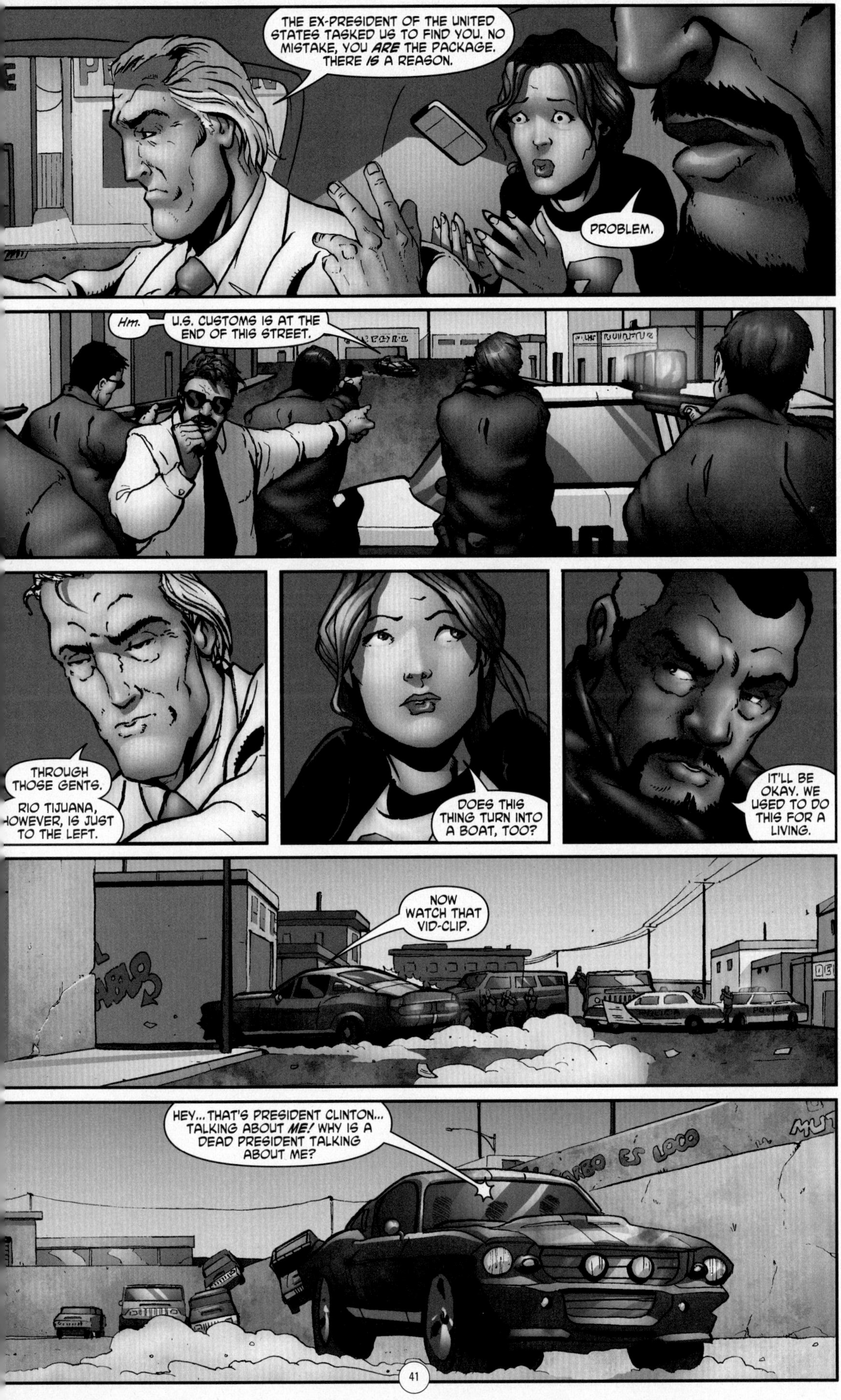
THE EX-PRESIDENT OF THE UNITED STATES TASKED US TO FIND YOU. NO MISTAKE, YOU *ARE* THE PACKAGE. THERE *IS* A REASON.
PROBLEM.
Hm.
U.S. CUSTOMS IS AT THE END OF THIS STREET.
THROUGH THOSE GENTS.
RIO TIJUANA, HOWEVER, IS JUST TO THE LEFT.
DOES THIS THING TURN INTO A BOAT, TOO?
IT'LL BE OKAY. WE USED TO DO THIS FOR A LIVING.
NOW WATCH THAT VID-CLIP.
HEY... THAT'S PRESIDENT CLINTON... TALKING ABOUT *ME!* WHY IS A DEAD PRESIDENT TALKING ABOUT ME?

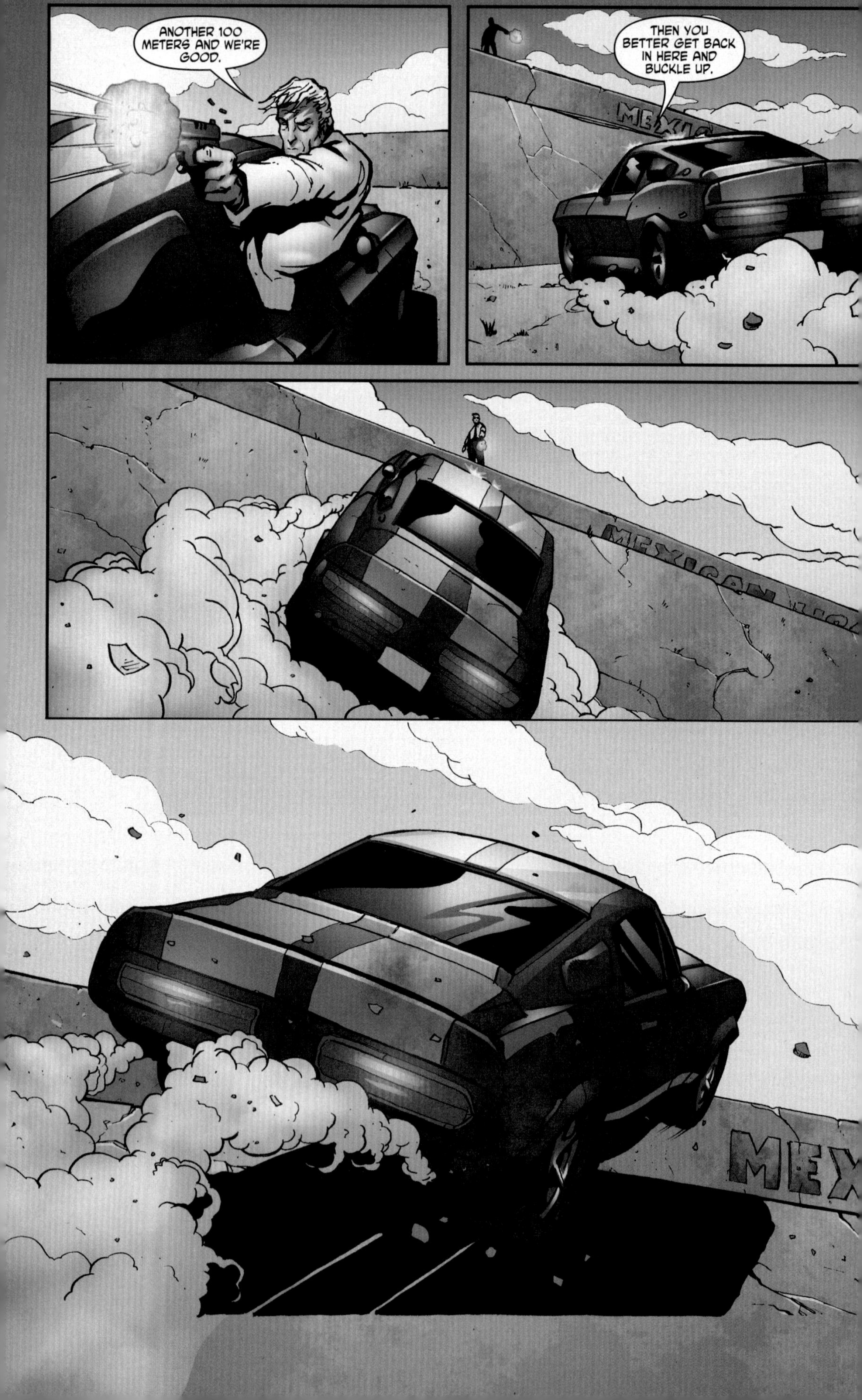
ANOTHER 100 METERS AND WE'RE GOOD.
THEN YOU BETTER GET BACK IN HERE AND BUCKLE UP.
MEXICAN

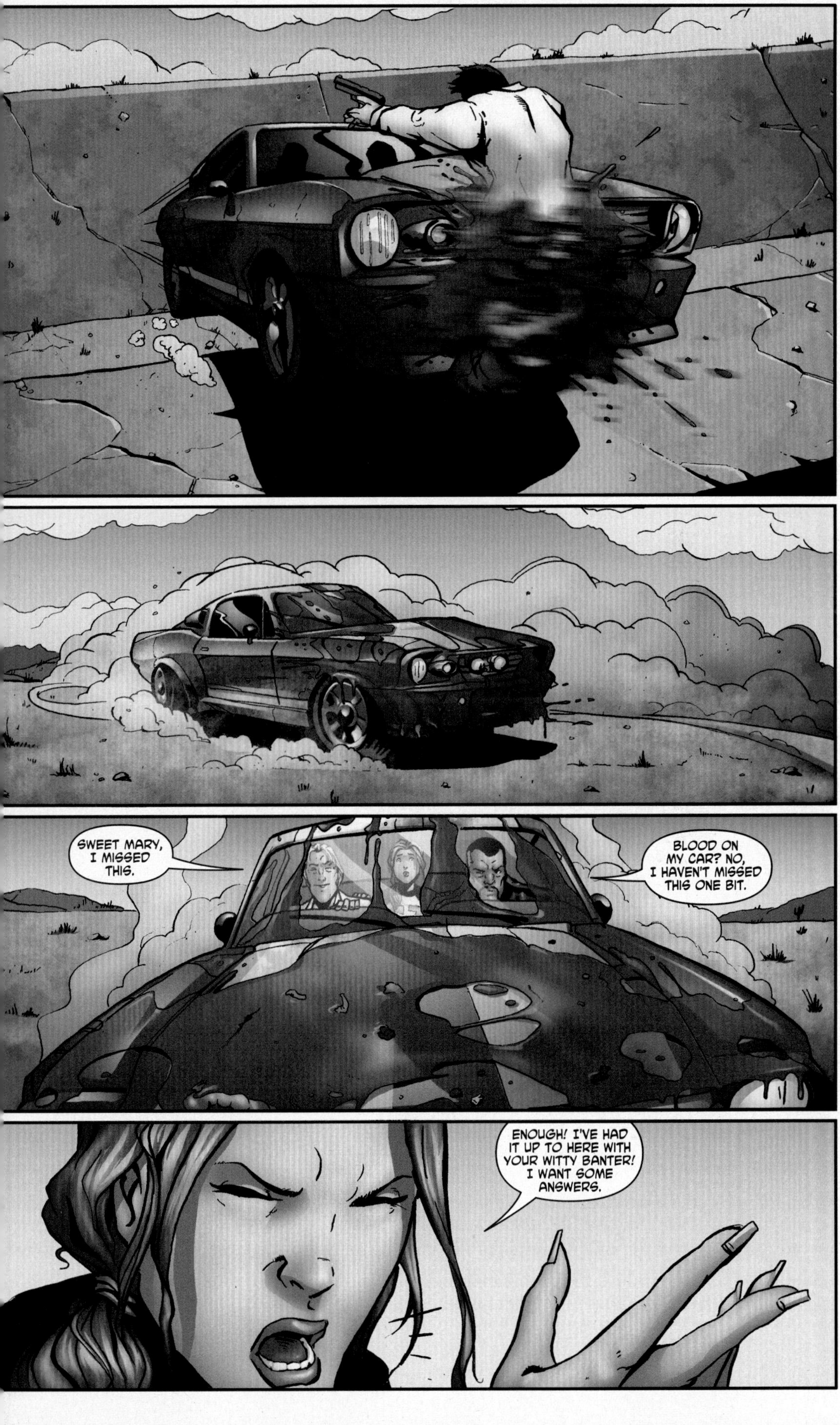
SWEET MARY, I MISSED THIS.
BLOOD ON MY CAR? NO, I HAVEN'T MISSED THIS ONE BIT.
ENOUGH! I'VE HAD IT UP TO HERE WITH YOUR WITTY BANTER! I WANT SOME ANSWERS.

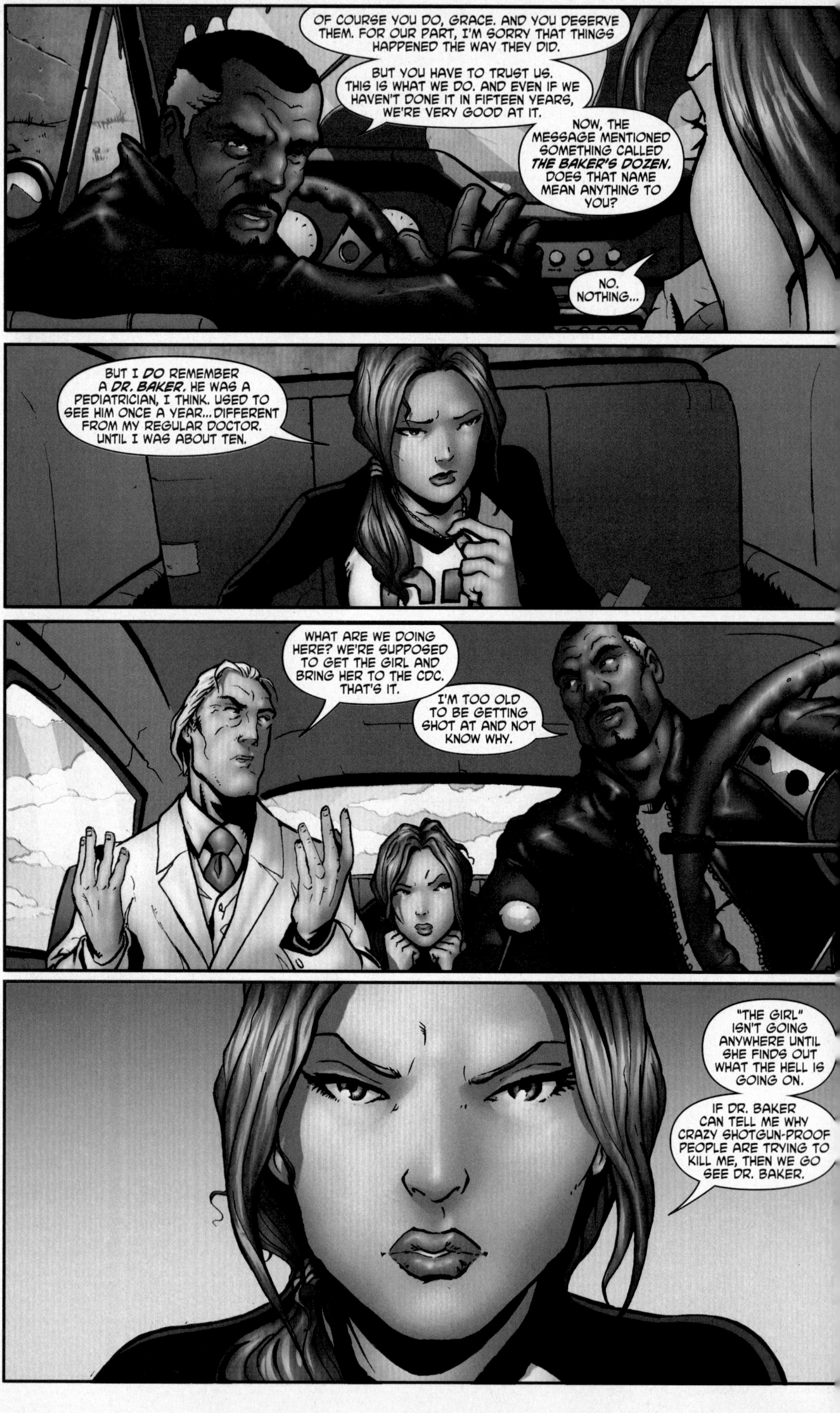
OF COURSE YOU DO, GRACE. AND YOU DESERVE THEM. FOR OUR PART, I'M SORRY THAT THINGS HAPPENED THE WAY THEY DID.
BUT YOU HAVE TO TRUST US. THIS IS WHAT WE DO. AND EVEN IF WE HAVEN'T DONE IT IN FIFTEEN YEARS, WE'RE VERY GOOD AT IT.
NOW, THE MESSAGE MENTIONED SOMETHING CALLED THE BAKER'S DOZEN. DOES THAT NAME MEAN ANYTHING TO YOU?
NO. NOTHING...
BUT I DO REMEMBER A DR. BAKER. HE WAS A PEDIATRICIAN, I THINK. USED TO SEE HIM ONCE A YEAR...DIFFERENT FROM MY REGULAR DOCTOR. UNTIL I WAS ABOUT TEN.
WHAT ARE WE DOING HERE? WE'RE SUPPOSED TO GET THE GIRL AND BRING HER TO THE CDC. THAT'S IT.
I'M TOO OLD TO BE GETTING SHOT AT AND NOT KNOW WHY.
"THE GIRL" ISN'T GOING ANYWHERE UNTIL SHE FINDS OUT WHAT THE HELL IS GOING ON.
IF DR. BAKER CAN TELL ME WHY CRAZY SHOTGUN-PROOF PEOPLE ARE TRYING TO KILL ME, THEN WE GO SEE DR. BAKER.

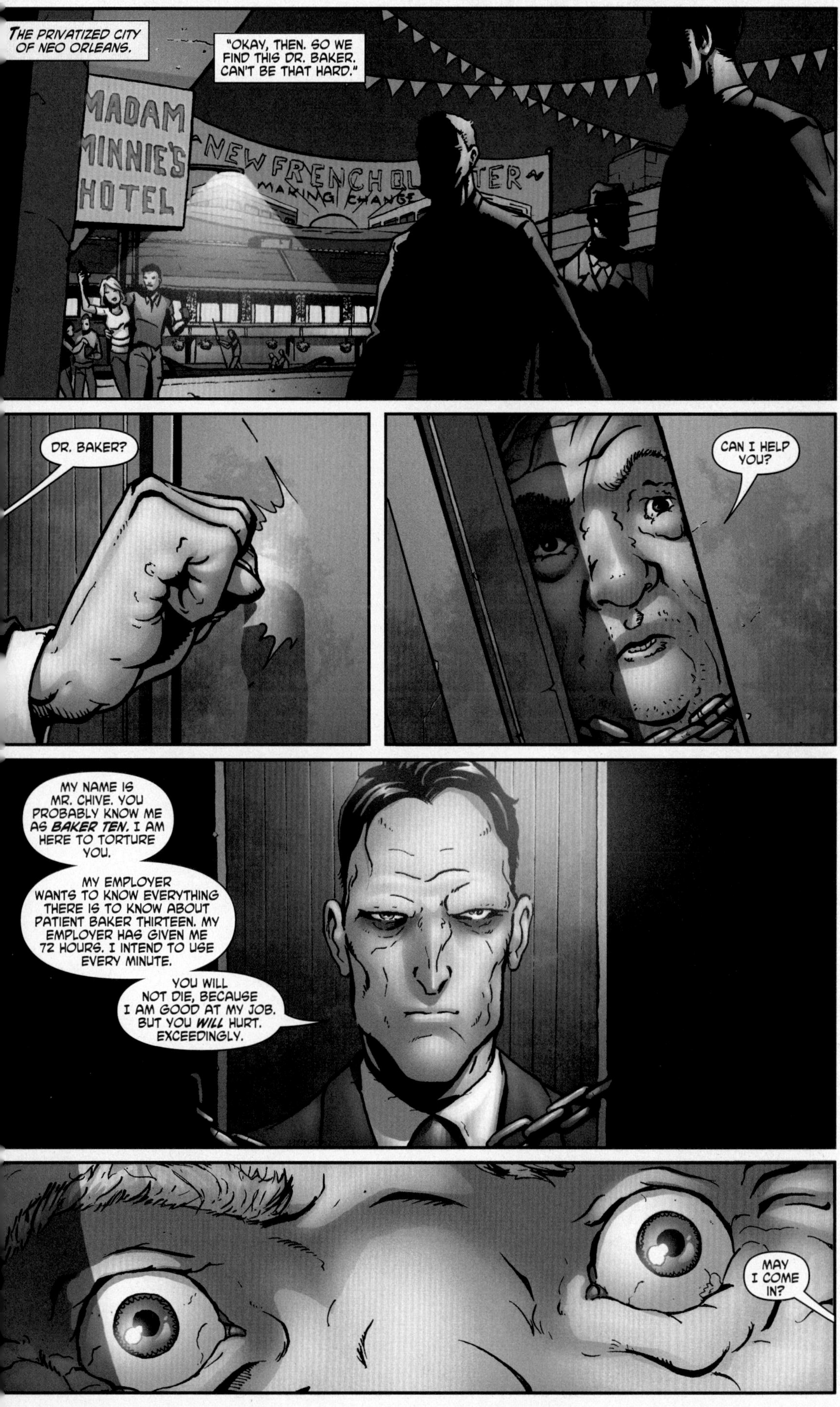
THE PRIVATIZED CITY OF NEO ORLEANS.
"OKAY, THEN. SO WE FIND THIS DR. BAKER. CAN'T BE THAT HARD."
MADAM MINNIE'S HOTEL
NEW FRENCH QUARTER
MAKING CHANGE
DR. BAKER?
CAN I HELP YOU?
MY NAME IS MR. CHIVE. YOU PROBABLY KNOW ME AS *BAKER TEN.* I AM HERE TO TORTURE YOU.
MY EMPLOYER WANTS TO KNOW EVERYTHING THERE IS TO KNOW ABOUT PATIENT BAKER THIRTEEN. MY EMPLOYER HAS GIVEN ME 72 HOURS. I INTEND TO USE EVERY MINUTE.
YOU WILL NOT DIE, BECAUSE I AM GOOD AT MY JOB. BUT YOU *WILL* HURT. EXCEEDINGLY.
MAY I COME IN?

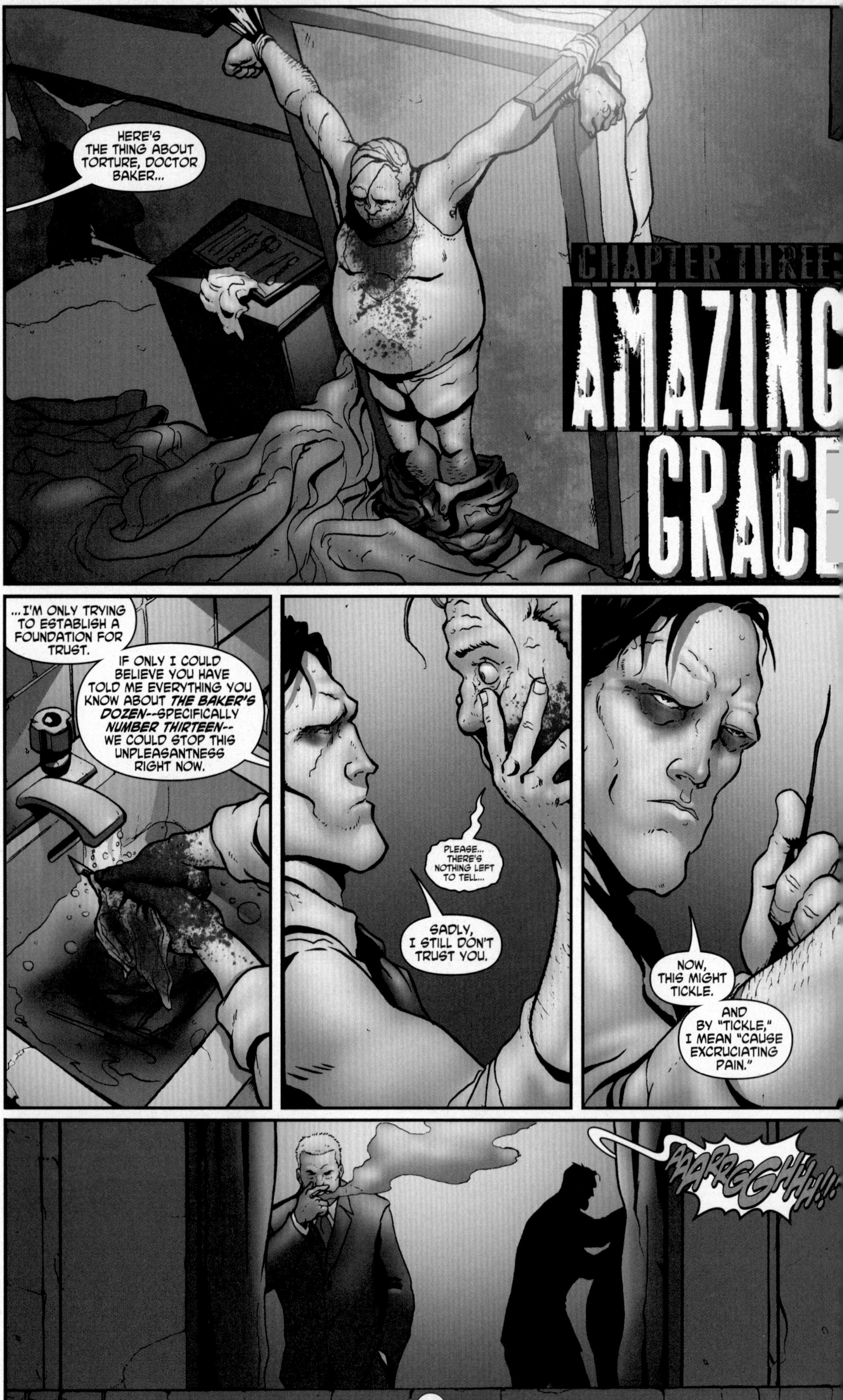
HERE'S THE THING ABOUT TORTURE, DOCTOR BAKER...
CHAPTER THREE
AMAZING GRACE
...I'M ONLY TRYING TO ESTABLISH A FOUNDATION FOR TRUST.
IF ONLY I COULD BELIEVE YOU HAVE TOLD ME EVERYTHING YOU KNOW ABOUT *THE BAKER'S DOZEN*--SPECIFICALLY *NUMBER THIRTEEN*--WE COULD STOP THIS UNPLEASANTNESS RIGHT NOW.
PLEASE... THERE'S NOTHING LEFT TO TELL...
SADLY, I STILL DON'T TRUST YOU.
NOW, THIS MIGHT TICKLE.
AND BY "TICKLE," I MEAN "CAUSE EXCRUCIATING PAIN."
AAARRGGHHH!!

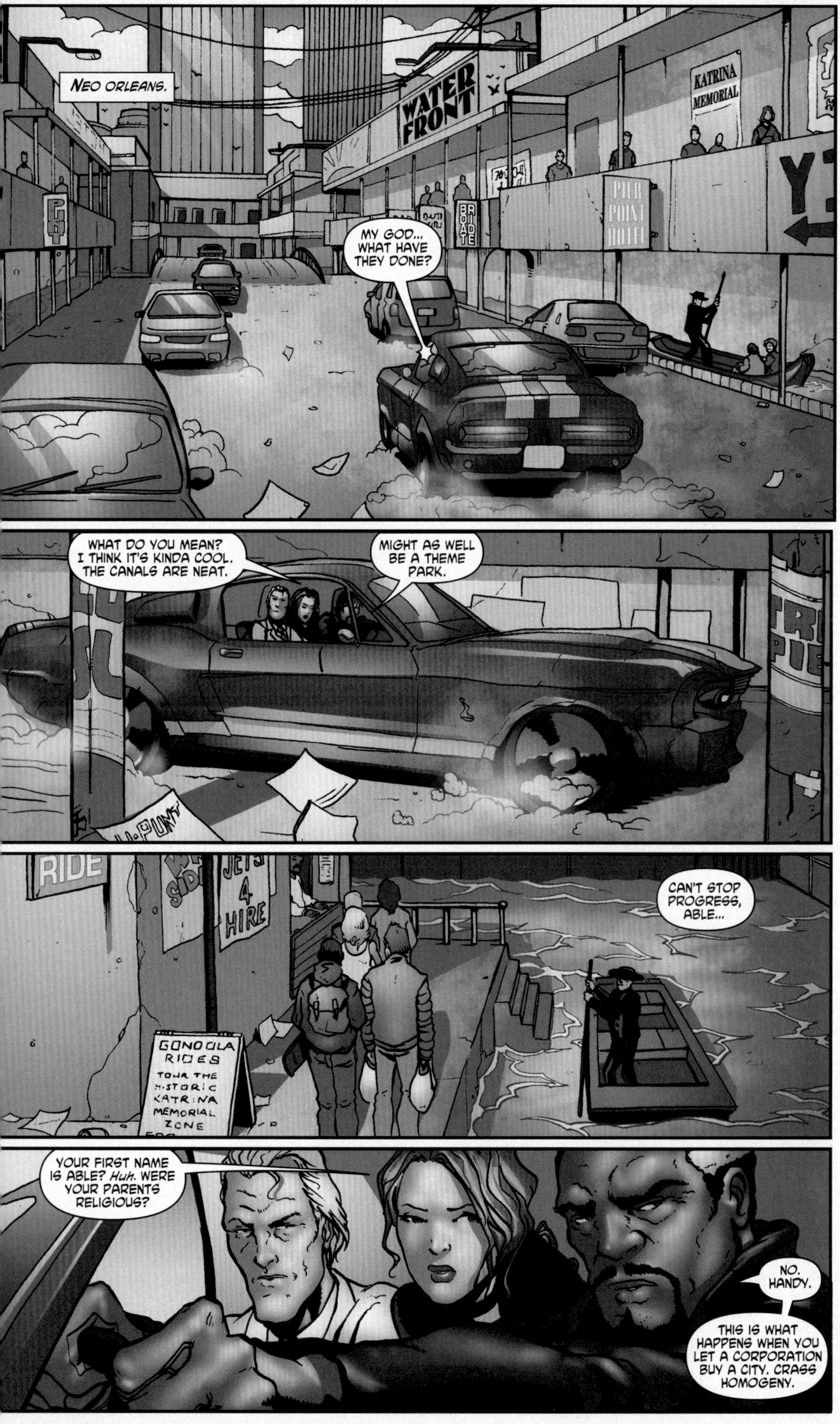
NEO ORLEANS.
WATER FRONT
KATRINA MEMORIAL
PIER POINT HOTEL
MY GOD... WHAT HAVE THEY DONE?
WHAT DO YOU MEAN? I THINK IT'S KINDA COOL. THE CANALS ARE NEAT.
MIGHT AS WELL BE A THEME PARK.
RIDE
JETS 4 HIRE
CAN'T STOP PROGRESS, ABLE...
GONDOLA RIDES TOUR THE HISTORIC KATRINA MEMORIAL ZONE
YOUR FIRST NAME IS ABLE? *Huh.* WERE YOUR PARENTS RELIGIOUS?
NO. HANDY.
THIS IS WHAT HAPPENS WHEN YOU LET A CORPORATION BUY A CITY. CRASS HOMOGENY.

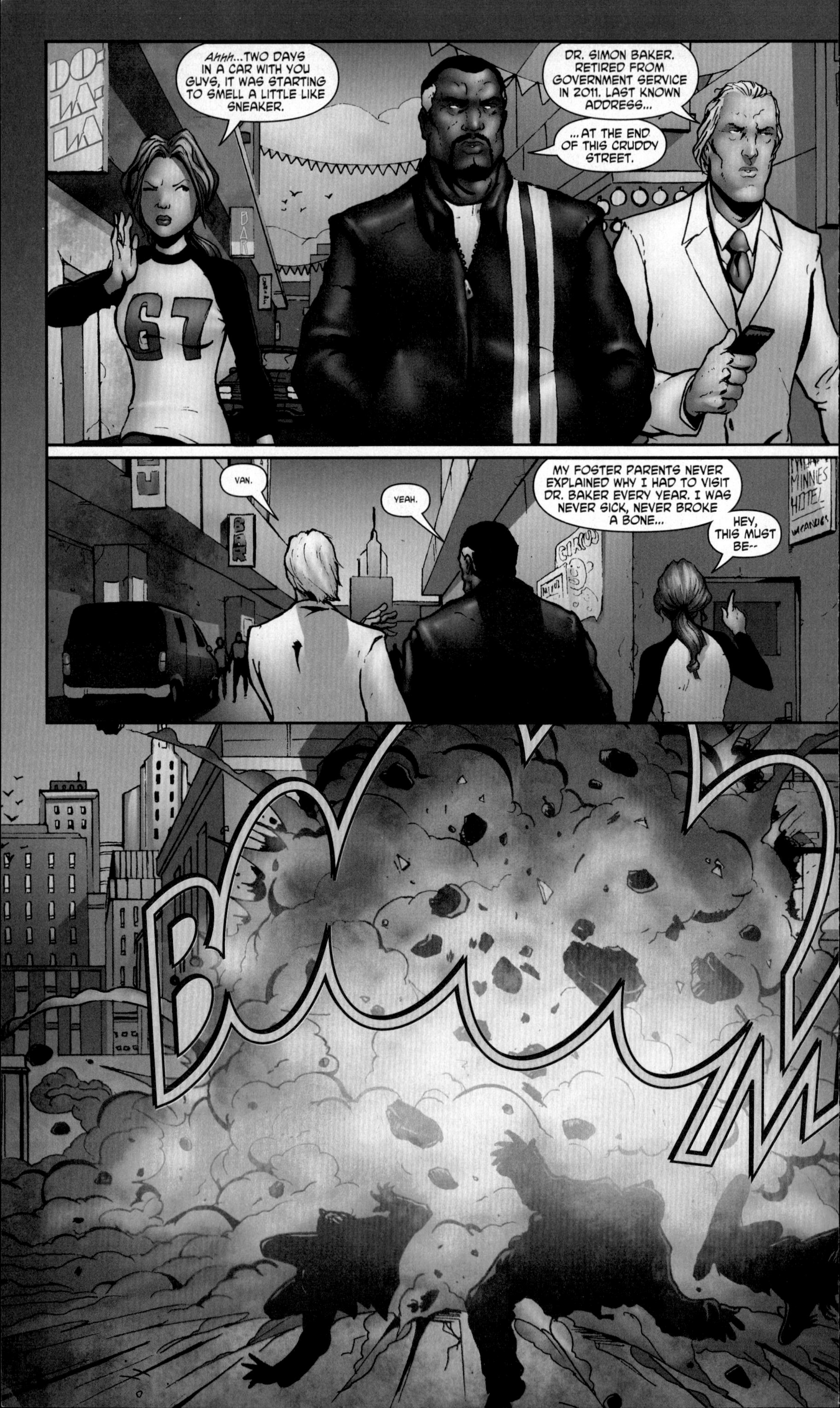

DO-WA-WA
Ahhh...TWO DAYS IN A CAR WITH YOU GUYS, IT WAS STARTING TO SMELL A LITTLE LIKE SNEAKER.
DR. SIMON BAKER. RETIRED FROM GOVERNMENT SERVICE IN 2011. LAST KNOWN ADDRESS...
...AT THE END OF THIS CRUDDY STREET.
BAR
67
VAN.
YEAH.
MY FOSTER PARENTS NEVER EXPLAINED WHY I HAD TO VISIT DR. BAKER EVERY YEAR. I WAS NEVER SICK, NEVER BROKE A BONE...
HEY, THIS MUST BE--
MINNIES HOTEL
BAR
BOOM

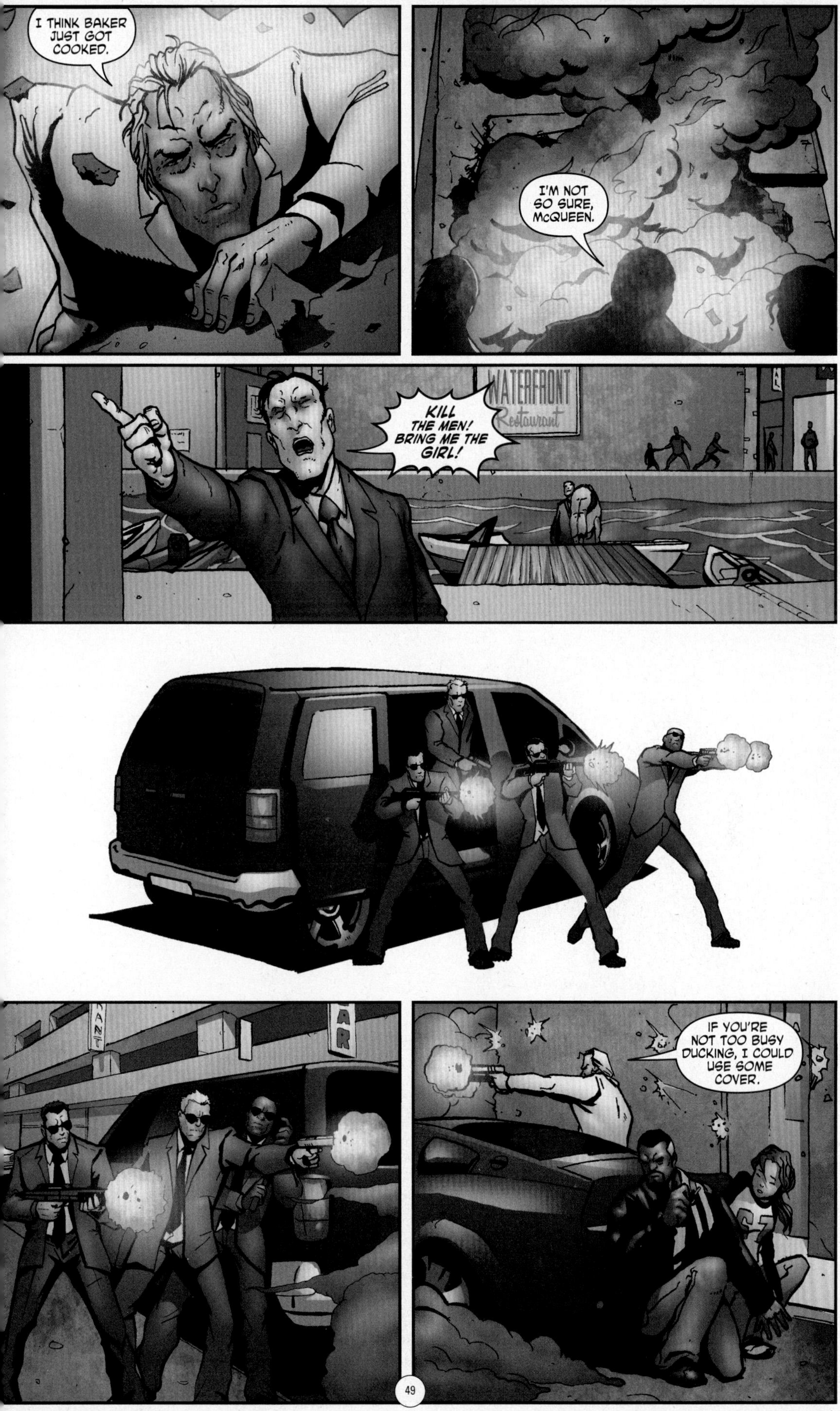
I THINK BAKER JUST GOT COOKED.
I'M NOT SO SURE, McQUEEN.
WATERFRONT Restaurant
KILL THE MEN! BRING ME THE GIRL!
IF YOU'RE NOT TOO BUSY DUCKING, I COULD USE SOME COVER.

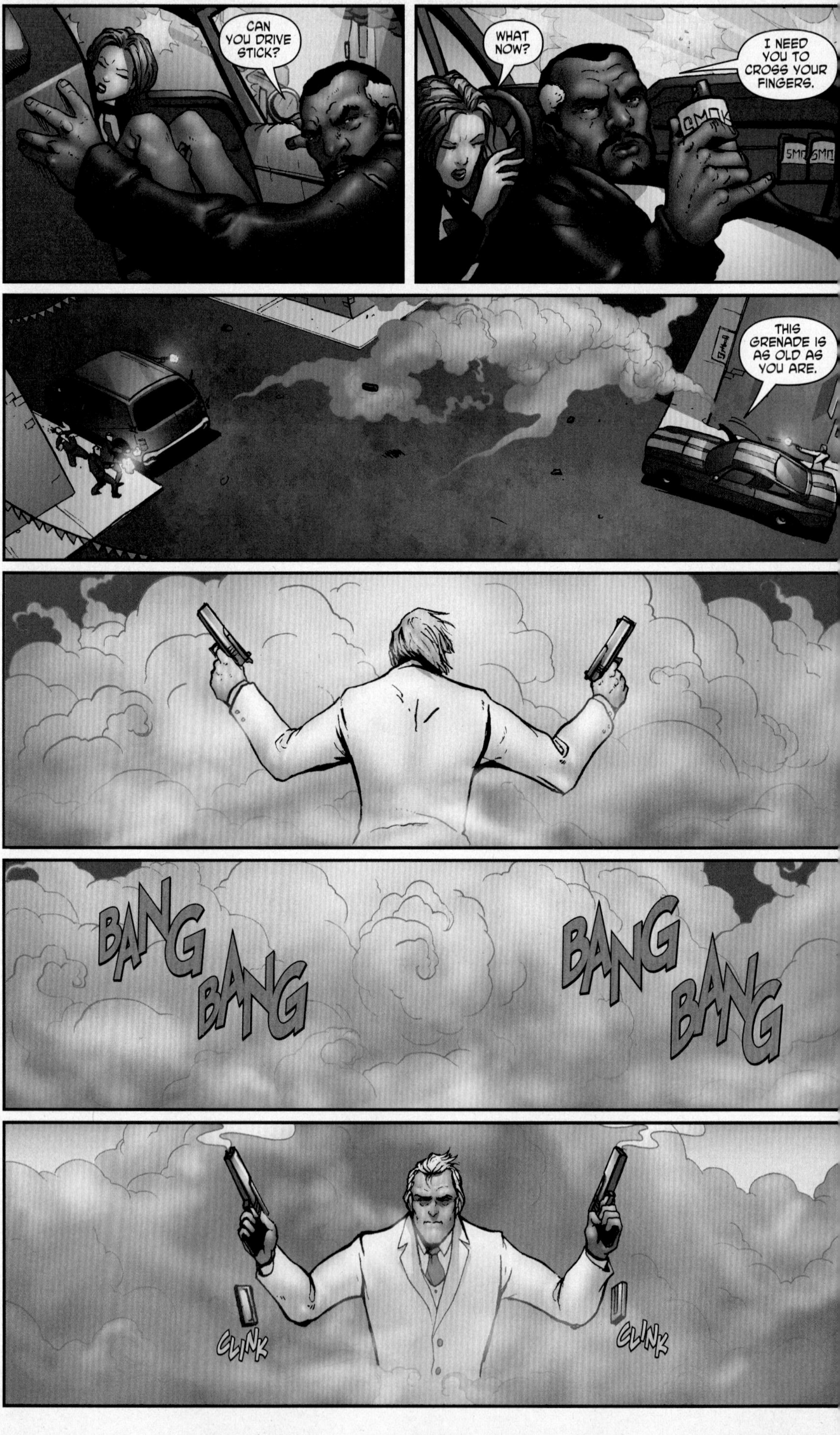
CAN YOU DRIVE STICK?
WHAT NOW?
I NEED YOU TO CROSS YOUR FINGERS.
THIS GRENADE IS AS OLD AS YOU ARE.
BANG
BANG
BANG
BANG
CLINK
CLINK

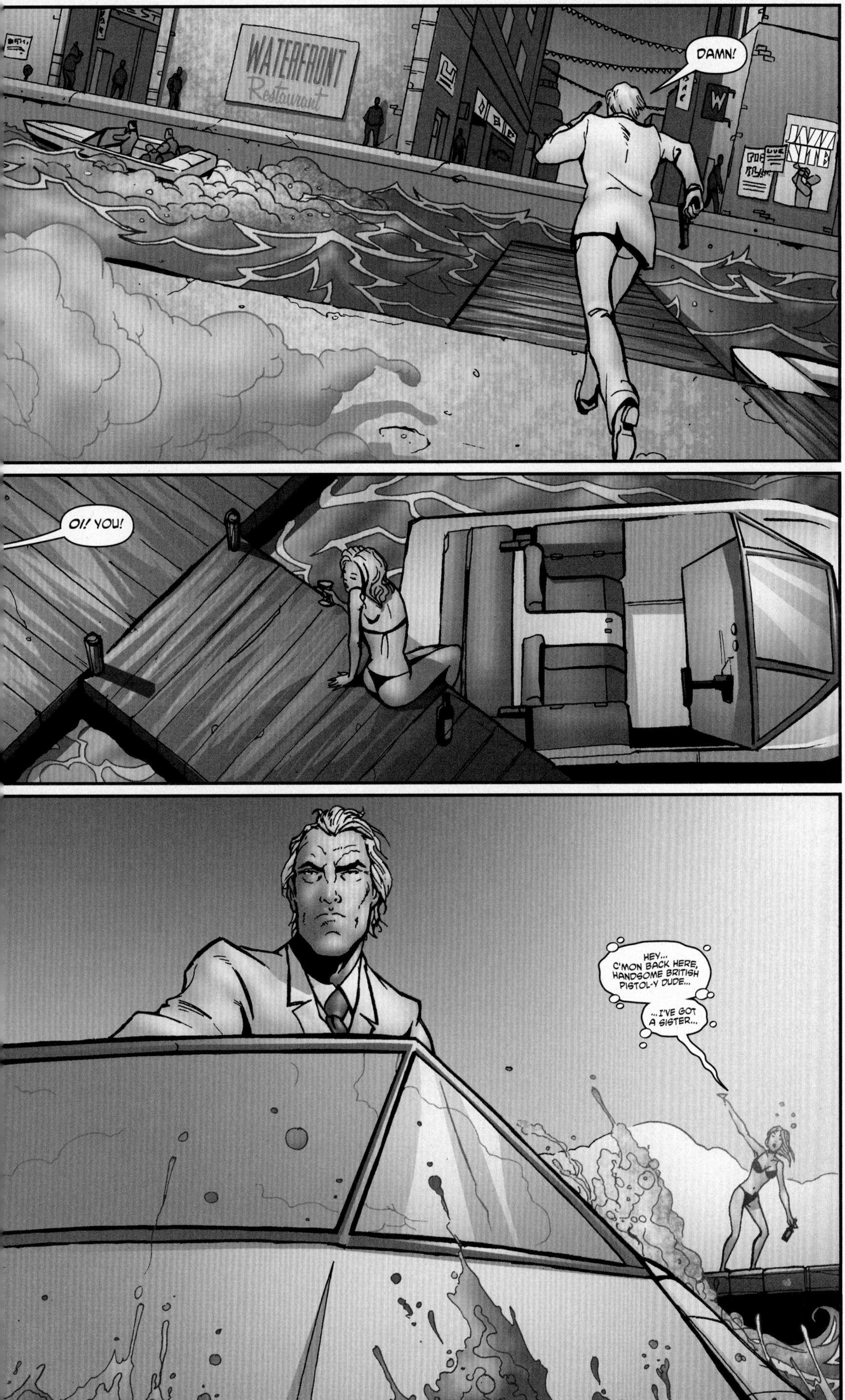
WATERFRONT
Restaurant
DAMN!
OI! YOU!
HEY... C'MON BACK HERE, HANDSOME BRITISH PISTOL-Y DUDE...
...I'VE GOT A SISTER...

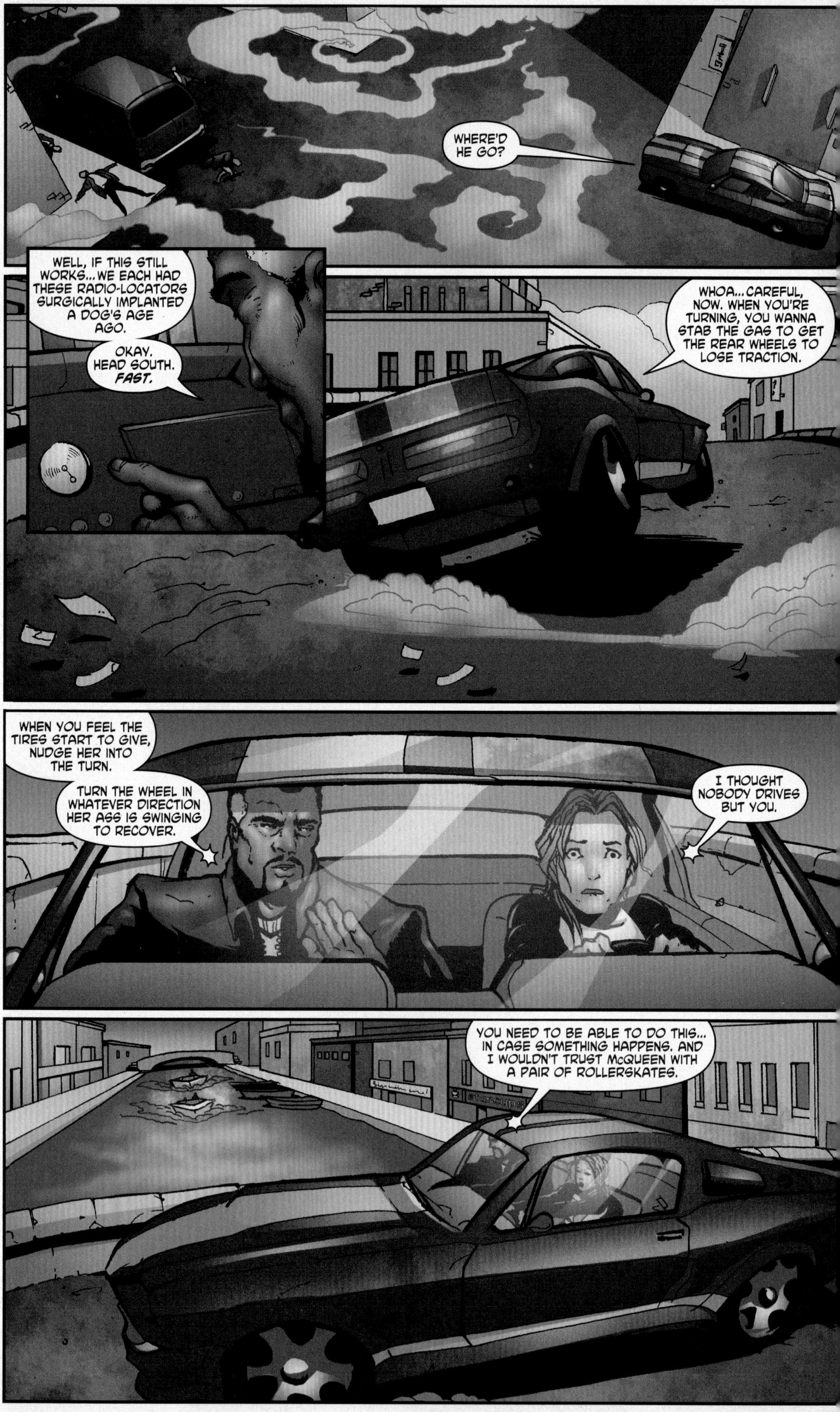
WHERE'D HE GO?
WELL, IF THIS STILL WORKS...WE EACH HAD THESE RADIO-LOCATORS SURGICALLY IMPLANTED A DOG'S AGE AGO.
OKAY. HEAD SOUTH. *FAST.*
WHOA...CAREFUL, NOW. WHEN YOU'RE TURNING, YOU WANNA STAB THE GAS TO GET THE REAR WHEELS TO LOSE TRACTION.
WHEN YOU FEEL THE TIRES START TO GIVE, NUDGE HER INTO THE TURN.
TURN THE WHEEL IN WHATEVER DIRECTION HER ASS IS SWINGING TO RECOVER.
I THOUGHT NOBODY DRIVES BUT YOU.
YOU NEED TO BE ABLE TO DO THIS... IN CASE SOMETHING HAPPENS. AND I WOULDN'T TRUST McQUEEN WITH A PAIR OF ROLLERSKATES.

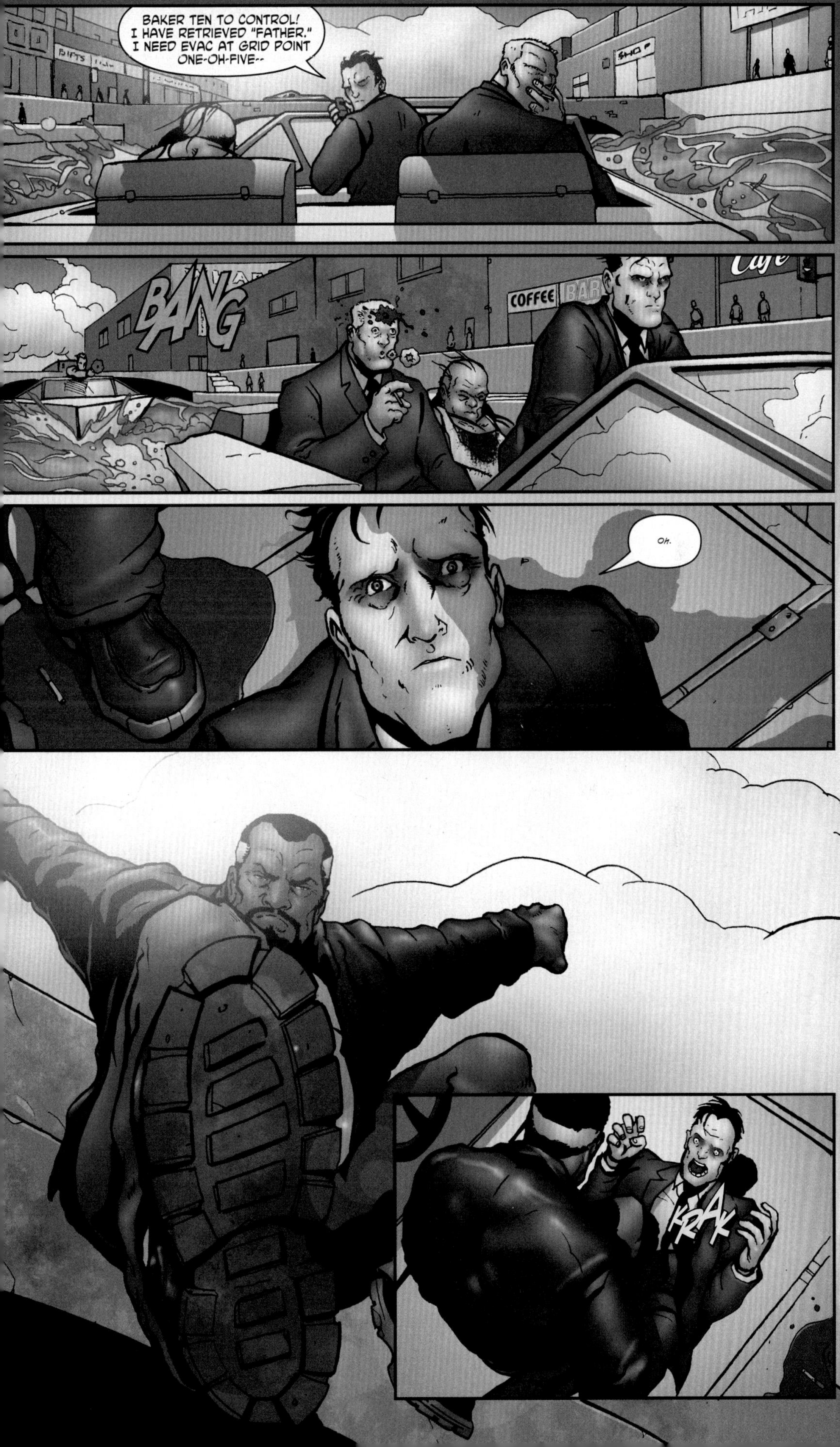

BAKER TEN TO CONTROL! I HAVE RETRIEVED "FATHER." I NEED EVAC AT GRID POINT ONE-OH-FIVE--
BANG
COFFEE BAR
Oh.
KRAK

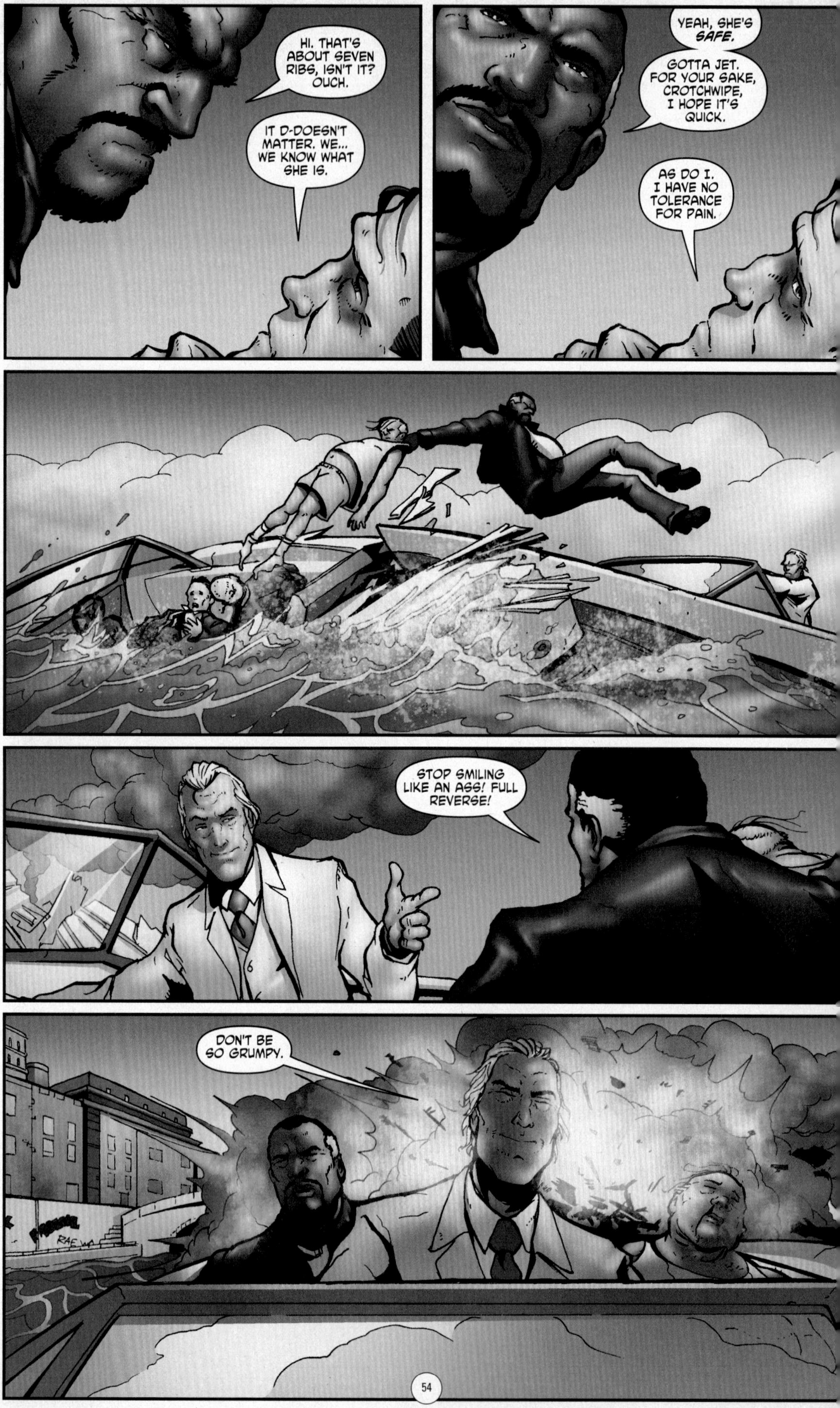
HI. THAT'S ABOUT SEVEN RIBS, ISN'T IT? OUCH.
IT D-DOESN'T MATTER. WE... WE KNOW WHAT SHE IS.
YEAH, SHE'S *SAFE.*
GOTTA JET. FOR YOUR SAKE, CROTCHWIPE, I HOPE IT'S QUICK.
AS DO I. I HAVE NO TOLERANCE FOR PAIN.
STOP SMILING LIKE AN ASS! FULL REVERSE!
DON'T BE SO GRUMPY.

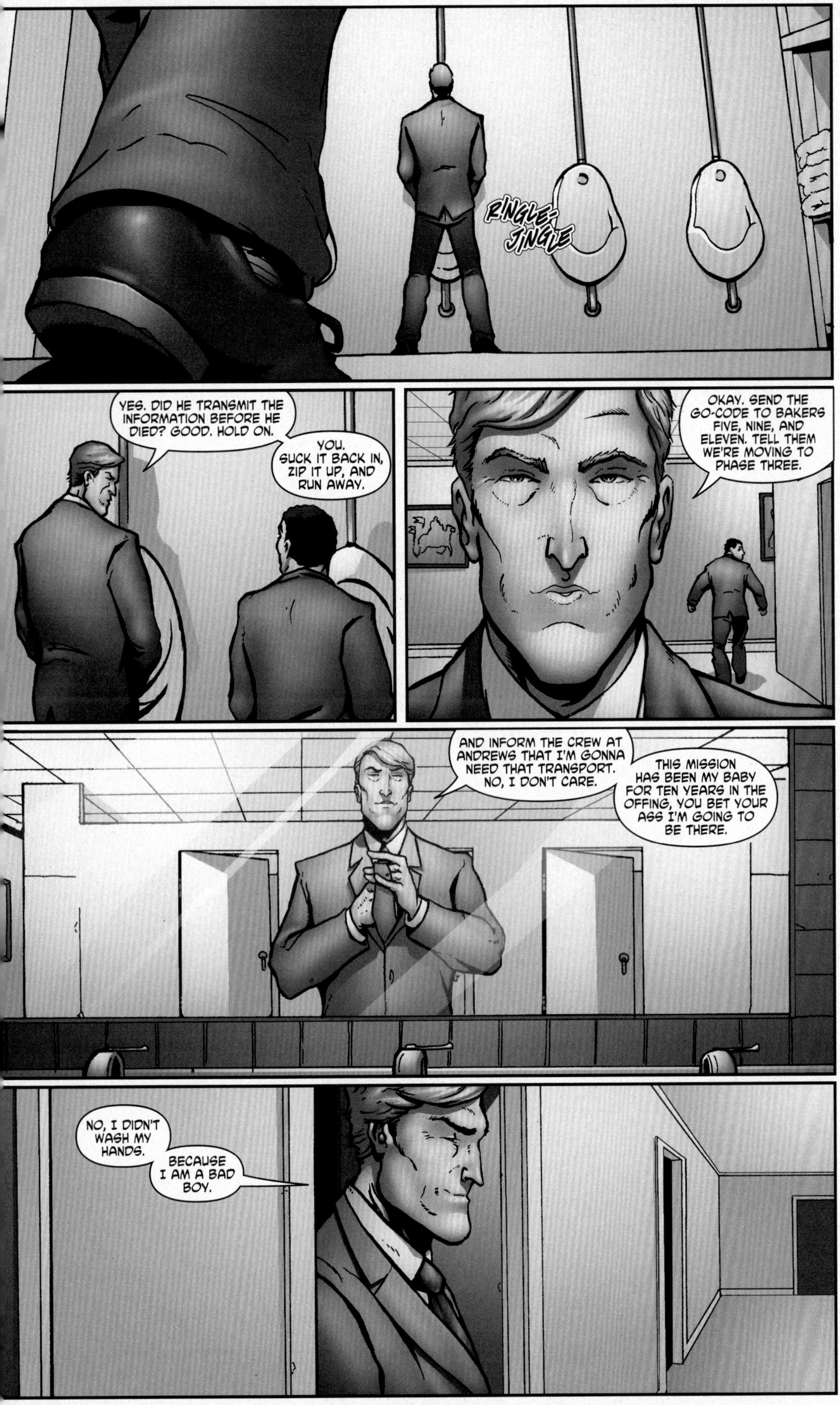
RINGLE-JINGLE
YES. DID HE TRANSMIT THE INFORMATION BEFORE HE DIED? GOOD. HOLD ON.
YOU. SUCK IT BACK IN, ZIP IT UP, AND RUN AWAY.
OKAY. SEND THE GO-CODE TO BAKERS FIVE, NINE, AND ELEVEN. TELL THEM WE'RE MOVING TO PHASE THREE.
AND INFORM THE CREW AT ANDREWS THAT I'M GONNA NEED THAT TRANSPORT. NO, I DON'T CARE.
THIS MISSION HAS BEEN MY BABY FOR TEN YEARS IN THE OFFING, YOU BET YOUR ASS I'M GOING TO BE THERE.
NO, I DIDN'T WASH MY HANDS.
BECAUSE I AM A BAD BOY.

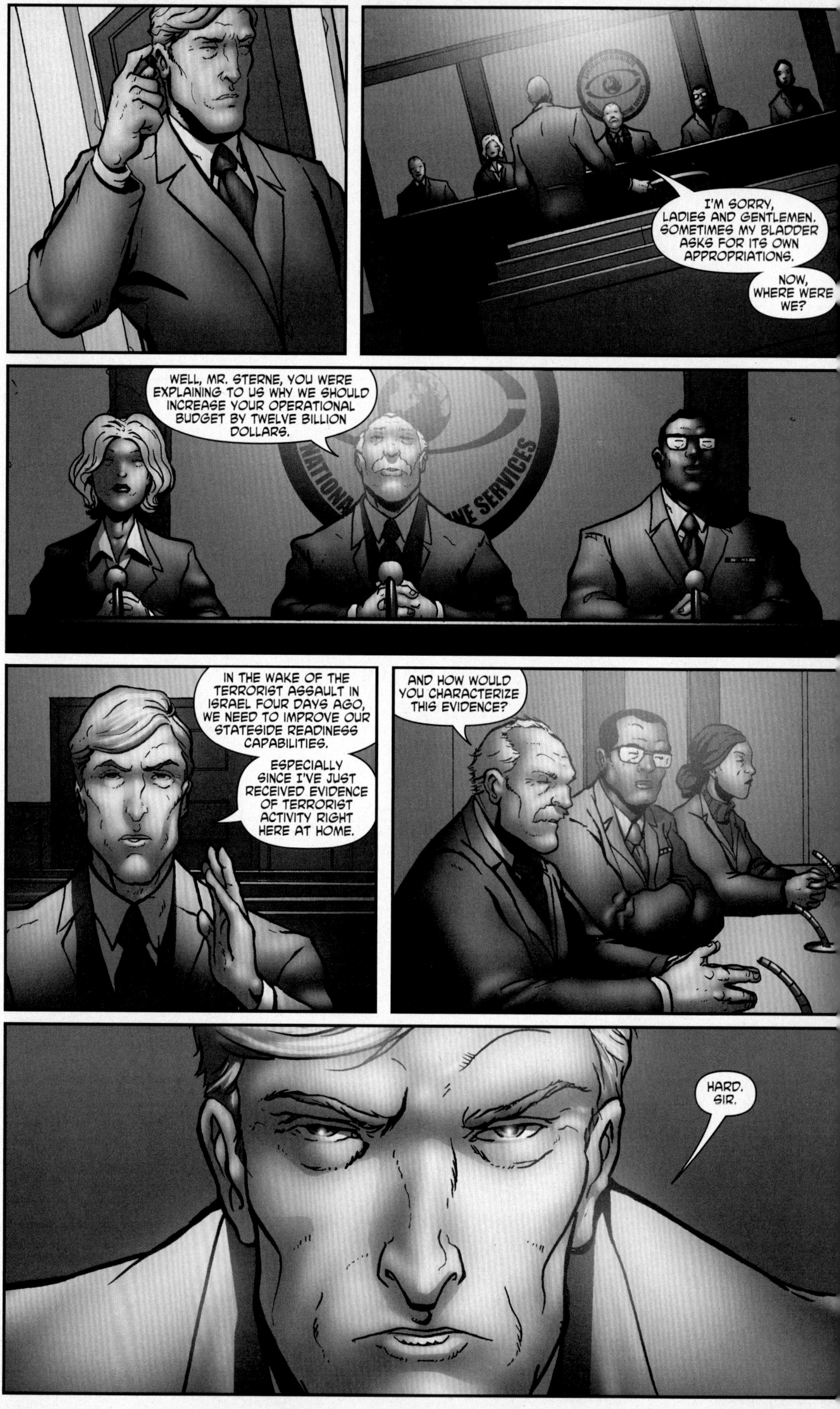
I'M SORRY, LADIES AND GENTLEMEN. SOMETIMES MY BLADDER ASKS FOR ITS OWN APPROPRIATIONS.
NOW, WHERE WERE WE?
WELL, MR. STERNE, YOU WERE EXPLAINING TO US WHY WE SHOULD INCREASE YOUR OPERATIONAL BUDGET BY TWELVE BILLION DOLLARS.
IN THE WAKE OF THE TERRORIST ASSAULT IN ISRAEL FOUR DAYS AGO, WE NEED TO IMPROVE OUR STATESIDE READINESS CAPABILITIES.
ESPECIALLY SINCE I'VE JUST RECEIVED EVIDENCE OF TERRORIST ACTIVITY RIGHT HERE AT HOME.
AND HOW WOULD YOU CHARACTERIZE THIS EVIDENCE?
HARD. SIR.

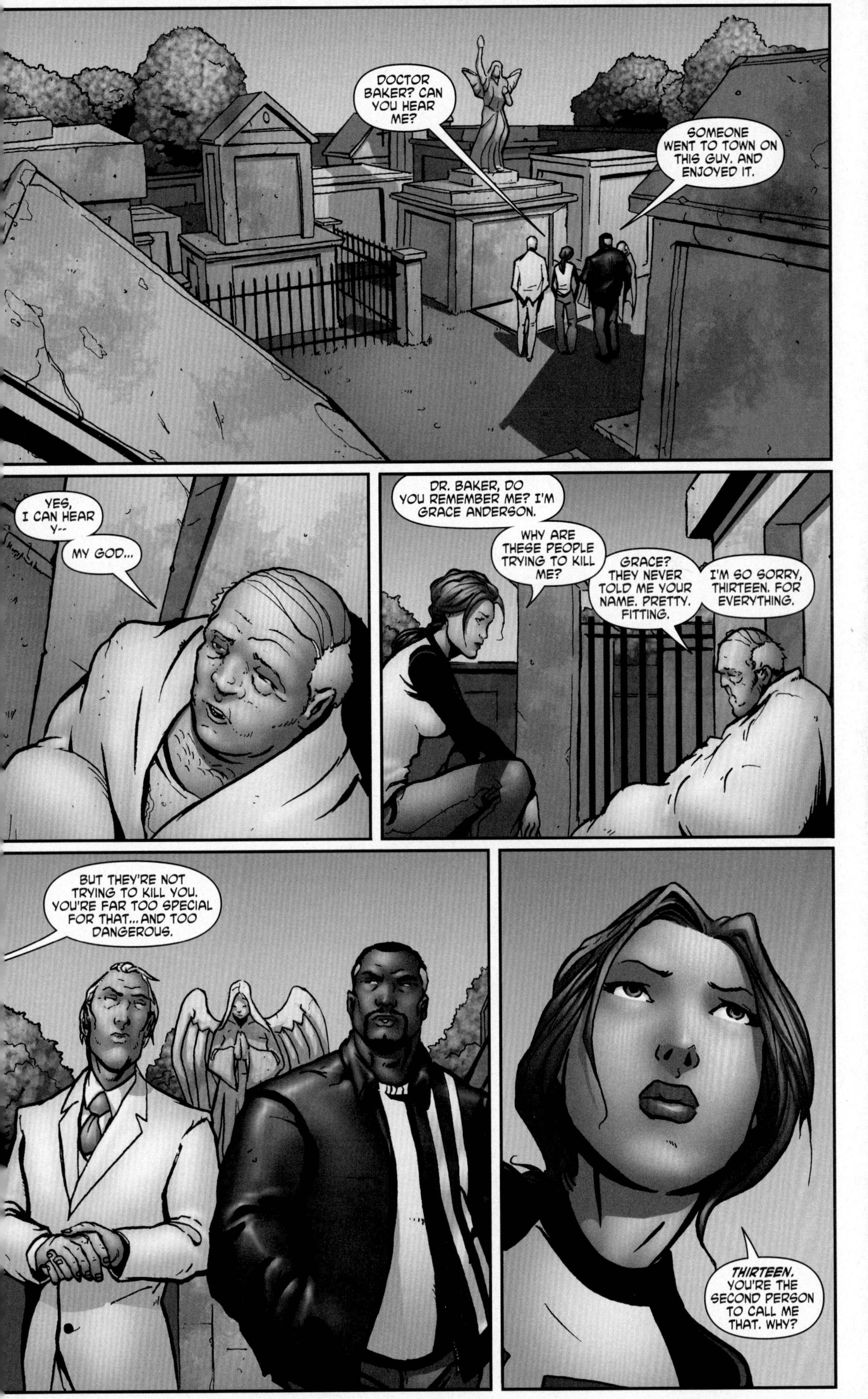
DOCTOR BAKER? CAN YOU HEAR ME?
SOMEONE WENT TO TOWN ON THIS GUY. AND ENJOYED IT.
YES, I CAN HEAR Y--
MY GOD...
DR. BAKER, DO YOU REMEMBER ME? I'M GRACE ANDERSON.
WHY ARE THESE PEOPLE TRYING TO KILL ME?
GRACE? THEY NEVER TOLD ME YOUR NAME. PRETTY. FITTING.
I'M SO SORRY, THIRTEEN. FOR EVERYTHING.
BUT THEY'RE NOT TRYING TO KILL YOU. YOU'RE FAR TOO SPECIAL FOR THAT... AND TOO DANGEROUS.
THIRTEEN. YOU'RE THE SECOND PERSON TO CALL ME THAT. WHY?

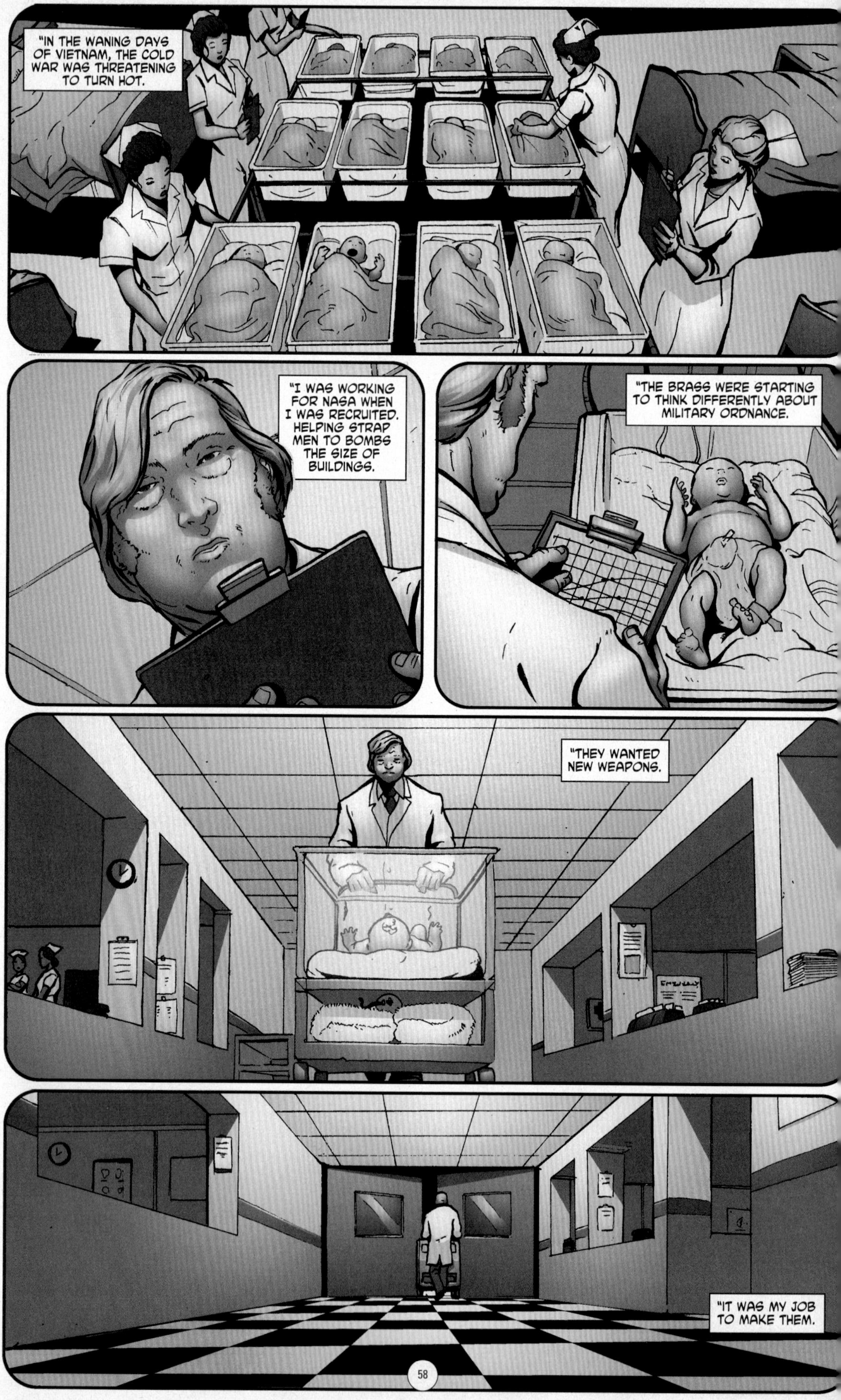
"IN THE WANING DAYS OF VIETNAM, THE COLD WAR WAS THREATENING TO TURN HOT.
"I WAS WORKING FOR NASA WHEN I WAS RECRUITED. HELPING STRAP MEN TO BOMBS THE SIZE OF BUILDINGS.
"THE BRASS WERE STARTING TO THINK DIFFERENTLY ABOUT MILITARY ORDNANCE.
"THEY WANTED NEW WEAPONS.
"IT WAS MY JOB TO MAKE THEM.

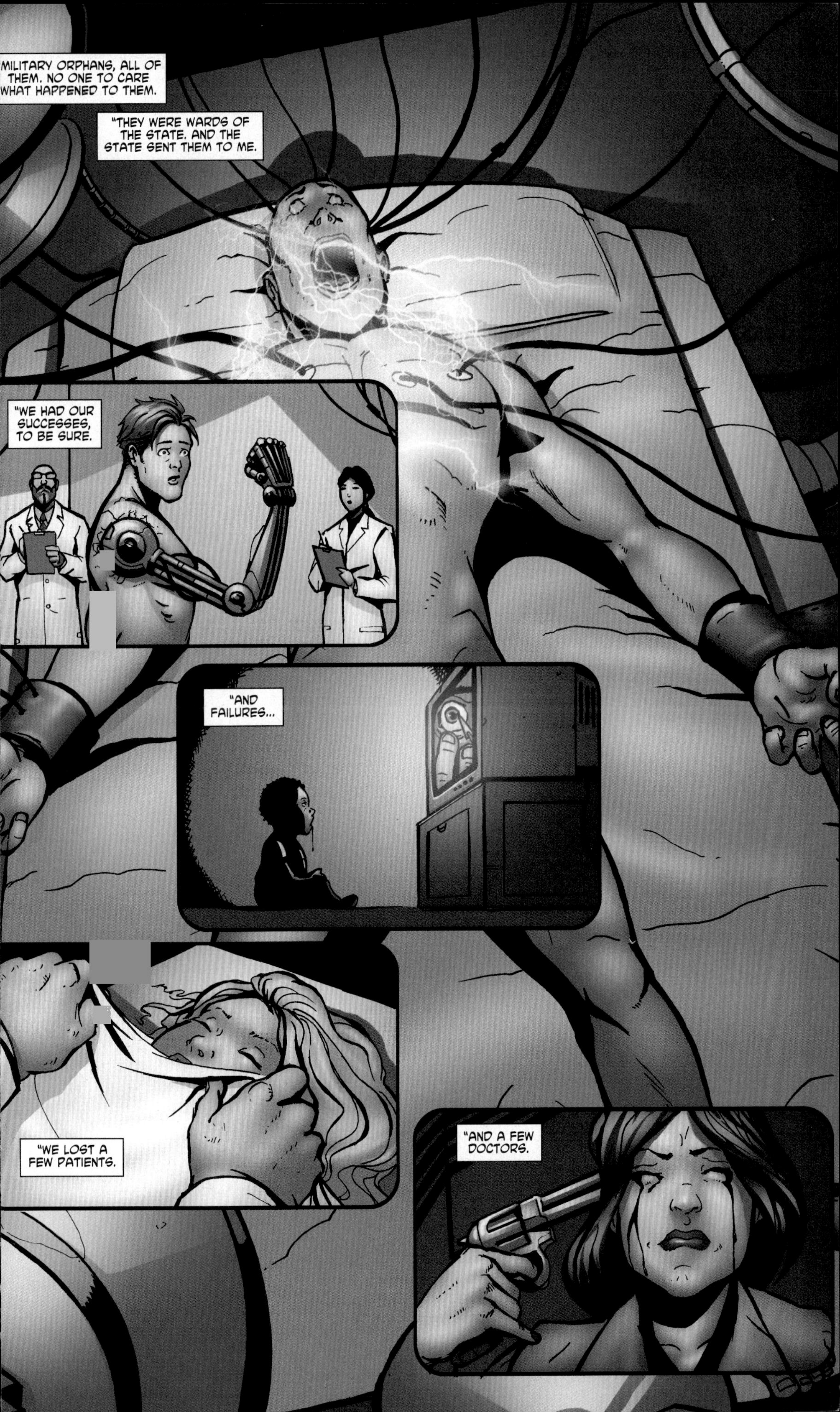
MILITARY ORPHANS, ALL OF THEM. NO ONE TO CARE WHAT HAPPENED TO THEM.
"THEY WERE WARDS OF THE STATE. AND THE STATE SENT THEM TO ME.
"WE HAD OUR SUCCESSES, TO BE SURE.
"AND FAILURES...
"WE LOST A FEW PATIENTS.
"AND A FEW DOCTORS.

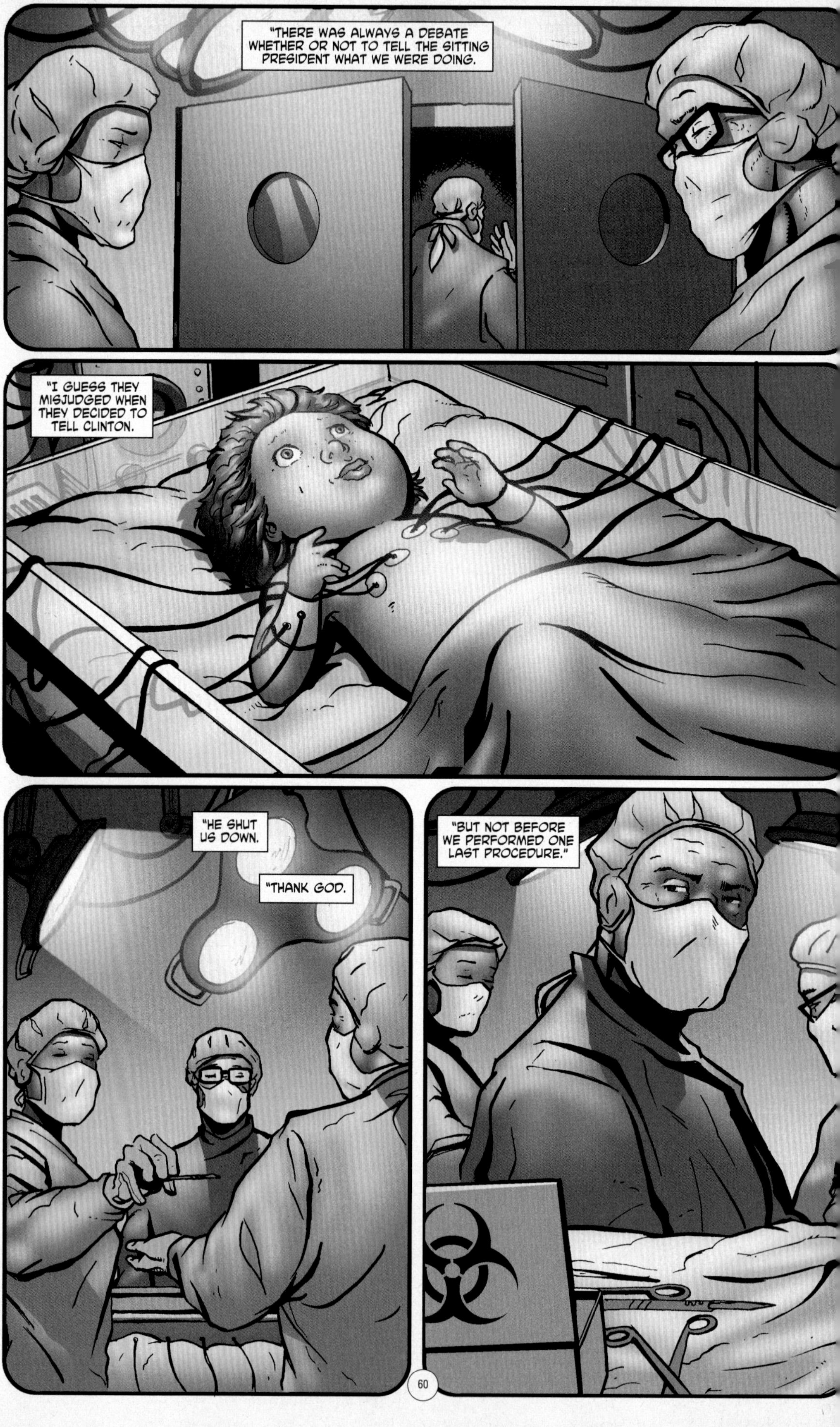
"THERE WAS ALWAYS A DEBATE WHETHER OR NOT TO TELL THE SITTING PRESIDENT WHAT WE WERE DOING.
"I GUESS THEY MISJUDGED WHEN THEY DECIDED TO TELL CLINTON.
"HE SHUT US DOWN.
"THANK GOD.
"BUT NOT BEFORE WE PERFORMED ONE LAST PROCEDURE."

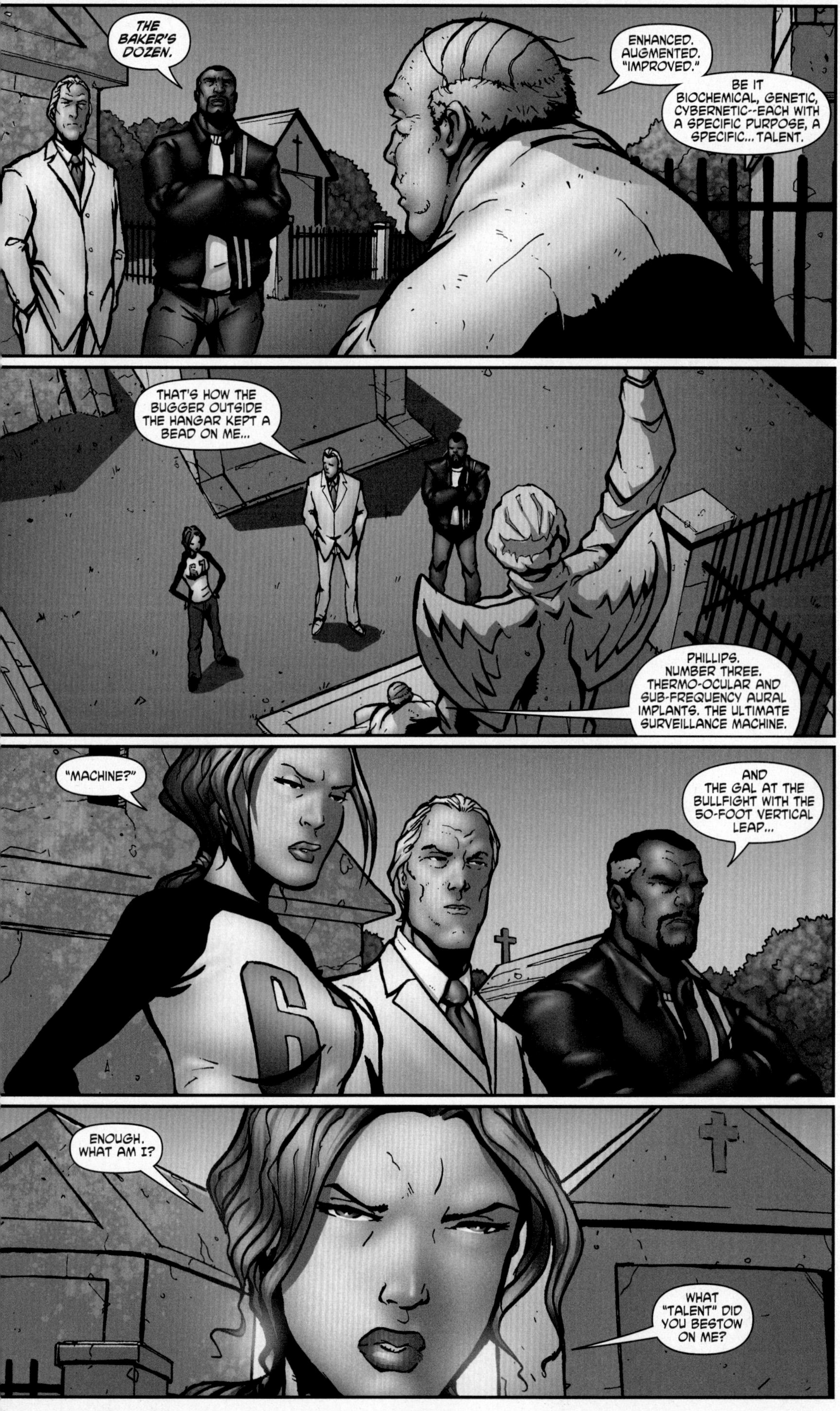
THE BAKER'S DOZEN.
ENHANCED. AUGMENTED. "IMPROVED."
BE IT BIOCHEMICAL, GENETIC, CYBERNETIC--EACH WITH A SPECIFIC PURPOSE, A SPECIFIC... TALENT.
THAT'S HOW THE BUGGER OUTSIDE THE HANGAR KEPT A BEAD ON ME...
PHILLIPS. NUMBER THREE. THERMO-OCULAR AND SUB-FREQUENCY AURAL IMPLANTS. THE ULTIMATE SURVEILLANCE MACHINE.
"MACHINE?"
AND THE GAL AT THE BULLFIGHT WITH THE 50-FOOT VERTICAL LEAP...
ENOUGH. WHAT AM I?
WHAT "TALENT" DID YOU BESTOW ON ME?

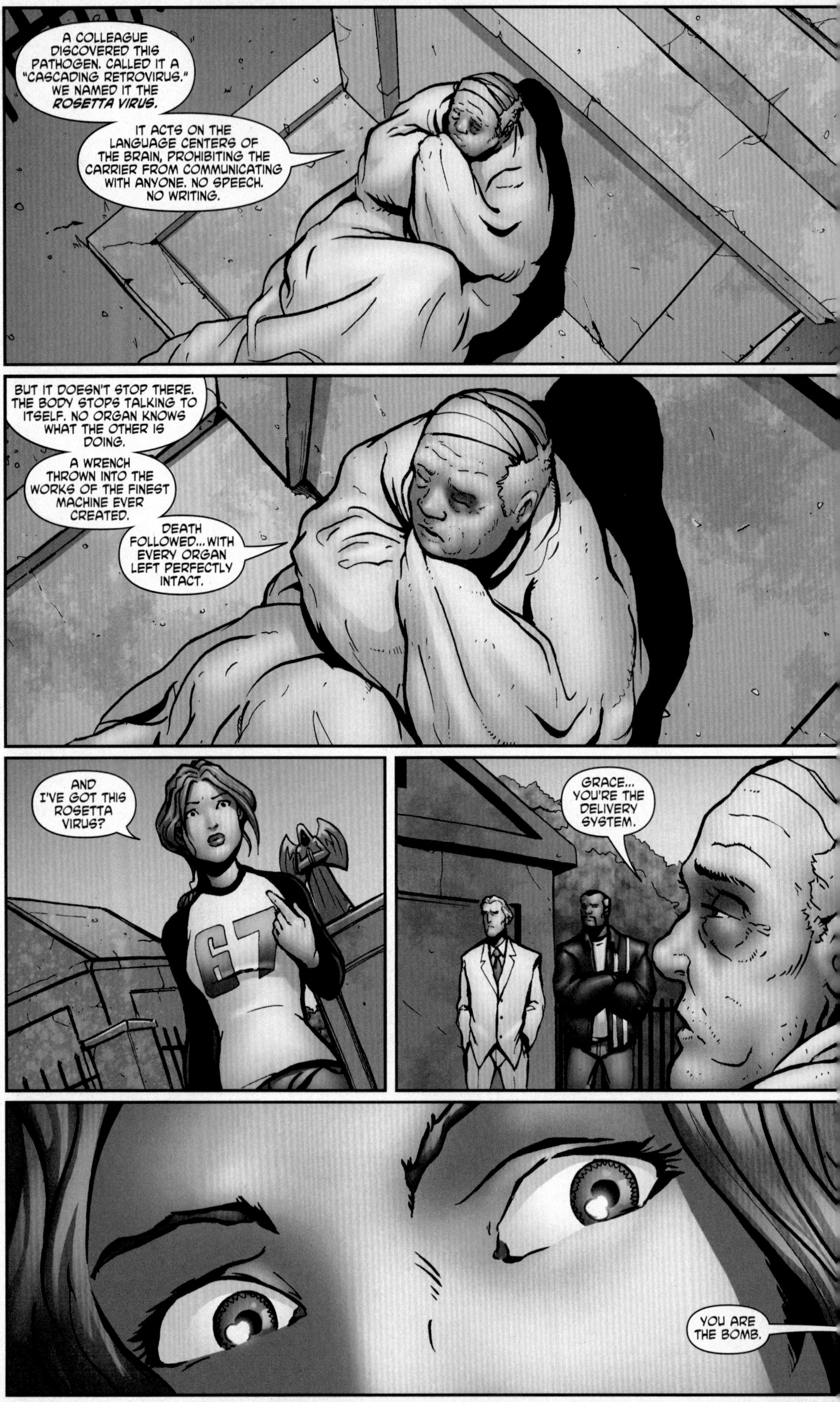
A COLLEAGUE DISCOVERED THIS PATHOGEN. CALLED IT A "CASCADING RETROVIRUS." WE NAMED IT THE *ROSETTA VIRUS.*
IT ACTS ON THE LANGUAGE CENTERS OF THE BRAIN, PROHIBITING THE CARRIER FROM COMMUNICATING WITH ANYONE. NO SPEECH. NO WRITING.
BUT IT DOESN'T STOP THERE. THE BODY STOPS TALKING TO ITSELF. NO ORGAN KNOWS WHAT THE OTHER IS DOING.
A WRENCH THROWN INTO THE WORKS OF THE FINEST MACHINE EVER CREATED.
DEATH FOLLOWED... WITH EVERY ORGAN LEFT PERFECTLY INTACT.
AND I'VE GOT THIS ROSETTA VIRUS?
GRACE... YOU'RE THE DELIVERY SYSTEM.
YOU ARE THE BOMB.

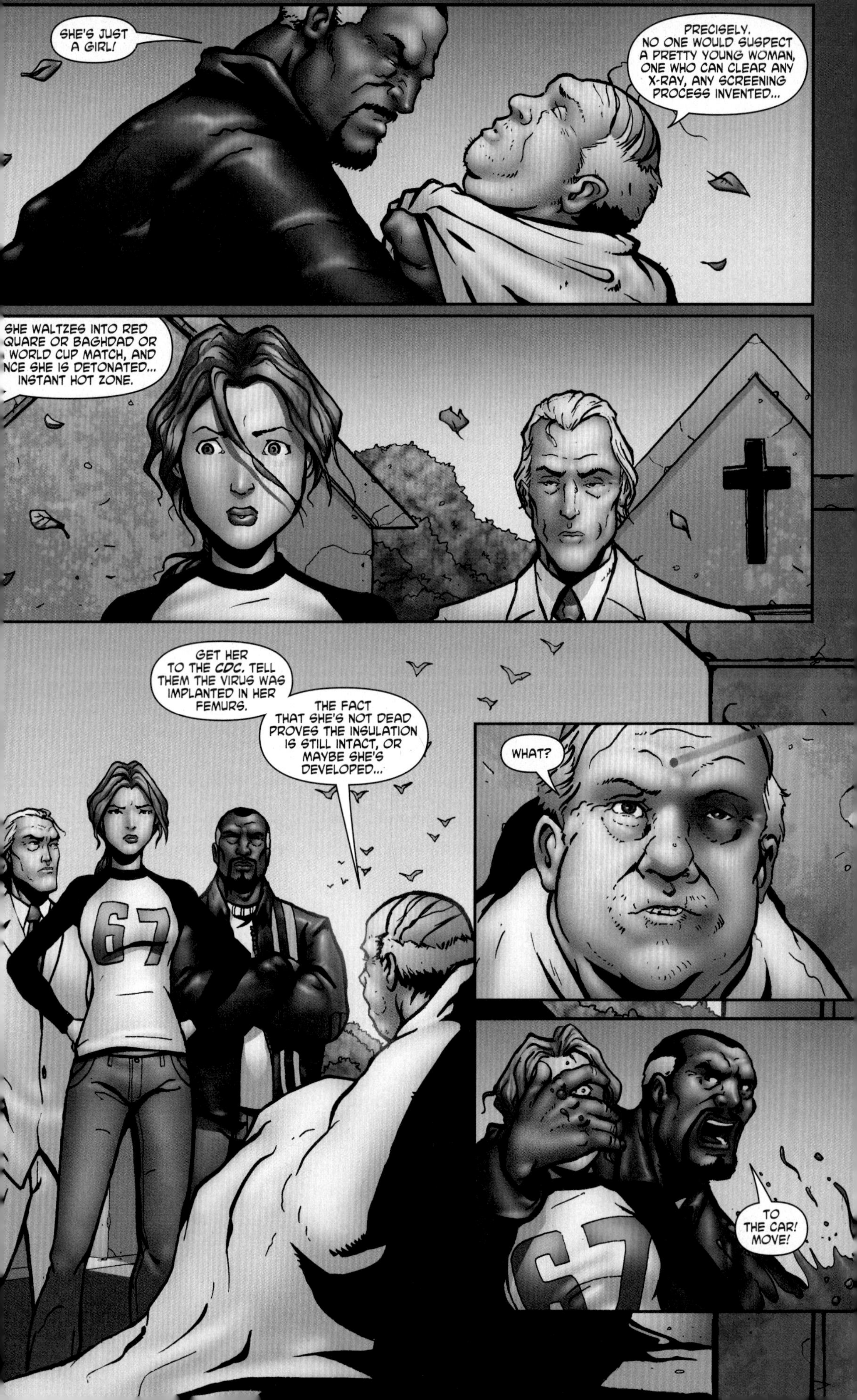
SHE'S JUST A GIRL!
PRECISELY. NO ONE WOULD SUSPECT A PRETTY YOUNG WOMAN, ONE WHO CAN CLEAR ANY X-RAY, ANY SCREENING PROCESS INVENTED...
SHE WALTZES INTO RED QUARE OR BAGHDAD OR WORLD CUP MATCH, AND NCE SHE IS DETONATED... INSTANT HOT ZONE.
GET HER TO THE CDC. TELL THEM THE VIRUS WAS IMPLANTED IN HER FEMURS.
THE FACT THAT SHE'S NOT DEAD PROVES THE INSULATION IS STILL INTACT, OR MAYBE SHE'S DEVELOPED...
WHAT?
TO THE CAR! MOVE!

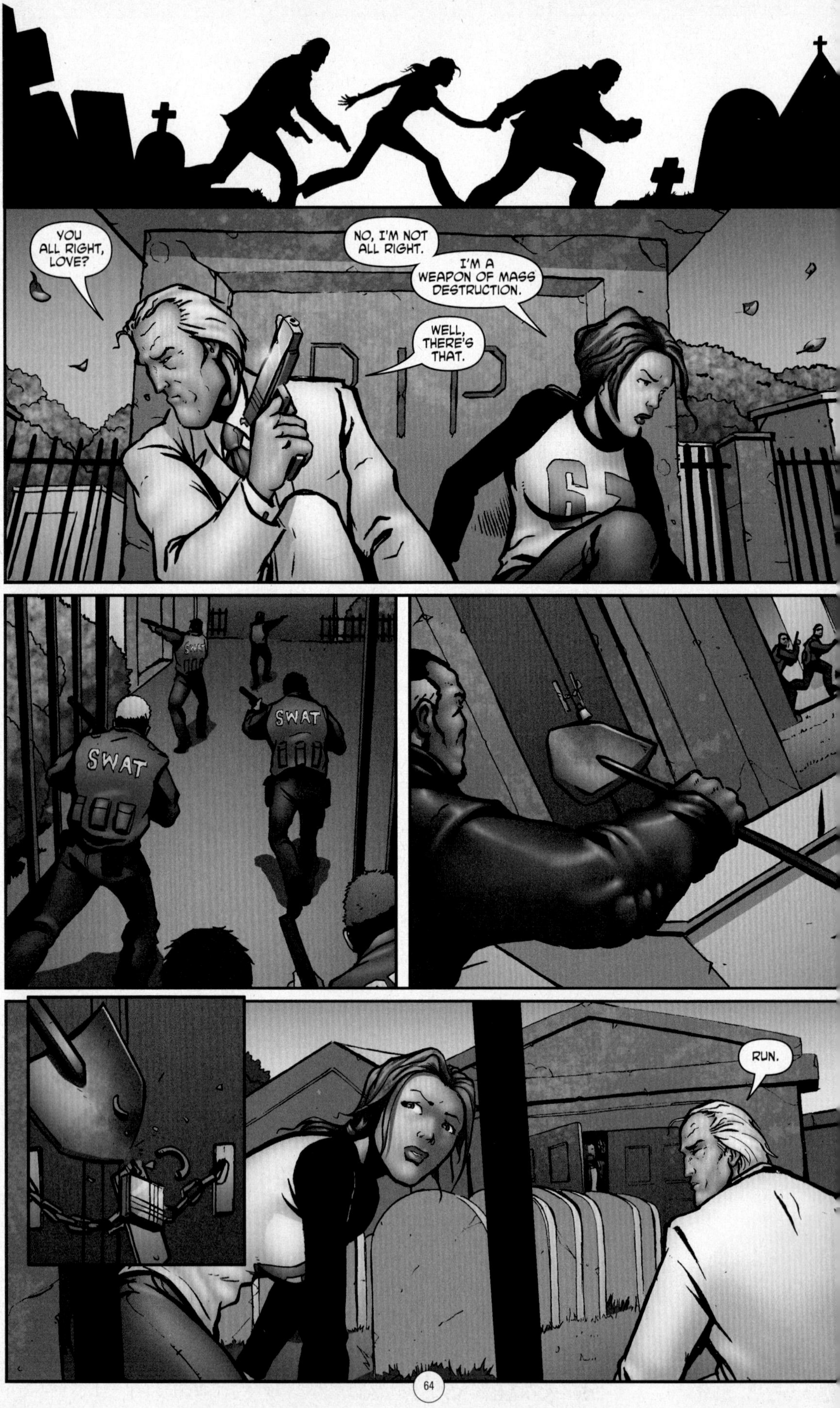
YOU ALL RIGHT, LOVE?
NO, I'M NOT ALL RIGHT.
I'M A WEAPON OF MASS DESTRUCTION.
WELL, THERE'S THAT.
SWAT
SWAT
SWAT
RUN.

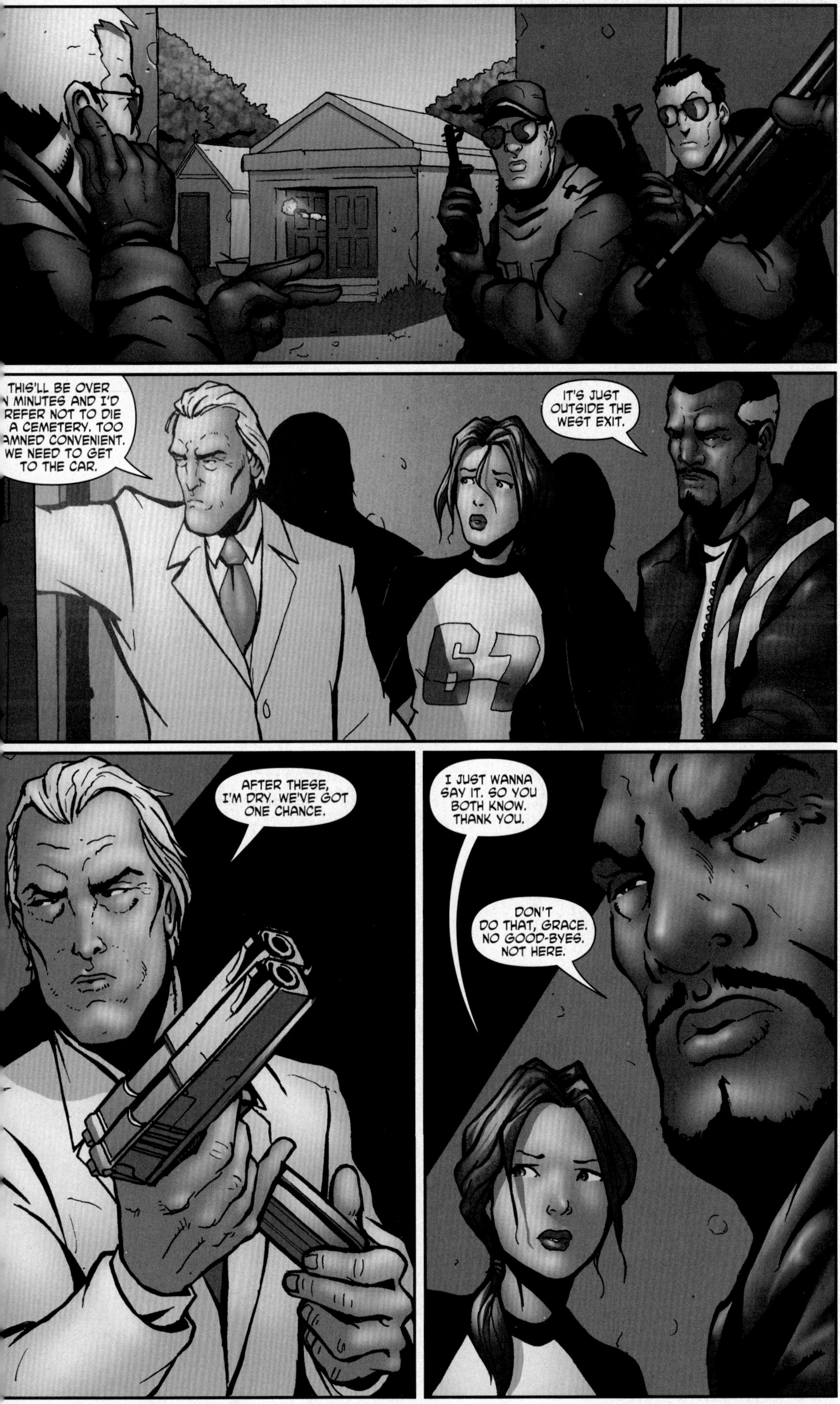

THIS'LL BE OVER N MINUTES AND I'D REFER NOT TO DIE A CEMETERY. TOO AMNED CONVENIENT. WE NEED TO GET TO THE CAR.
IT'S JUST OUTSIDE THE WEST EXIT.
67
AFTER THESE, I'M DRY. WE'VE GOT ONE CHANCE.
I JUST WANNA SAY IT. SO YOU BOTH KNOW. THANK YOU.
DON'T DO THAT, GRACE. NO GOOD-BYES. NOT HERE.

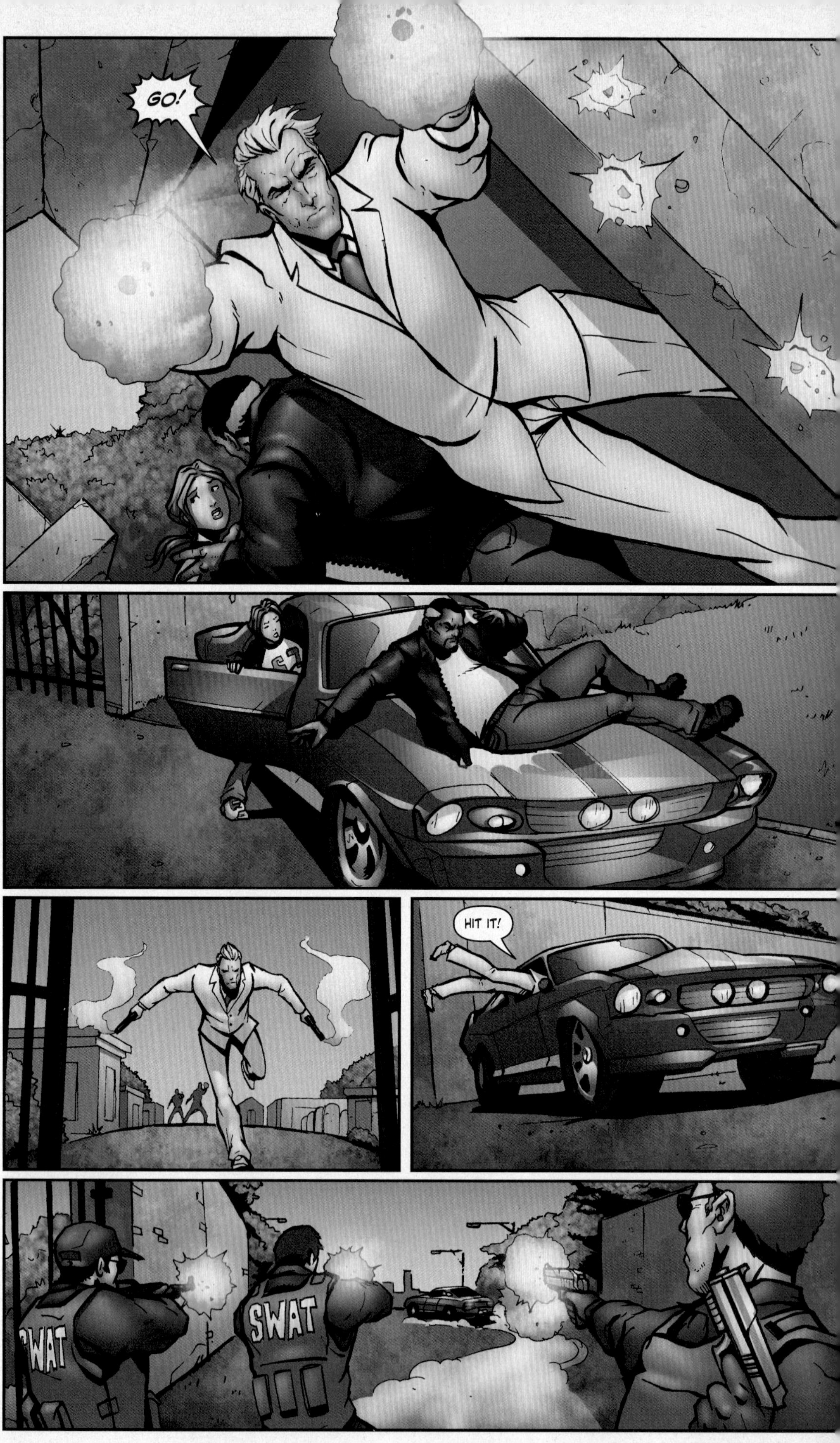
GO!
HIT IT!
SWAT
SWAT

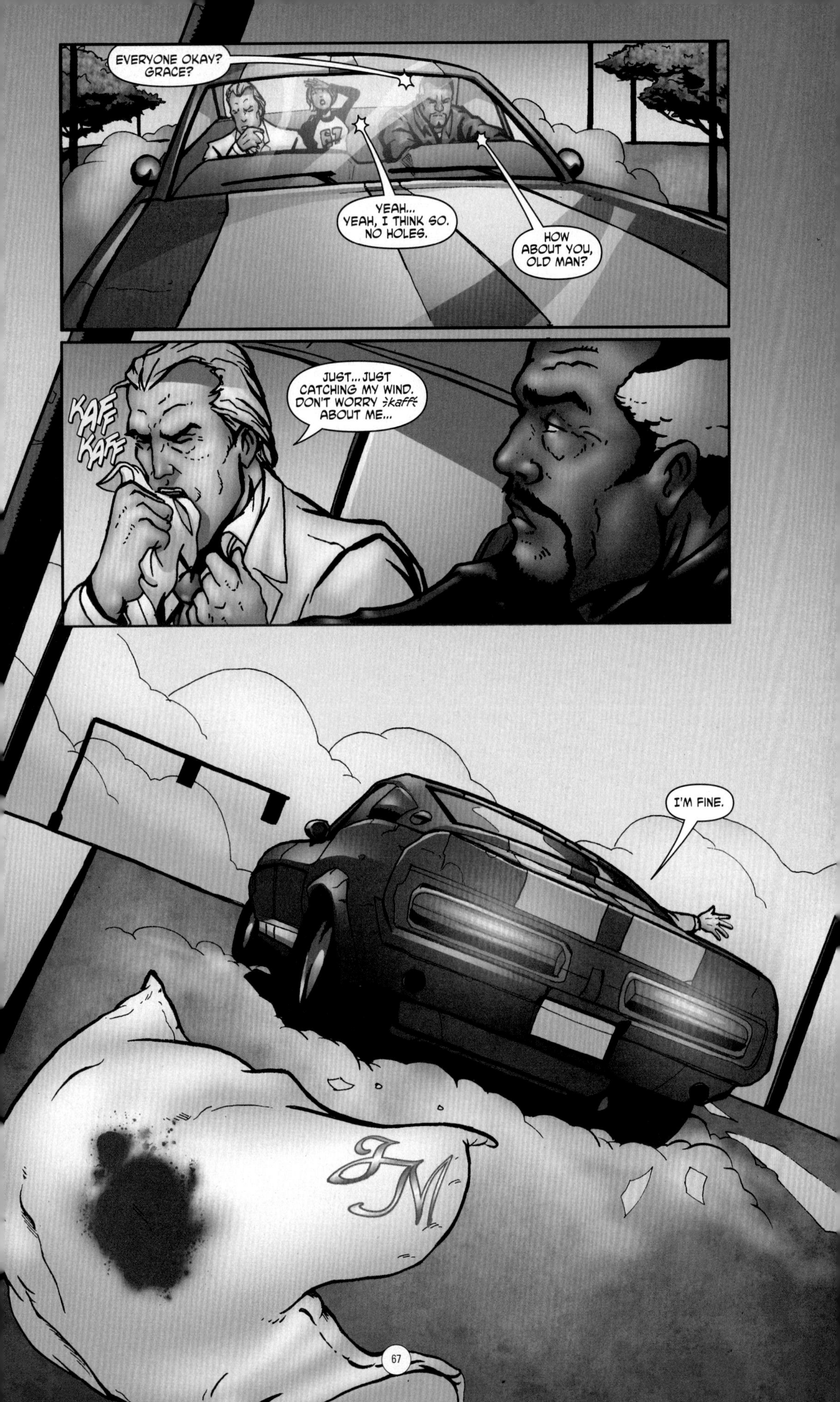
EVERYONE OKAY? GRACE?
YEAH... YEAH, I THINK SO. NO HOLES.
HOW ABOUT YOU, OLD MAN?
KAFF KAFF
JUST... JUST CATCHING MY WIND. DON'T WORRY ≯kaff≮ ABOUT ME...
I'M FINE.

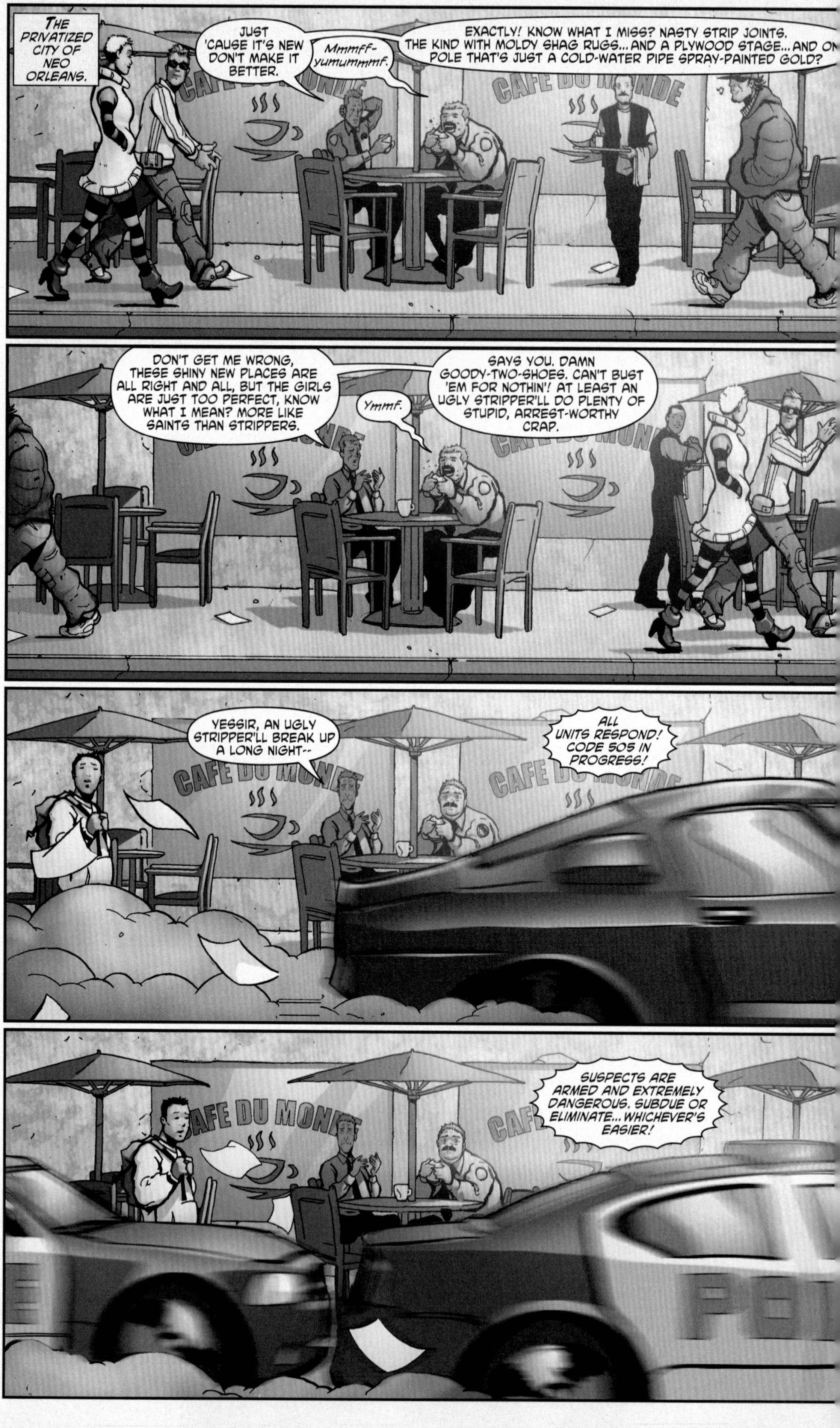
THE PRIVATIZED CITY OF NEO ORLEANS.
JUST 'CAUSE IT'S NEW DON'T MAKE IT BETTER.
Mmmff-yumummmf.
EXACTLY! KNOW WHAT I MISS? NASTY STRIP JOINTS. THE KIND WITH MOLDY SHAG RUGS... AND A PLYWOOD STAGE... AND ON POLE THAT'S JUST A COLD-WATER PIPE SPRAY-PAINTED GOLD?
CAFE DU MONDE
DON'T GET ME WRONG, THESE SHINY NEW PLACES ARE ALL RIGHT AND ALL, BUT THE GIRLS ARE JUST TOO PERFECT, KNOW WHAT I MEAN? MORE LIKE SAINTS THAN STRIPPERS.
Ymmf.
SAYS YOU. DAMN GOODY-TWO-SHOES. CAN'T BUST 'EM FOR NOTHIN'! AT LEAST AN UGLY STRIPPER'LL DO PLENTY OF STUPID, ARREST-WORTHY CRAP.
YESSIR, AN UGLY STRIPPER'LL BREAK UP A LONG NIGHT--
ALL UNITS RESPOND! CODE 505 IN PROGRESS!
CAFE DU MONDE
SUSPECTS ARE ARMED AND EXTREMELY DANGEROUS. SUBDUE OR ELIMINATE... WHICHEVER'S EASIER!

CHAPTER FOUR:
STERNE REPRISALS

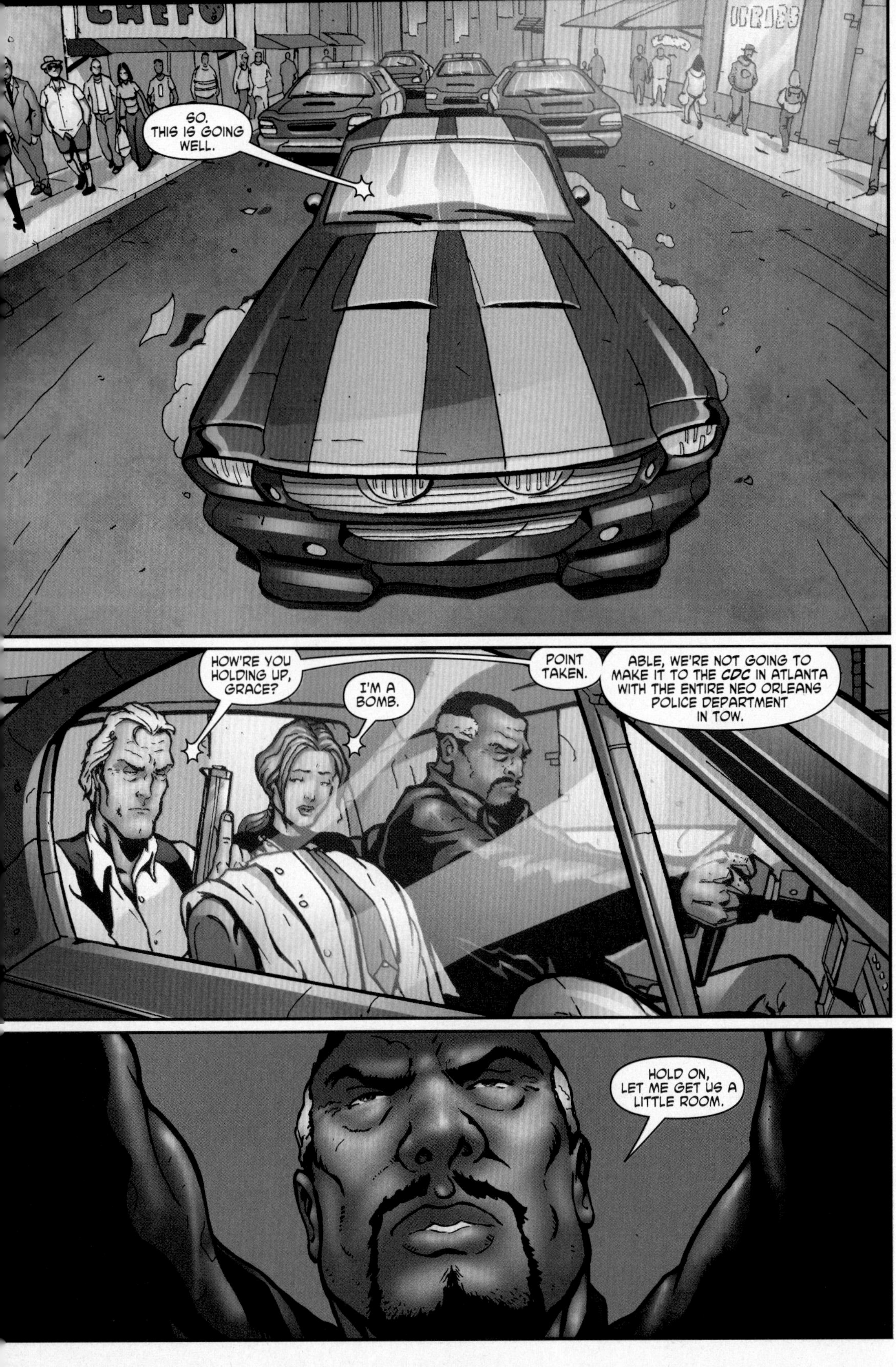
SO. THIS IS GOING WELL.
HOW'RE YOU HOLDING UP, GRACE?
I'M A BOMB.
POINT TAKEN.
ABLE, WE'RE NOT GOING TO MAKE IT TO THE CDC IN ATLANTA WITH THE ENTIRE NEO ORLEANS POLICE DEPARTMENT IN TOW.
HOLD ON, LET ME GET US A LITTLE ROOM.

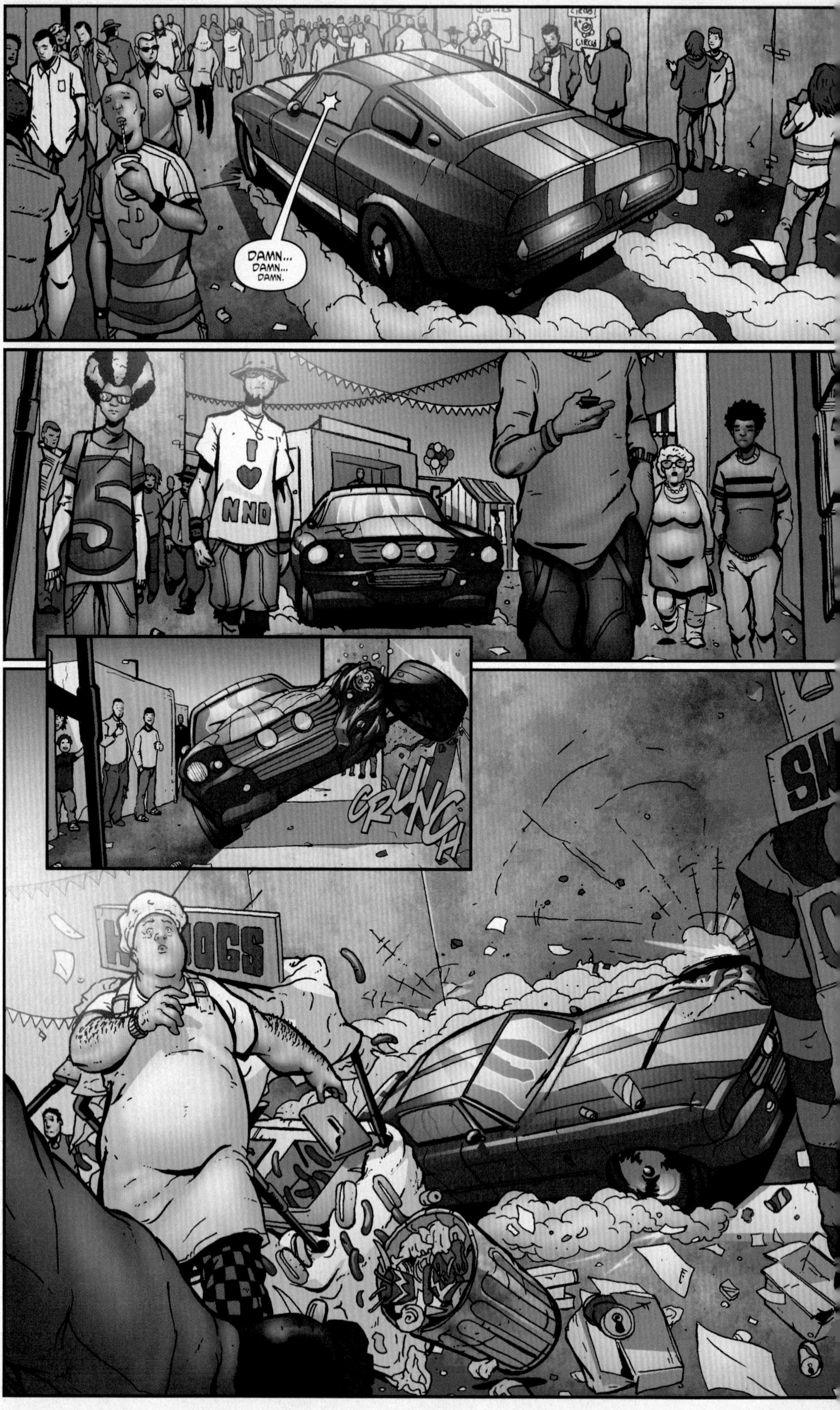
DAMN... DAMN... DAMN.
CRUNCH

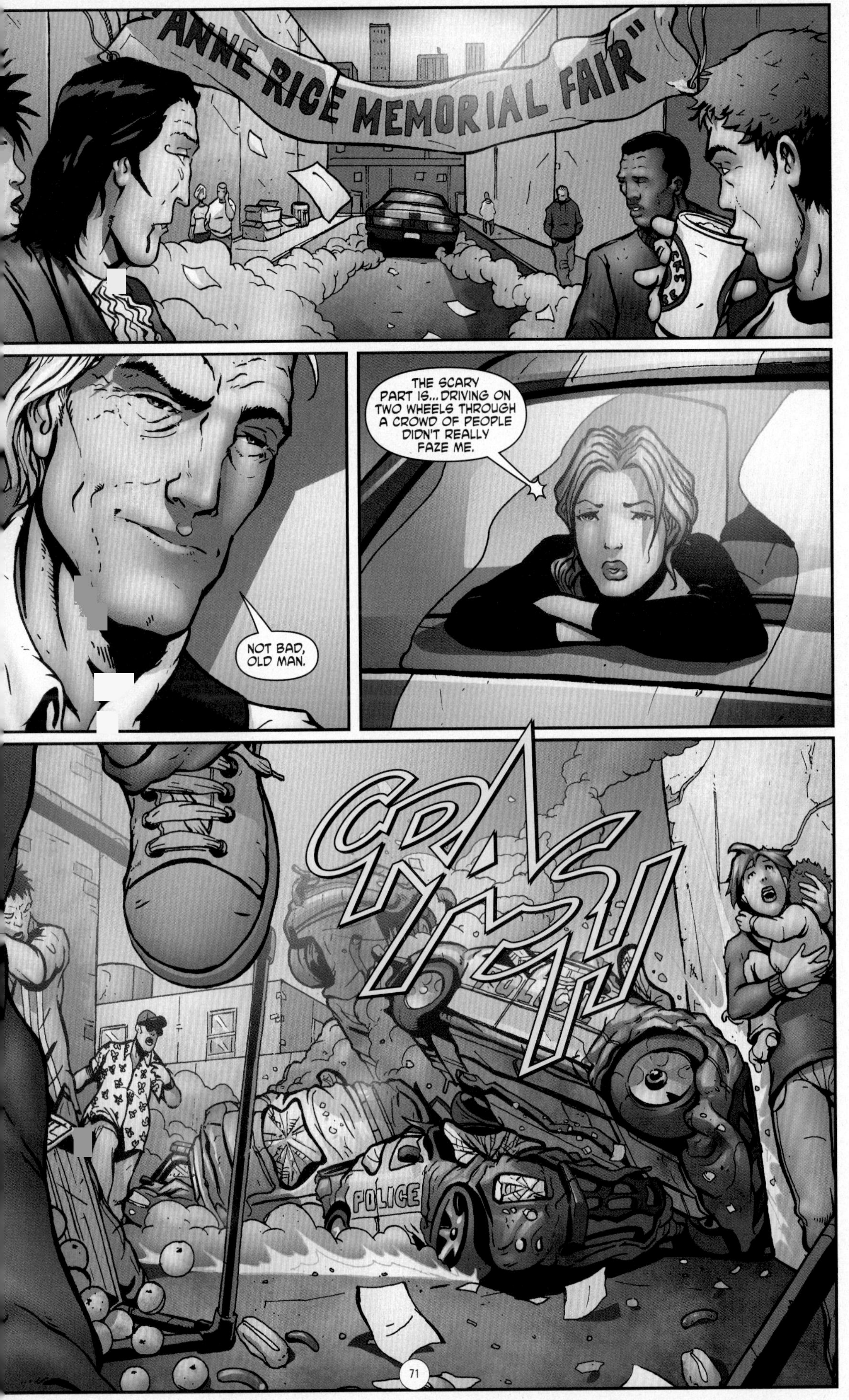
"ANNE RICE MEMORIAL FAIR"
NOT BAD, OLD MAN.
THE SCARY PART IS...DRIVING ON TWO WHEELS THROUGH A CROWD OF PEOPLE DIDN'T REALLY FAZE ME.
CRASH
POLICE
POLICE

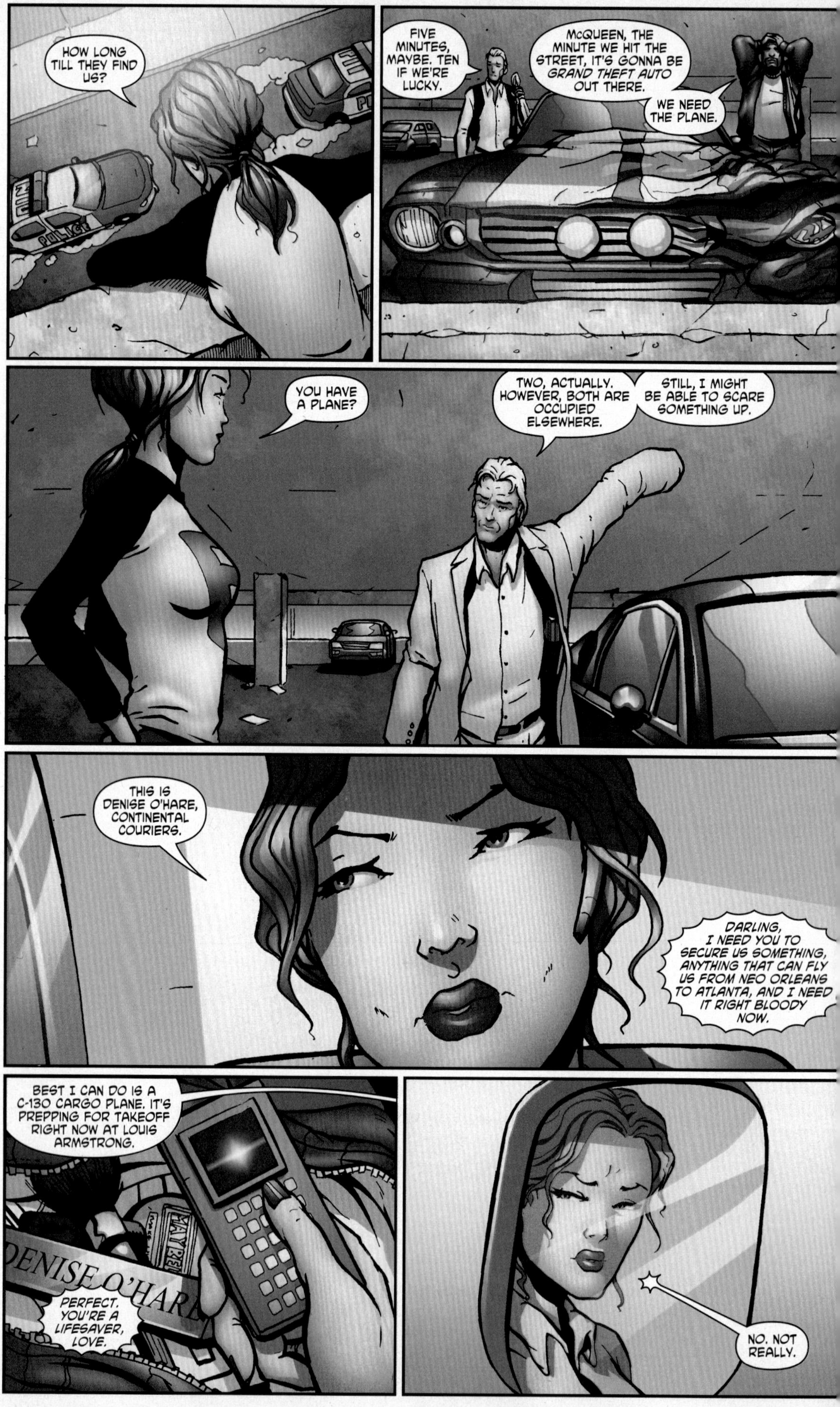
HOW LONG TILL THEY FIND US?
FIVE MINUTES, MAYBE. TEN IF WE'RE LUCKY.
McQUEEN, THE MINUTE WE HIT THE STREET, IT'S GONNA BE *GRAND THEFT AUTO* OUT THERE.
WE NEED THE PLANE.
YOU HAVE A PLANE?
TWO, ACTUALLY. HOWEVER, BOTH ARE OCCUPIED ELSEWHERE.
STILL, I MIGHT BE ABLE TO SCARE SOMETHING UP.
THIS IS DENISE O'HARE, CONTINENTAL COURIERS.
DARLING, I NEED YOU TO SECURE US SOMETHING, ANYTHING THAT CAN FLY US FROM NEO ORLEANS TO ATLANTA, AND I NEED IT RIGHT BLOODY NOW.
BEST I CAN DO IS A C-130 CARGO PLANE. IT'S PREPPING FOR TAKEOFF RIGHT NOW AT LOUIS ARMSTRONG.
DENISE O'HARE
PERFECT. YOU'RE A LIFESAVER, LOVE.
NO. NOT REALLY.

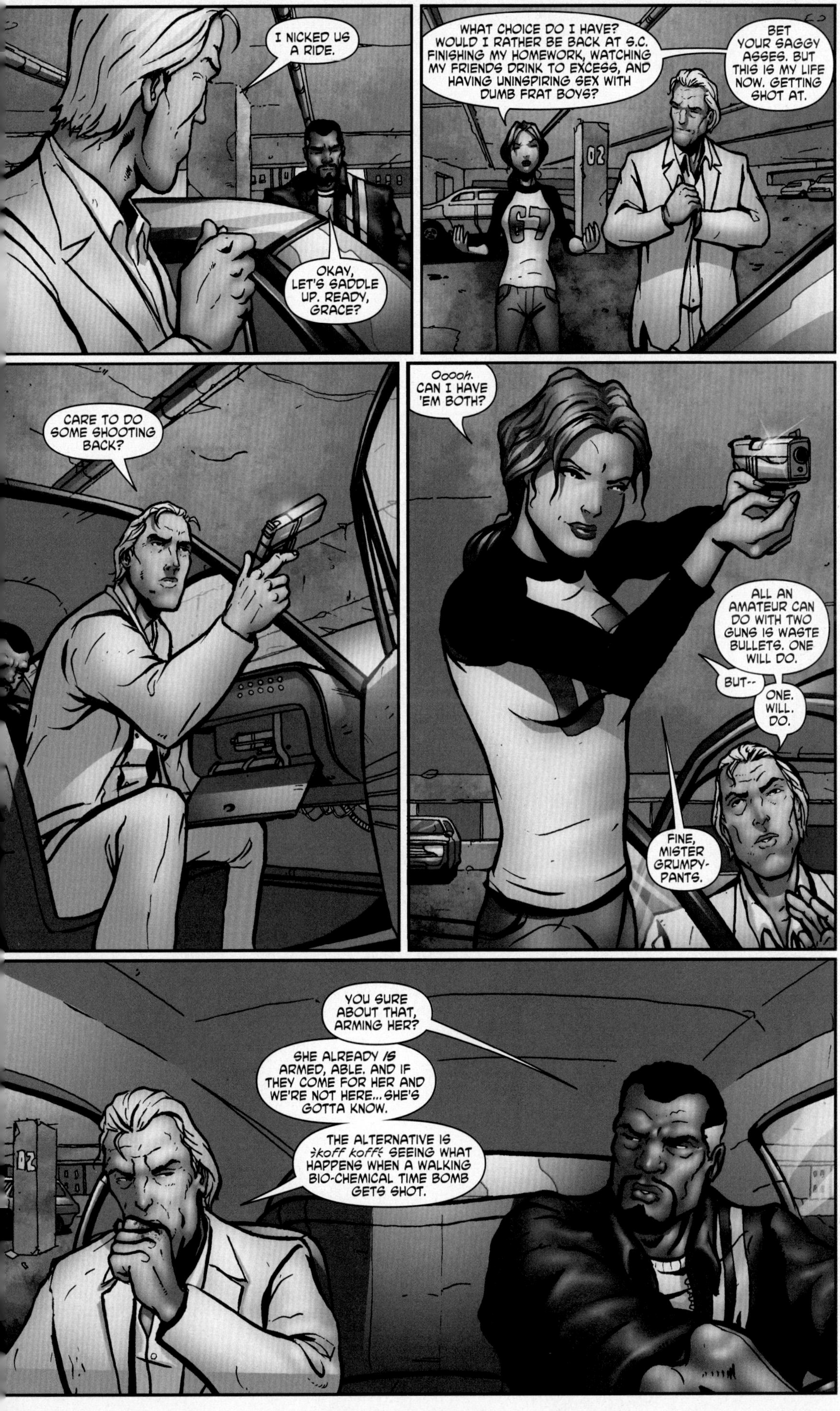
I NICKED US A RIDE.
OKAY, LET'S SADDLE UP. READY, GRACE?
WHAT CHOICE DO I HAVE? WOULD I RATHER BE BACK AT S.C. FINISHING MY HOMEWORK, WATCHING MY FRIENDS DRINK TO EXCESS, AND HAVING UNINSPIRING SEX WITH DUMB FRAT BOYS?
BET YOUR SAGGY ASSES. BUT THIS IS MY LIFE NOW. GETTING SHOT AT.
02
67
CARE TO DO SOME SHOOTING BACK?
Ooooh. CAN I HAVE 'EM BOTH?
ALL AN AMATEUR CAN DO WITH TWO GUNS IS WASTE BULLETS. ONE WILL DO.
BUT--
ONE. WILL. DO.
FINE, MISTER GRUMPY-PANTS.
YOU SURE ABOUT THAT, ARMING HER?
SHE ALREADY IS ARMED, ABLE. AND IF THEY COME FOR HER AND WE'RE NOT HERE... SHE'S GOTTA KNOW.
THE ALTERNATIVE IS *koff koff* SEEING WHAT HAPPENS WHEN A WALKING BIO-CHEMICAL TIME BOMB GETS SHOT.
02

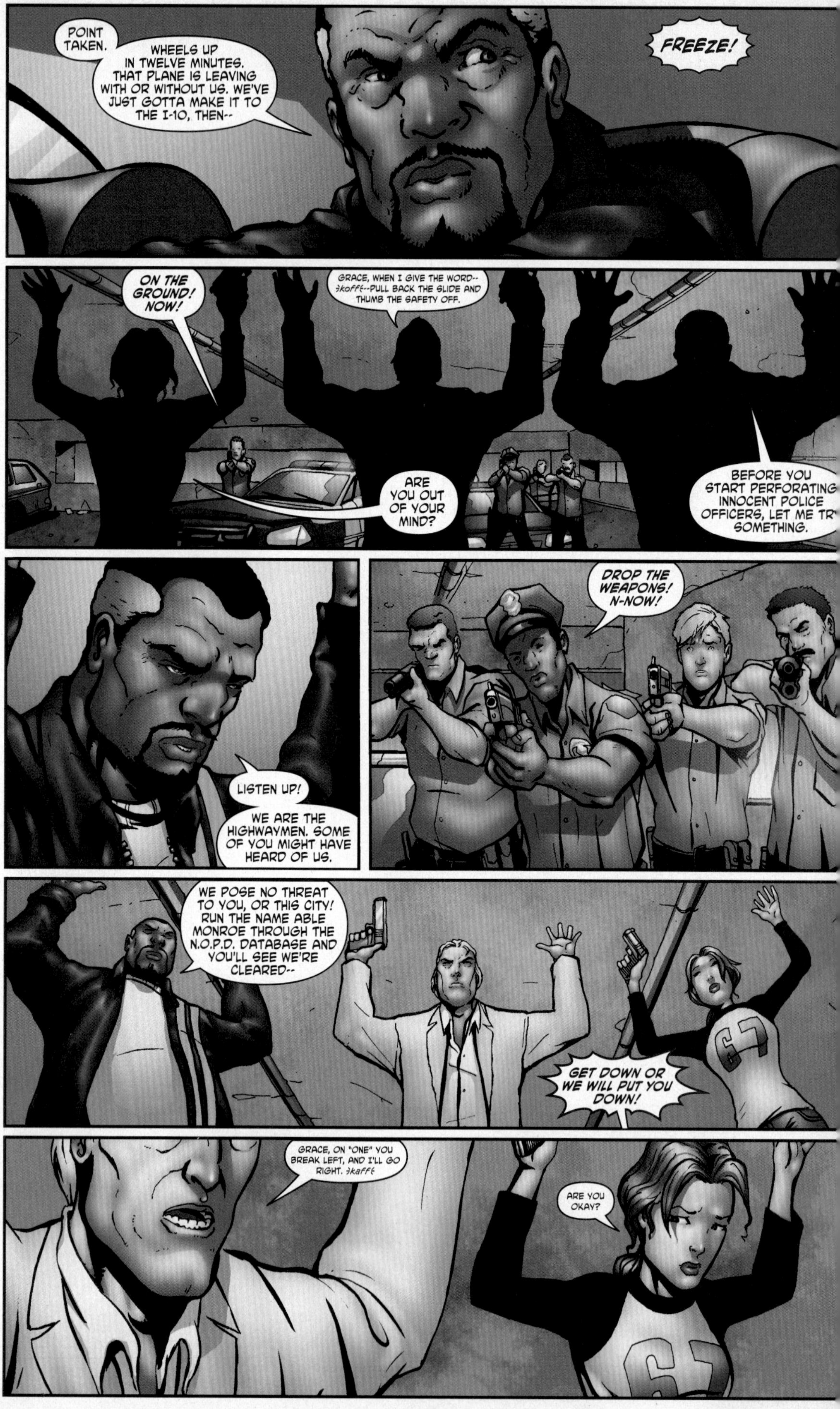
POINT TAKEN.
WHEELS UP IN TWELVE MINUTES. THAT PLANE IS LEAVING WITH OR WITHOUT US. WE'VE JUST GOTTA MAKE IT TO THE I-10, THEN--
FREEZE!
ON THE GROUND! NOW!
GRACE, WHEN I GIVE THE WORD-- *koff*--PULL BACK THE SLIDE AND THUMB THE SAFETY OFF.
ARE YOU OUT OF YOUR MIND?
BEFORE YOU START PERFORATING INNOCENT POLICE OFFICERS, LET ME TR SOMETHING.
LISTEN UP!
WE ARE THE HIGHWAYMEN. SOME OF YOU MIGHT HAVE HEARD OF US.
DROP THE WEAPONS! N-NOW!
WE POSE NO THREAT TO YOU, OR THIS CITY! RUN THE NAME ABLE MONROE THROUGH THE N.O.P.D. DATABASE AND YOU'LL SEE WE'RE CLEARED--
GET DOWN OR WE WILL PUT YOU DOWN!
GRACE, ON "ONE" YOU BREAK LEFT, AND I'LL GO RIGHT. *kaff*
ARE YOU OKAY?

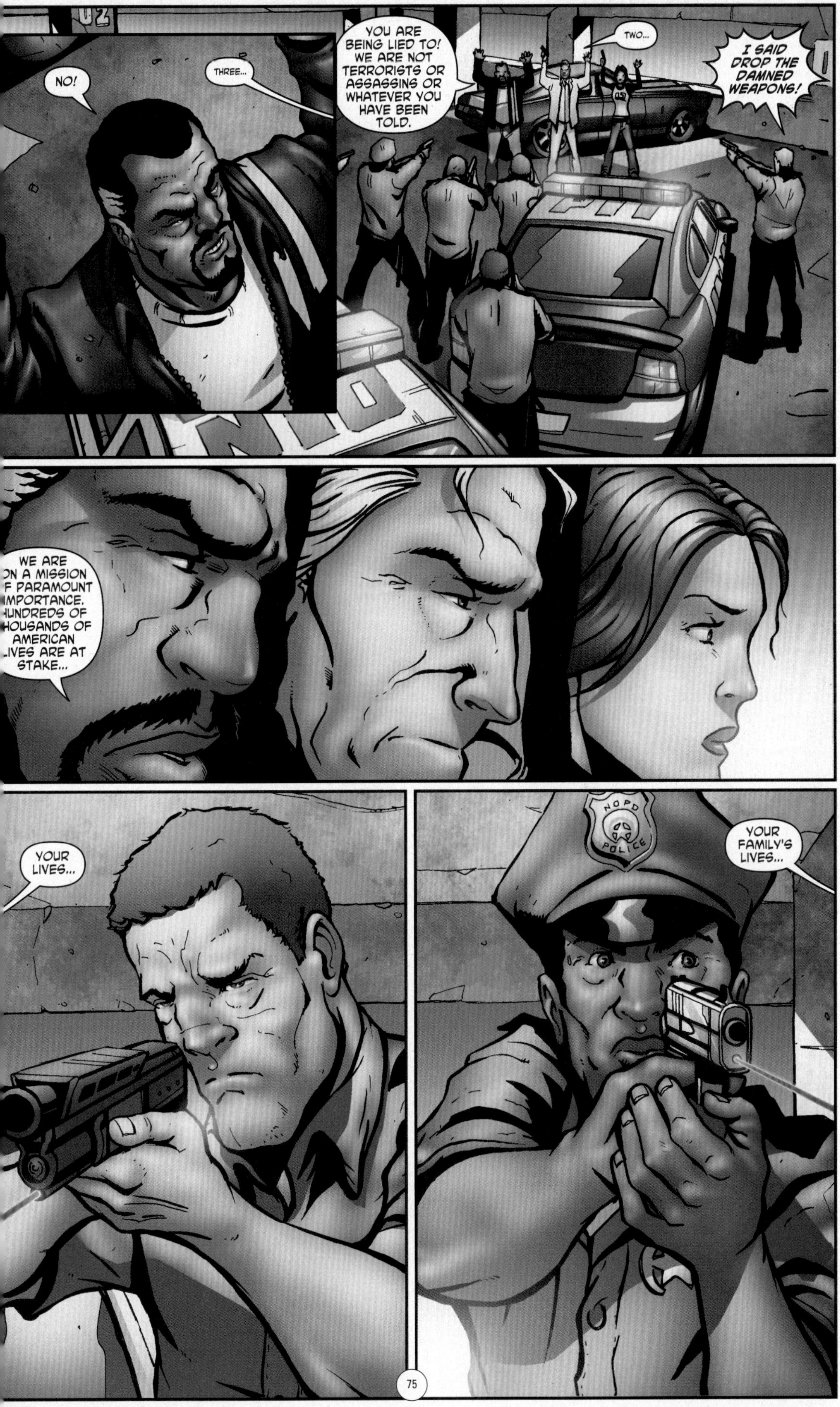
NO!
THREE...
YOU ARE BEING LIED TO! WE ARE NOT TERRORISTS OR ASSASSINS OR WHATEVER YOU HAVE BEEN TOLD.
TWO...
I SAID DROP THE DAMNED WEAPONS!
WE ARE ON A MISSION OF PARAMOUNT IMPORTANCE. HUNDREDS OF THOUSANDS OF AMERICAN LIVES ARE AT STAKE...
YOUR LIVES...
NOPD POLICE
YOUR FAMILY'S LIVES...

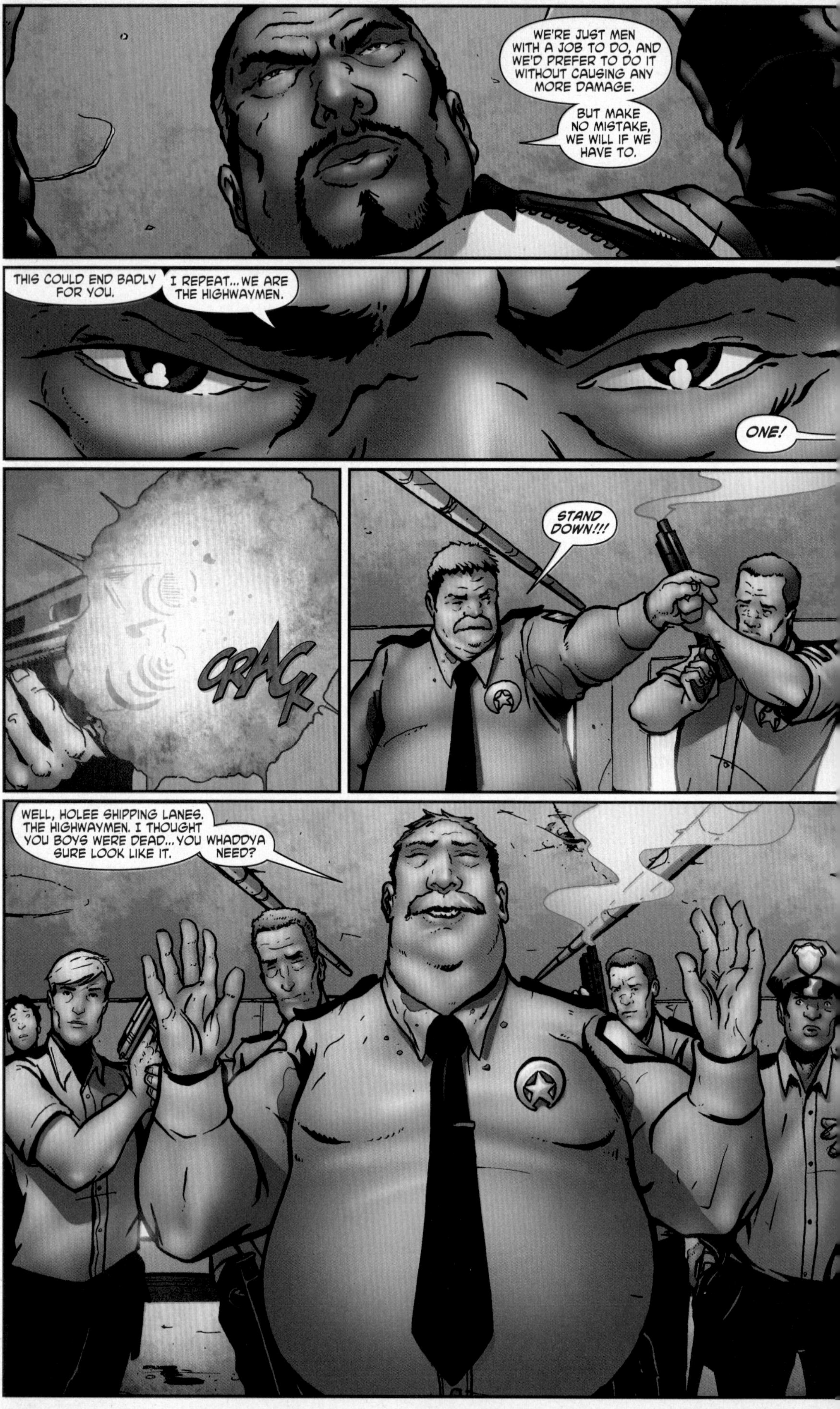

WE'RE JUST MEN WITH A JOB TO DO, AND WE'D PREFER TO DO IT WITHOUT CAUSING ANY MORE DAMAGE.
BUT MAKE NO MISTAKE, WE WILL IF WE HAVE TO.
THIS COULD END BADLY FOR YOU.
I REPEAT...WE ARE THE HIGHWAYMEN.
ONE!
CRACK
STAND DOWN!!!
WELL, HOLEE SHIPPING LANES. THE HIGHWAYMEN. I THOUGHT YOU BOYS WERE DEAD... YOU SURE LOOK LIKE IT.
WHADDYA NEED?

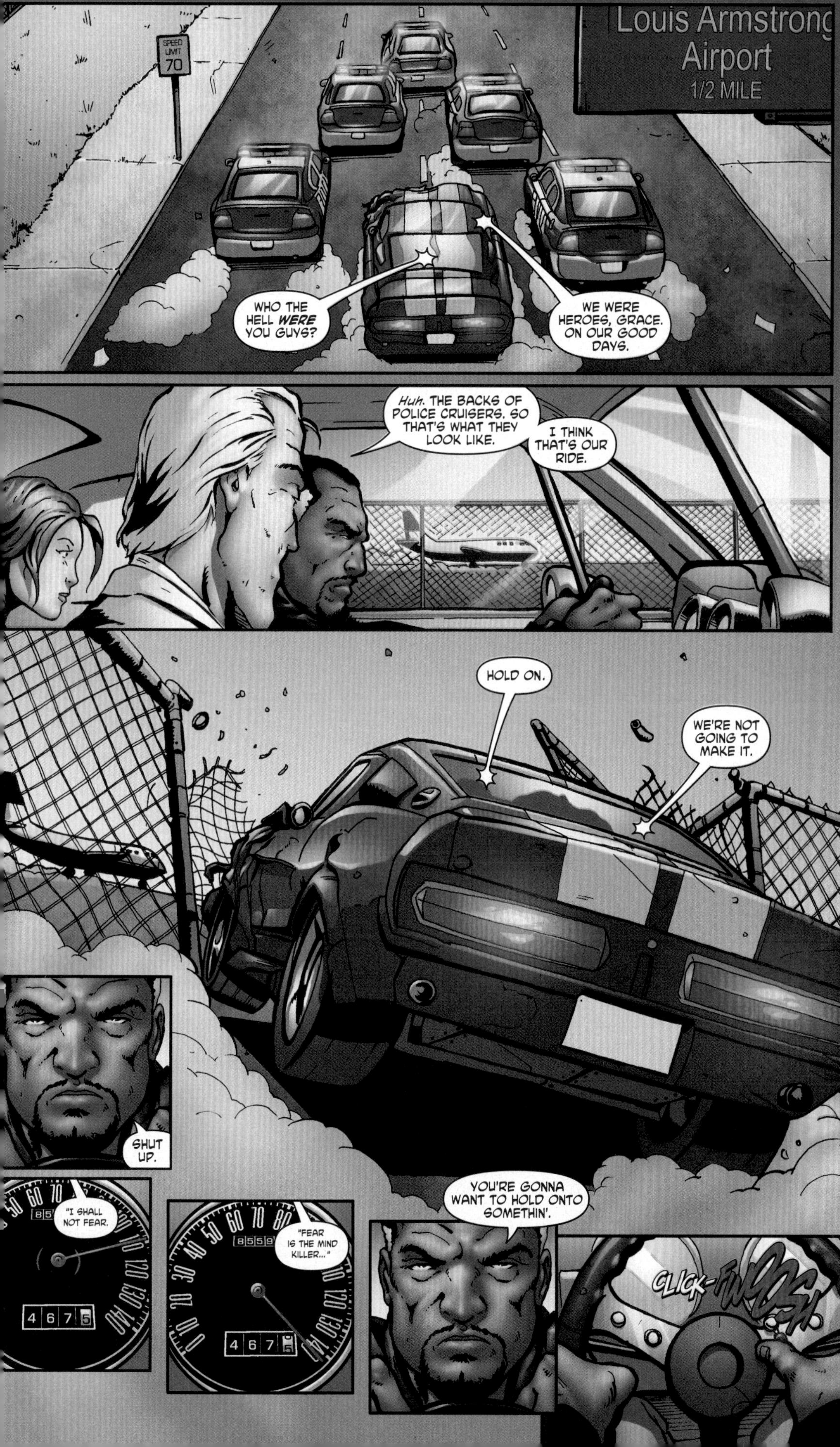
SPEED LIMIT 70
Louis Armstrong Airport 1/2 MILE
WHO THE HELL *WERE* YOU GUYS?
WE WERE HEROES, GRACE. ON OUR GOOD DAYS.
Huh. THE BACKS OF POLICE CRUISERS. SO THAT'S WHAT THEY LOOK LIKE.
I THINK THAT'S OUR RIDE.
HOLD ON.
WE'RE NOT GOING TO MAKE IT.
SHUT UP.
"I SHALL NOT FEAR.
"FEAR IS THE MIND KILLER..."
YOU'RE GONNA WANT TO HOLD ONTO SOMETHIN'.
CLICK-FWOOSH

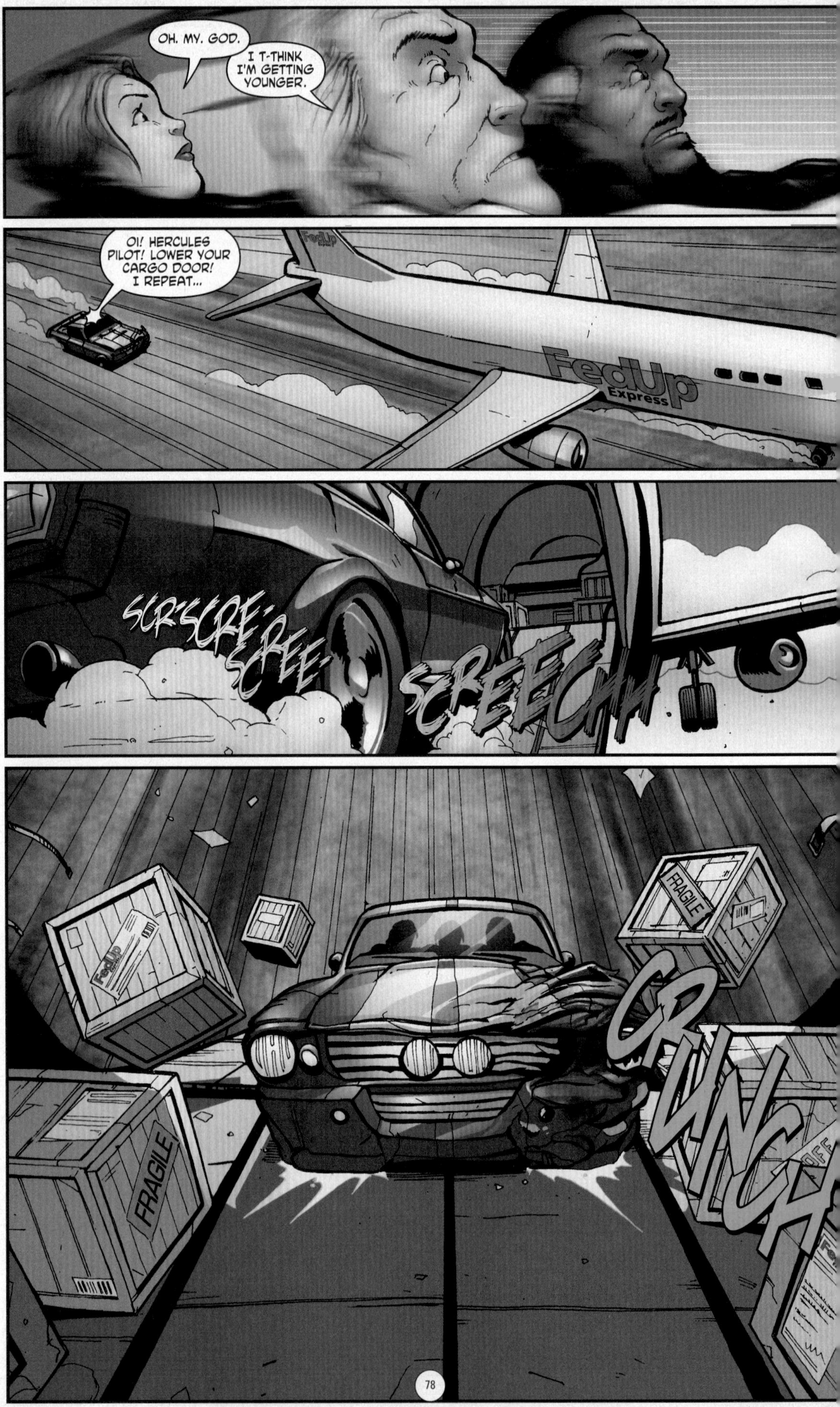
OH. MY. GOD.
I T-THINK I'M GETTING YOUNGER.
OI! HERCULES PILOT! LOWER YOUR CARGO DOOR! I REPEAT...
FedUp Express
SCR'SCRE'SCREE-SCREECHH
FRAGILE
FRAGILE
CRUNCH

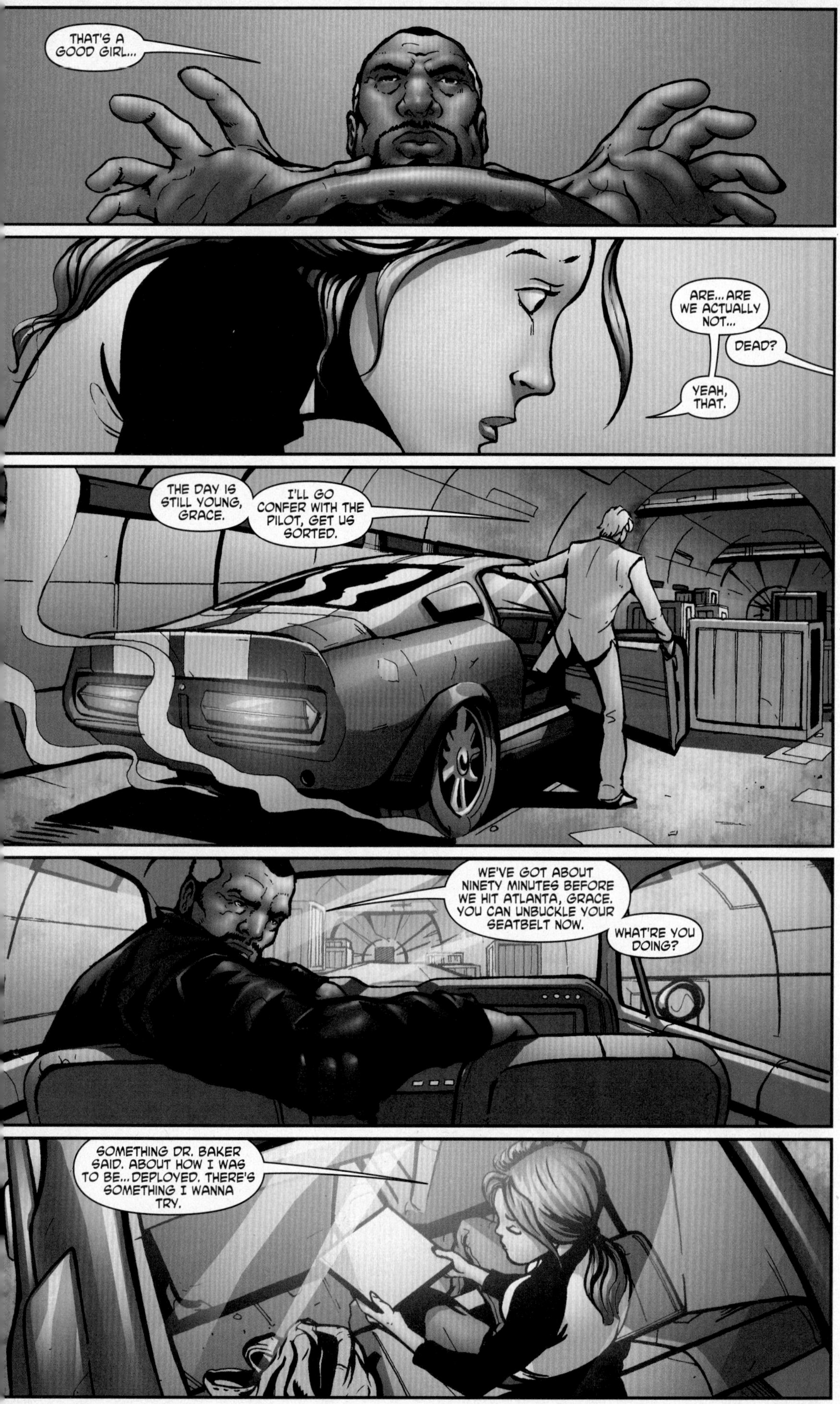
THAT'S A GOOD GIRL...
ARE...ARE WE ACTUALLY NOT...
DEAD?
YEAH, THAT.
THE DAY IS STILL YOUNG, GRACE.
I'LL GO CONFER WITH THE PILOT, GET US SORTED.
WE'VE GOT ABOUT NINETY MINUTES BEFORE WE HIT ATLANTA, GRACE. YOU CAN UNBUCKLE YOUR SEATBELT NOW.
WHAT'RE YOU DOING?
SOMETHING DR. BAKER SAID. ABOUT HOW I WAS TO BE...DEPLOYED. THERE'S SOMETHING I WANNA TRY.

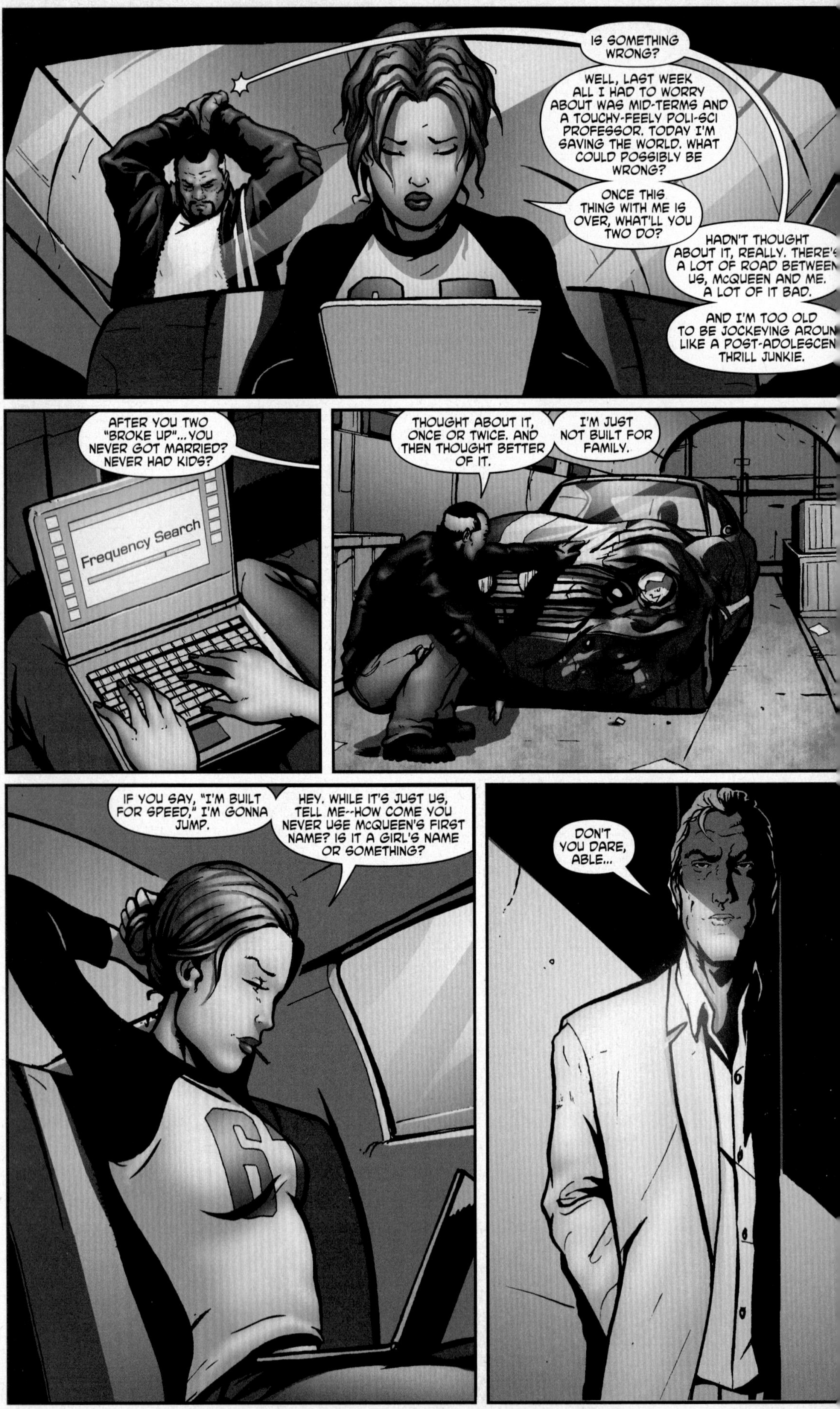
IS SOMETHING WRONG?
WELL, LAST WEEK ALL I HAD TO WORRY ABOUT WAS MID-TERMS AND A TOUCHY-FEELY POLI-SCI PROFESSOR. TODAY I'M SAVING THE WORLD. WHAT COULD POSSIBLY BE WRONG?
ONCE THIS THING WITH ME IS OVER, WHAT'LL YOU TWO DO?
HADN'T THOUGHT ABOUT IT, REALLY. THERE'S A LOT OF ROAD BETWEEN US, McQUEEN AND ME. A LOT OF IT BAD.
AND I'M TOO OLD TO BE JOCKEYING AROUN LIKE A POST-ADOLESCEN THRILL JUNKIE.
AFTER YOU TWO "BROKE UP"...YOU NEVER GOT MARRIED? NEVER HAD KIDS?
Frequency Search
THOUGHT ABOUT IT, ONCE OR TWICE. AND THEN THOUGHT BETTER OF IT.
I'M JUST NOT BUILT FOR FAMILY.
IF YOU SAY, "I'M BUILT FOR SPEED," I'M GONNA JUMP.
HEY. WHILE IT'S JUST US, TELL ME--HOW COME YOU NEVER USE McQUEEN'S FIRST NAME? IS IT A GIRL'S NAME OR SOMETHING?
DON'T YOU DARE, ABLE...

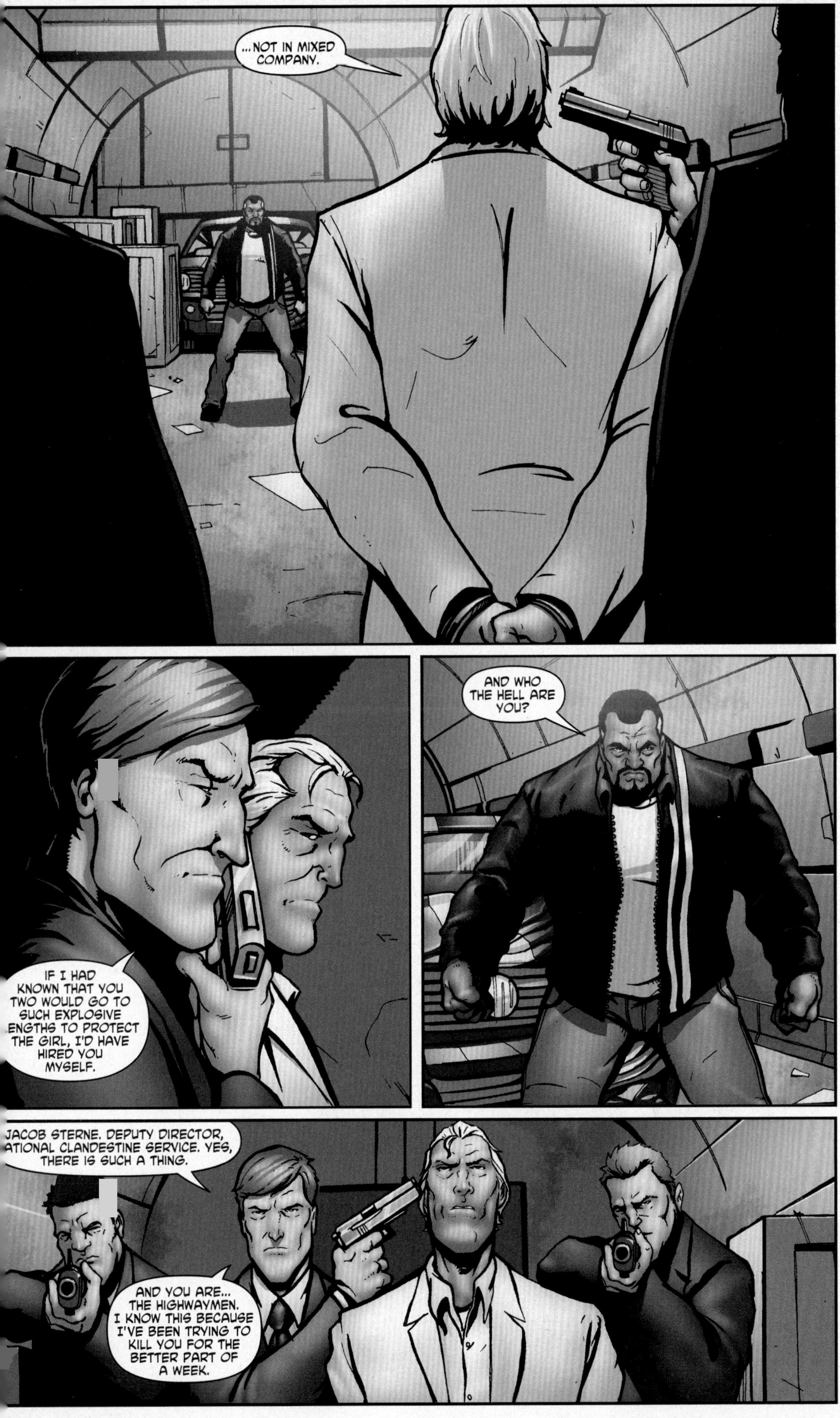
...NOT IN MIXED COMPANY.
IF I HAD KNOWN THAT YOU TWO WOULD GO TO SUCH EXPLOSIVE ENGTHS TO PROTECT THE GIRL, I'D HAVE HIRED YOU MYSELF.
AND WHO THE HELL ARE YOU?
JACOB STERNE. DEPUTY DIRECTOR, ATIONAL CLANDESTINE SERVICE. YES, THERE IS SUCH A THING.
AND YOU ARE... THE HIGHWAYMEN. I KNOW THIS BECAUSE I'VE BEEN TRYING TO KILL YOU FOR THE BETTER PART OF A WEEK.

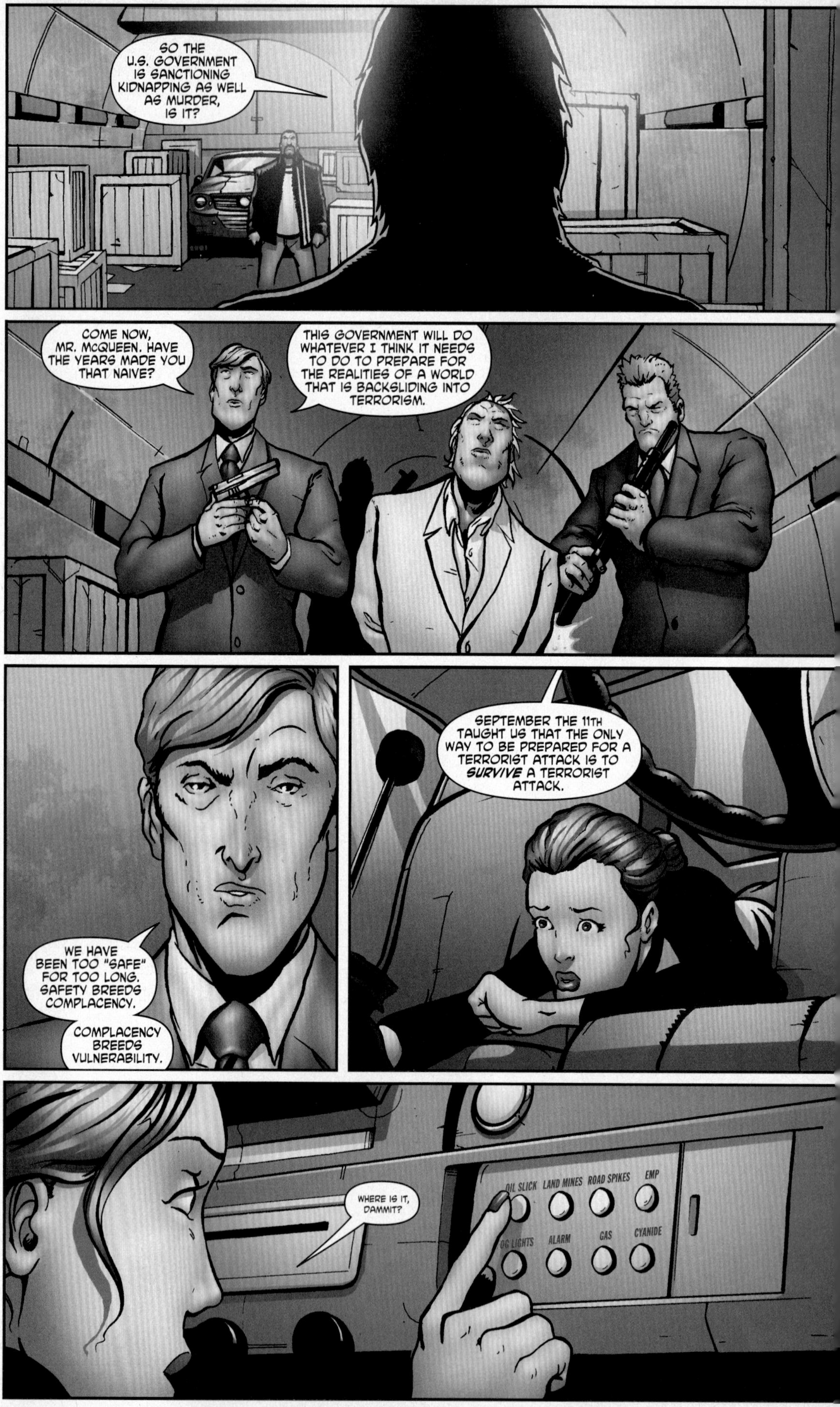
SO THE U.S. GOVERNMENT IS SANCTIONING KIDNAPPING AS WELL AS MURDER, IS IT?
COME NOW, MR. McQUEEN. HAVE THE YEARS MADE YOU THAT NAIVE?
THIS GOVERNMENT WILL DO WHATEVER I THINK IT NEEDS TO DO TO PREPARE FOR THE REALITIES OF A WORLD THAT IS BACKSLIDING INTO TERRORISM.
WE HAVE BEEN TOO "SAFE" FOR TOO LONG. SAFETY BREEDS COMPLACENCY.
COMPLACENCY BREEDS VULNERABILITY.
SEPTEMBER THE 11TH TAUGHT US THAT THE ONLY WAY TO BE PREPARED FOR A TERRORIST ATTACK IS TO *SURVIVE* A TERRORIST ATTACK.
WHERE IS IT, DAMMIT?
OIL SLICK
LAND MINES
ROAD SPIKES
EMP
OG LIGHTS
ALARM
GAS
CYANIDE

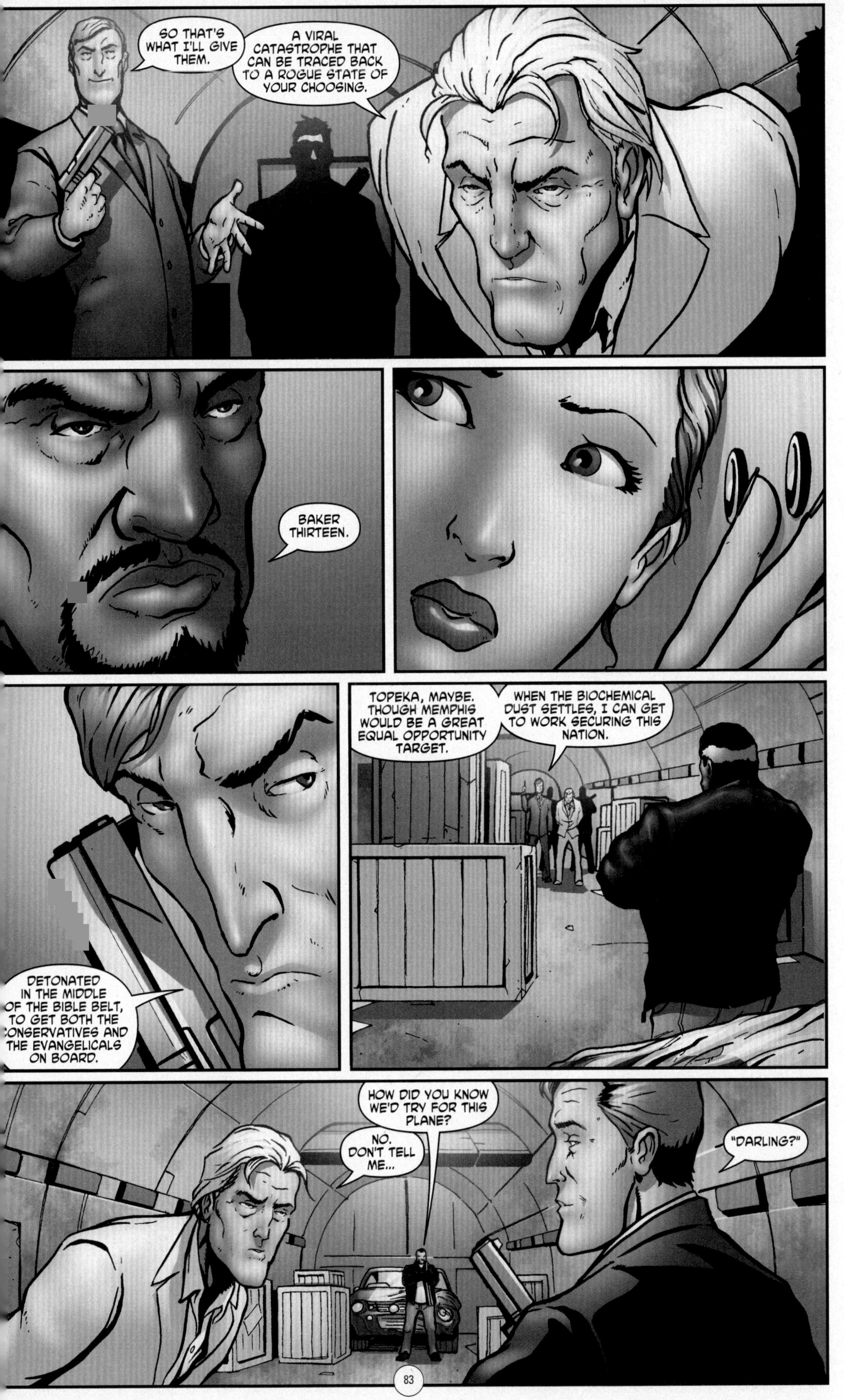
SO THAT'S WHAT I'LL GIVE THEM.
A VIRAL CATASTROPHE THAT CAN BE TRACED BACK TO A ROGUE STATE OF YOUR CHOOSING.
BAKER THIRTEEN.
DETONATED IN THE MIDDLE OF THE BIBLE BELT, TO GET BOTH THE CONSERVATIVES AND THE EVANGELICALS ON BOARD.
TOPEKA, MAYBE. THOUGH MEMPHIS WOULD BE A GREAT EQUAL OPPORTUNITY TARGET.
WHEN THE BIOCHEMICAL DUST SETTLES, I CAN GET TO WORK SECURING THIS NATION.
HOW DID YOU KNOW WE'D TRY FOR THIS PLANE?
NO. DON'T TELL ME...
"DARLING?"

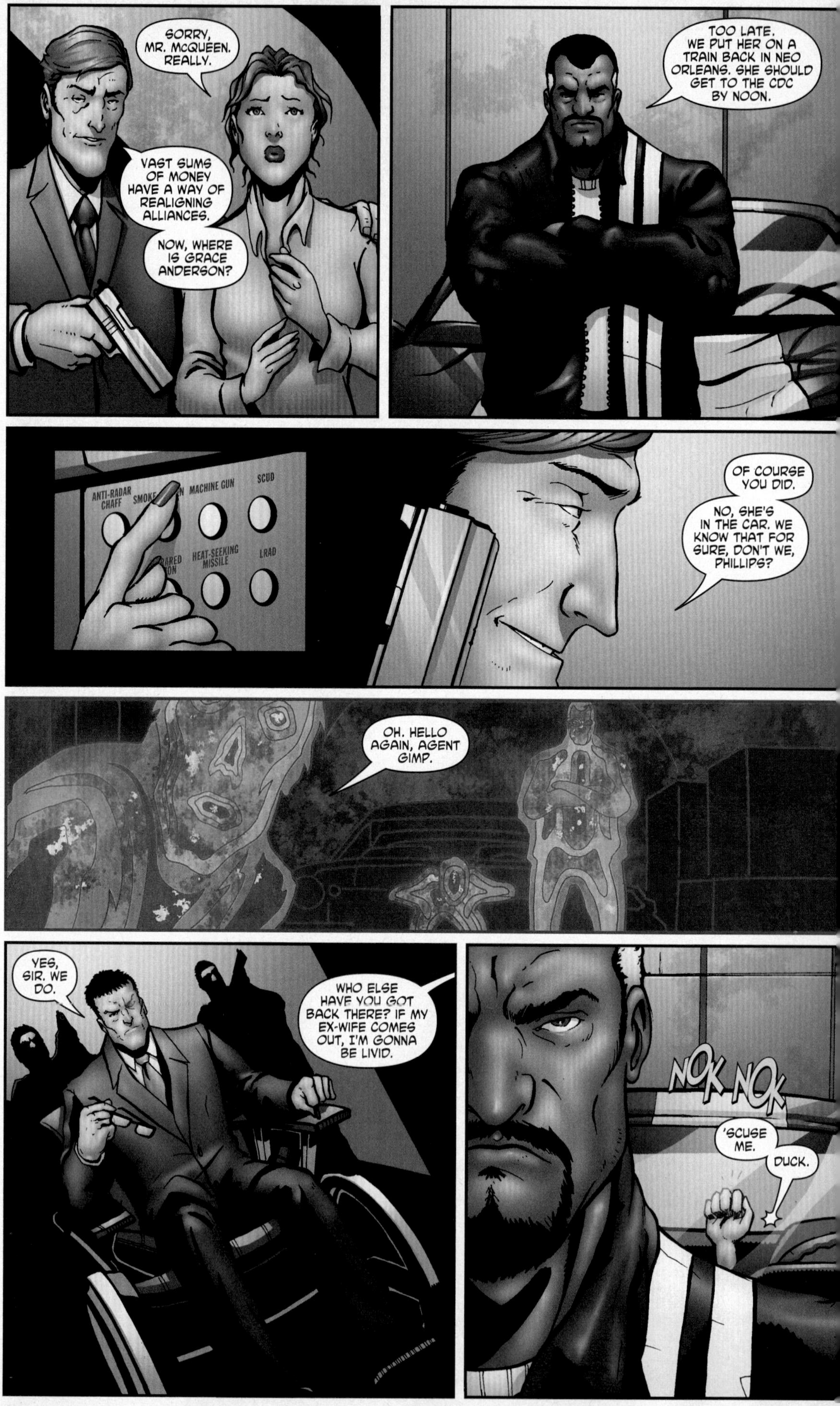
SORRY, MR. McQUEEN. REALLY.
VAST SUMS OF MONEY HAVE A WAY OF REALIGNING ALLIANCES.
NOW, WHERE IS GRACE ANDERSON?
TOO LATE. WE PUT HER ON A TRAIN BACK IN NEO ORLEANS. SHE SHOULD GET TO THE CDC BY NOON.
ANTI-RADAR CHAFF
SMOKE
MACHINE GUN
SCUD
HEAT-SEEKING MISSILE
LRAD
OF COURSE YOU DID.
NO, SHE'S IN THE CAR. WE KNOW THAT FOR SURE, DON'T WE, PHILLIPS?
OH. HELLO AGAIN, AGENT GIMP.
YES, SIR. WE DO.
WHO ELSE HAVE YOU GOT BACK THERE? IF MY EX-WIFE COMES OUT, I'M GONNA BE LIVID.
NOK NOK
'SCUSE ME.
DUCK.

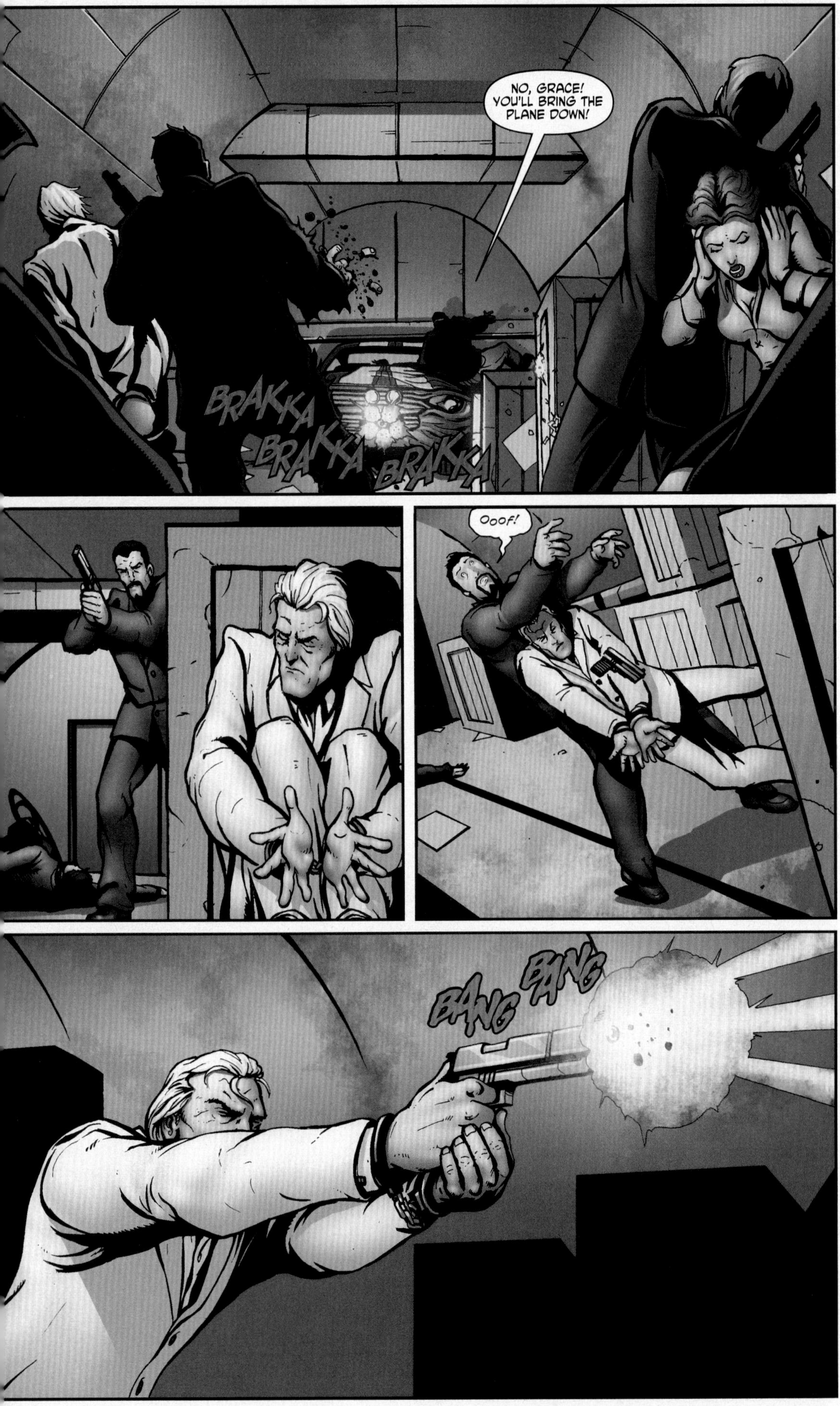

NO, GRACE! YOU'LL BRING THE PLANE DOWN!
BRAKKA
BRAKKA
BRAKKA
OOOF!
BANG
BANG

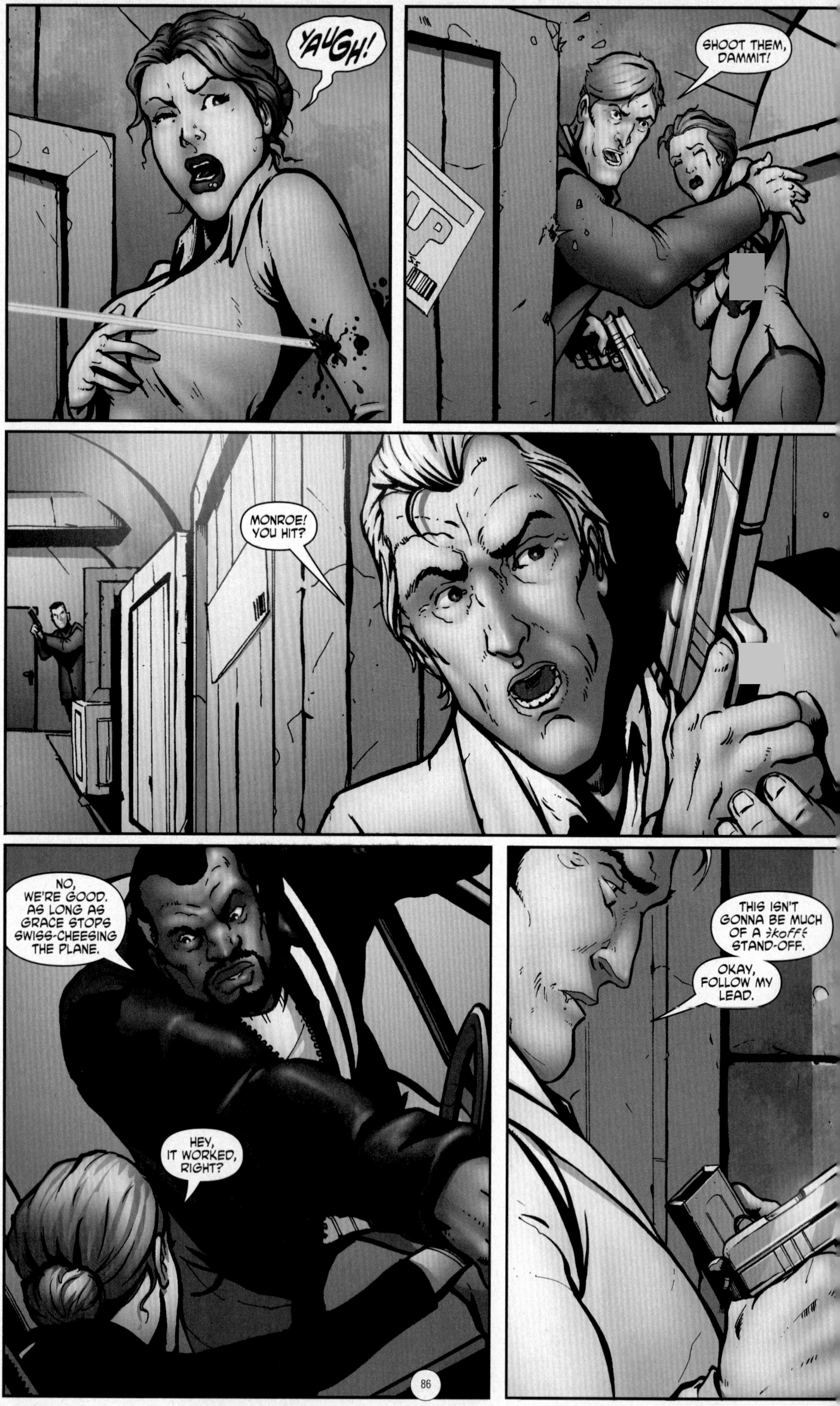
YAUGH!
SHOOT THEM, DAMMIT!
MONROE! YOU HIT?
NO, WE'RE GOOD. AS LONG AS GRACE STOPS SWISS-CHEESING THE PLANE.
HEY, IT WORKED, RIGHT?
THIS ISN'T GONNA BE MUCH OF A *koff* STAND-OFF.
OKAY, FOLLOW MY LEAD.

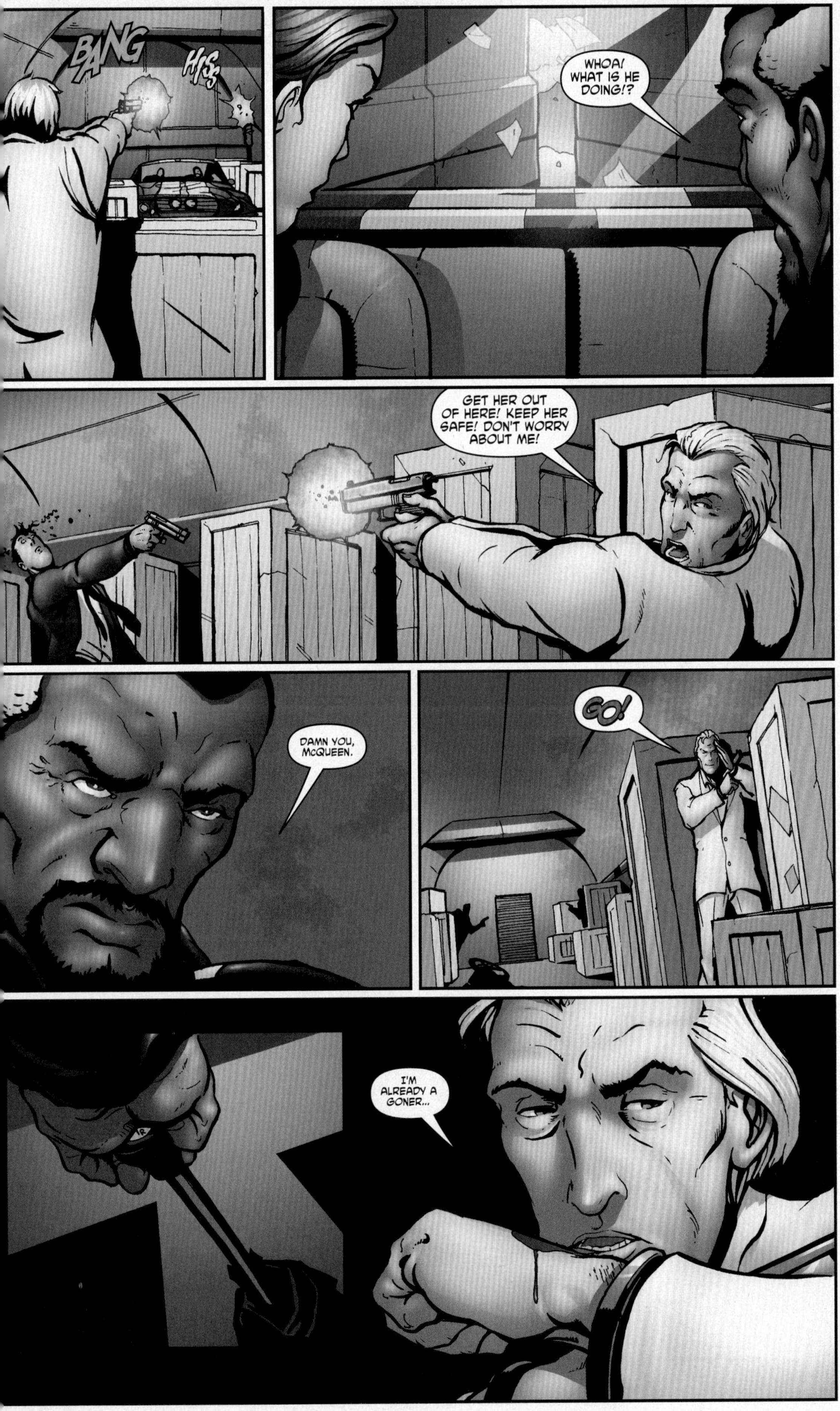
BANG
HISS
WHOA! WHAT IS HE DOING!?
GET HER OUT OF HERE! KEEP HER SAFE! DON'T WORRY ABOUT ME!
DAMN YOU, McQUEEN.
GO!
I'M ALREADY A GONER...

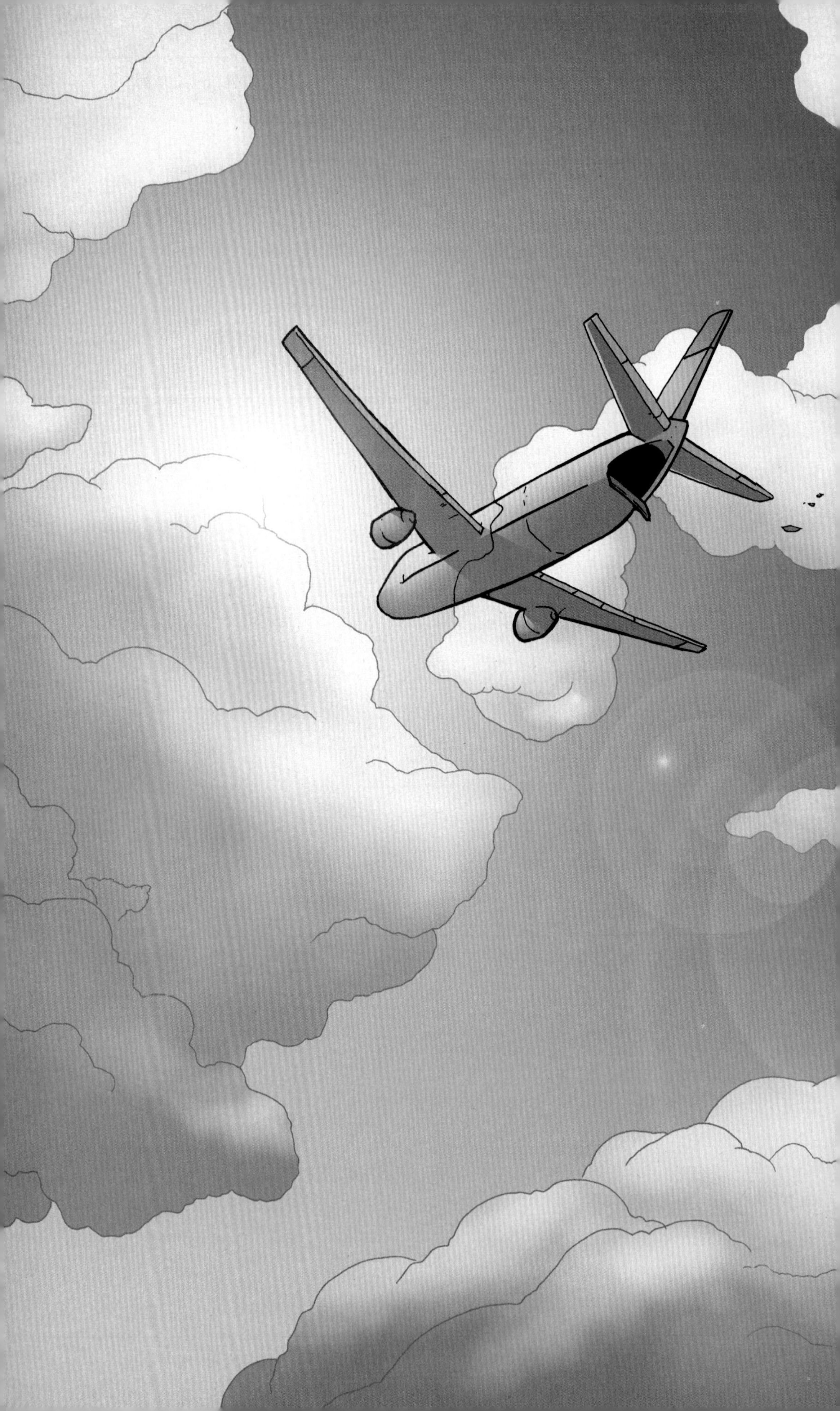

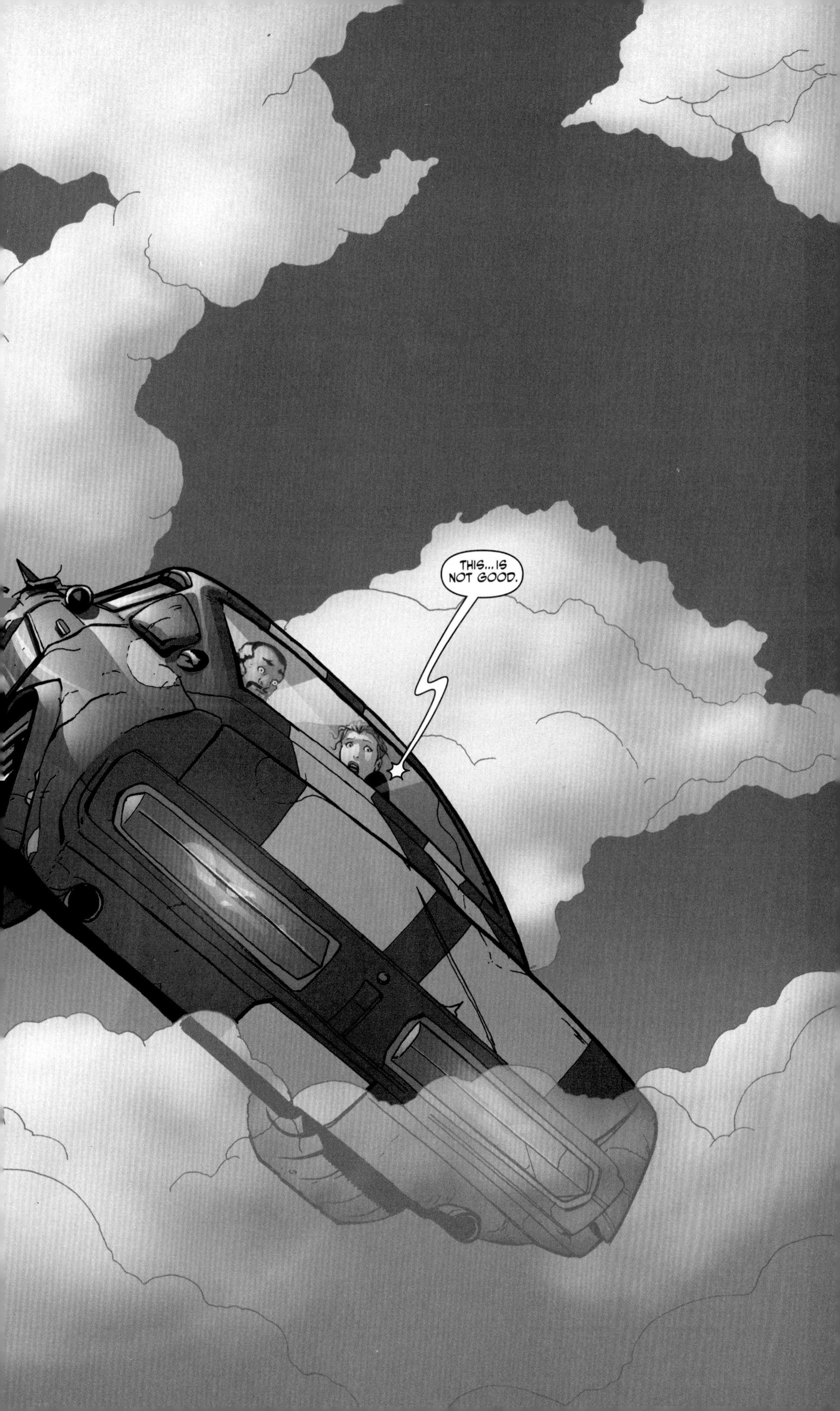
THIS... IS NOT GOOD.

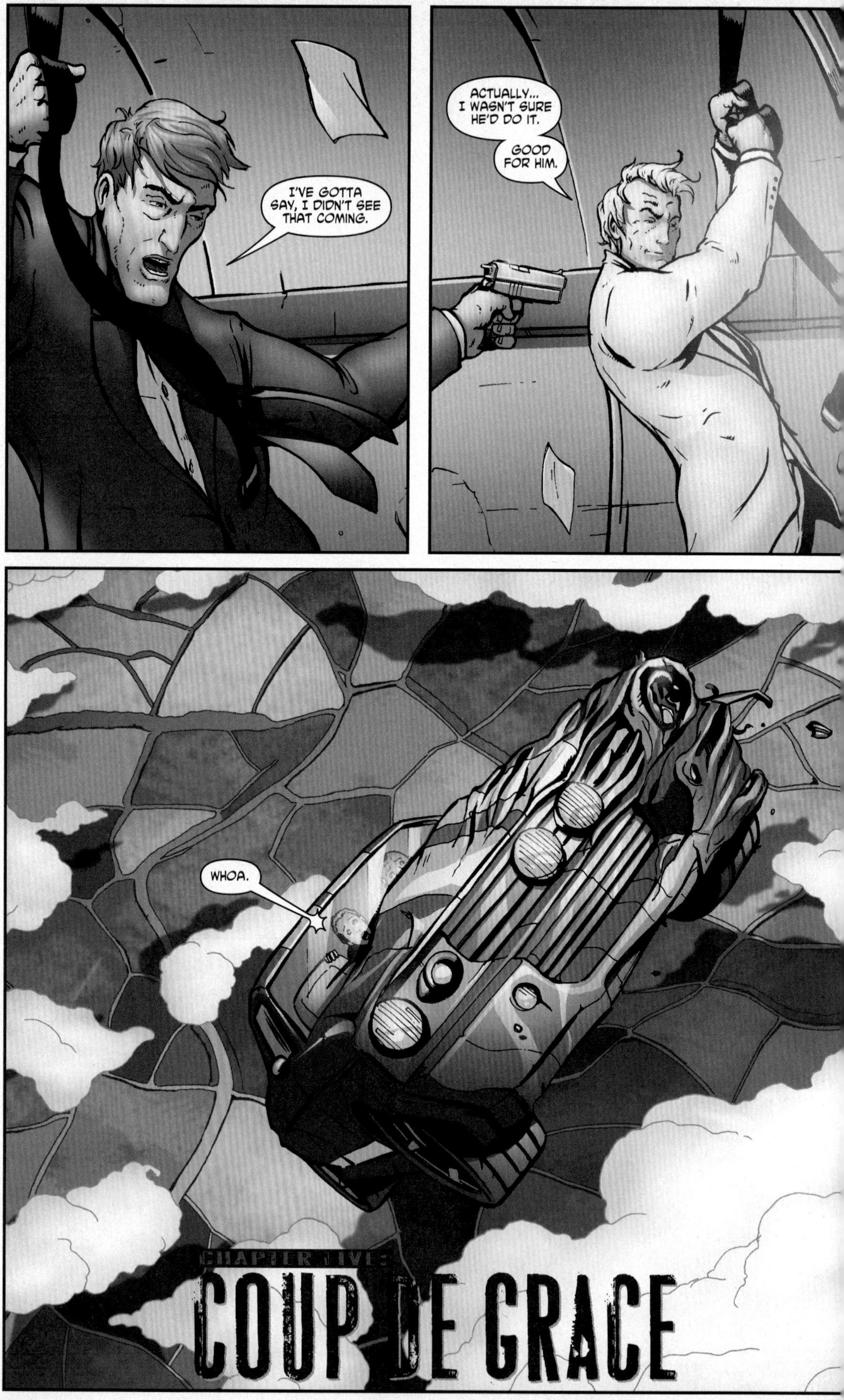
I'VE GOTTA SAY, I DIDN'T SEE THAT COMING.
ACTUALLY... I WASN'T SURE HE'D DO IT.
GOOD FOR HIM.
WHOA.
CHAPTER FIVE:
COUP DE GRACE

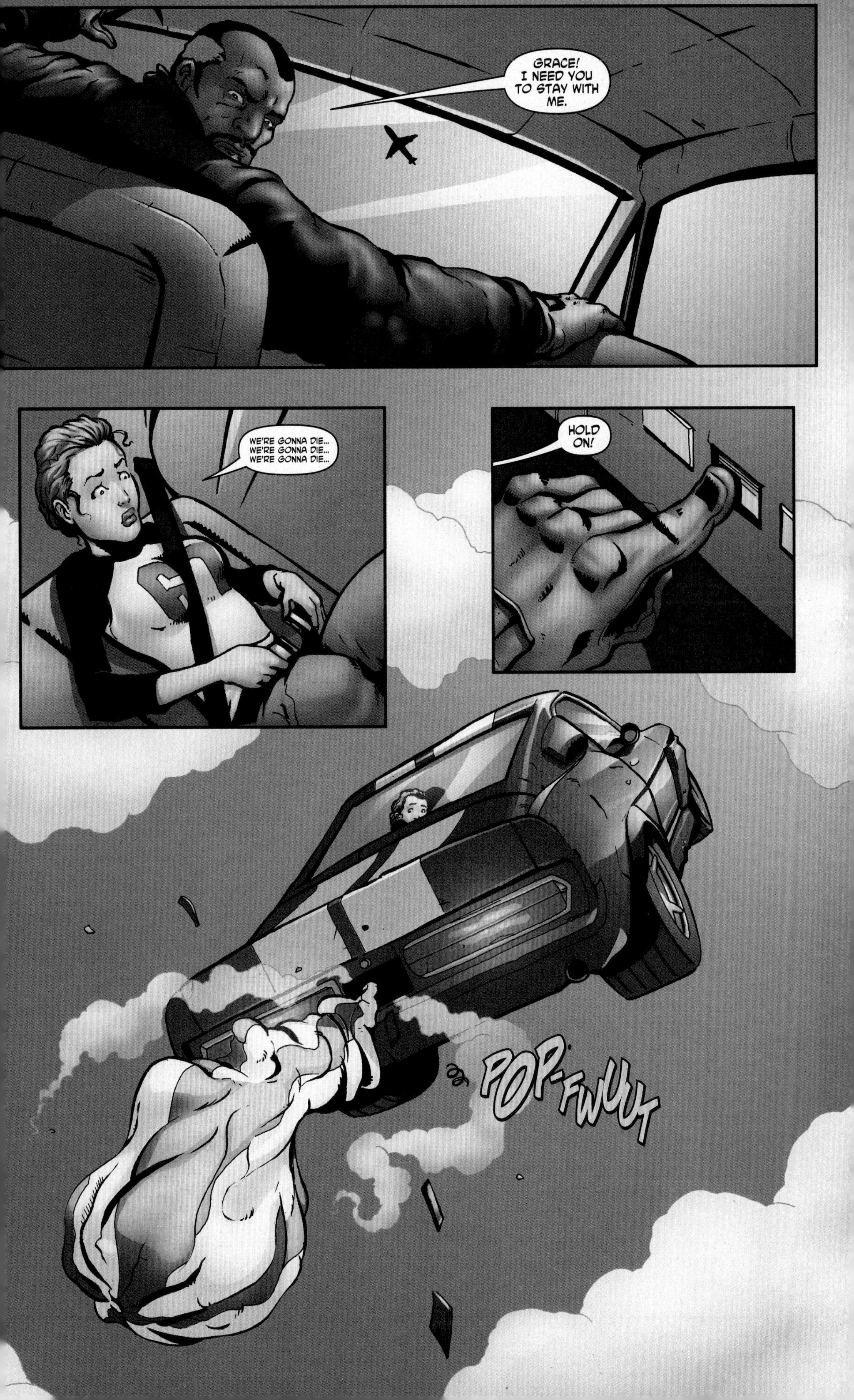
GRACE! I NEED YOU TO STAY WITH ME.
WE'RE GONNA DIE... WE'RE GONNA DIE... WE'RE GONNA DIE...
HOLD ON!
POP-FWUUK

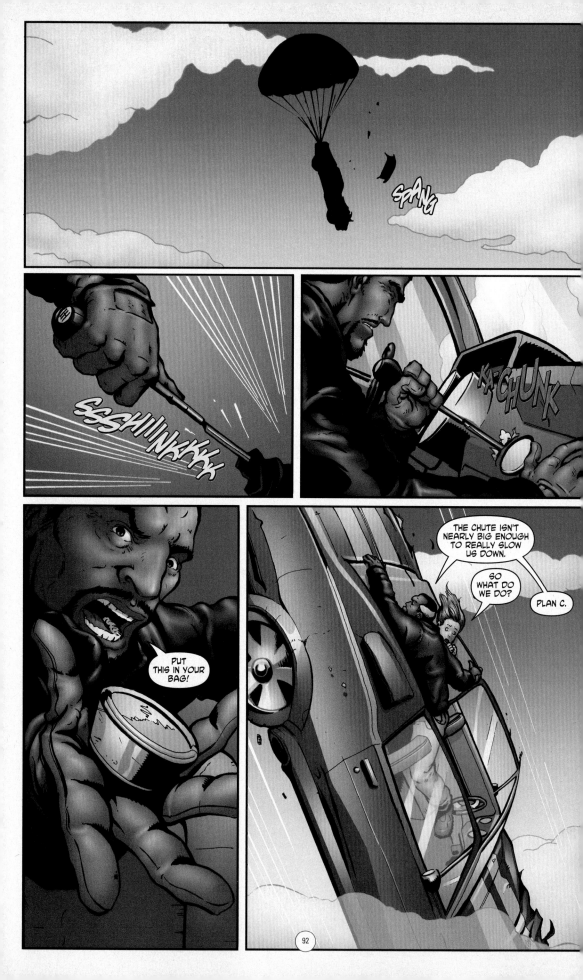

SPANG

SSSHIIINKKKK

KA-CHUNK

PUT THIS IN YOUR BAG!

THE CHUTE ISN'T NEARLY BIG ENOUGH TO REALLY SLOW US DOWN.

SO WHAT DO WE DO?

PLAN C.

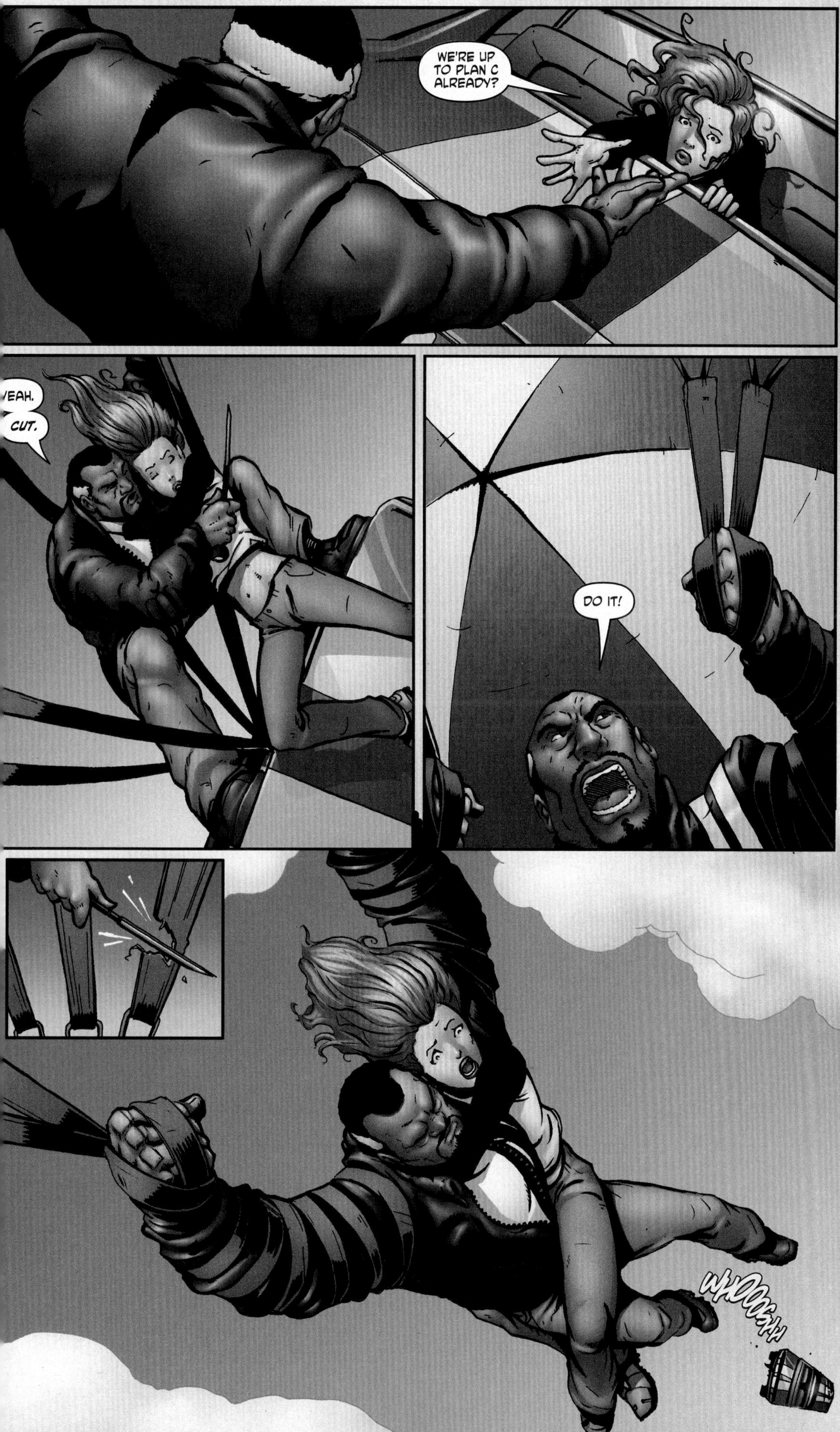
WE'RE UP TO PLAN C ALREADY?
YEAH.
CUT.
DO IT!
WHOOOSHH

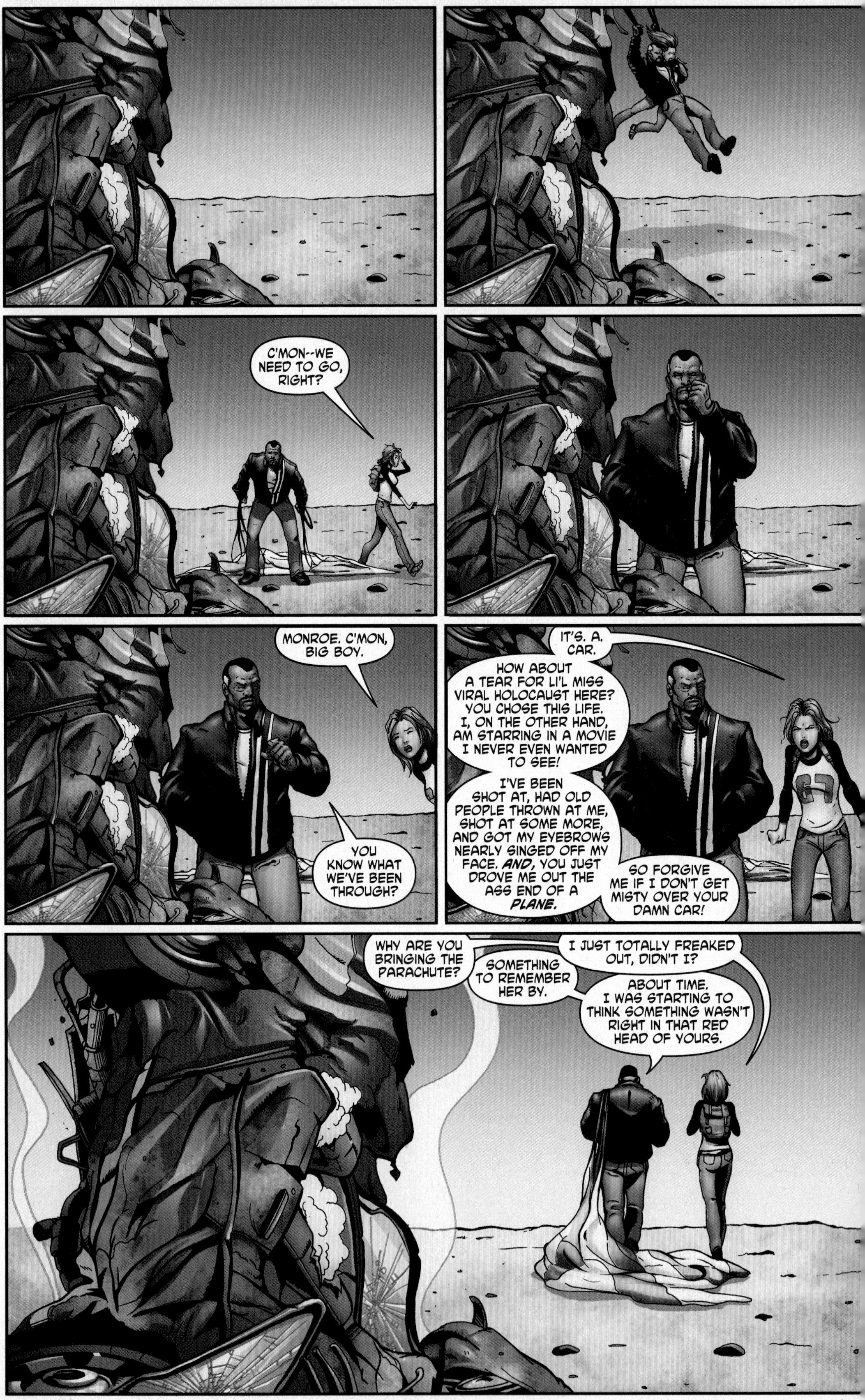
C'MON--WE NEED TO GO, RIGHT?
MONROE. C'MON, BIG BOY.
YOU KNOW WHAT WE'VE BEEN THROUGH?
IT'S. A. CAR.
HOW ABOUT A TEAR FOR LI'L MISS VIRAL HOLOCAUST HERE? YOU CHOSE THIS LIFE. I, ON THE OTHER HAND, AM STARRING IN A MOVIE I NEVER EVEN WANTED TO SEE!
I'VE BEEN SHOT AT, HAD OLD PEOPLE THROWN AT ME, SHOT AT SOME MORE, AND GOT MY EYEBROWS NEARLY SINGED OFF MY FACE. AND, YOU JUST DROVE ME OUT THE ASS END OF A PLANE.
SO FORGIVE ME IF I DON'T GET MISTY OVER YOUR DAMN CAR!
WHY ARE YOU BRINGING THE PARACHUTE?
SOMETHING TO REMEMBER HER BY.
I JUST TOTALLY FREAKED OUT, DIDN'T I?
ABOUT TIME. I WAS STARTING TO THINK SOMETHING WASN'T RIGHT IN THAT RED HEAD OF YOURS.

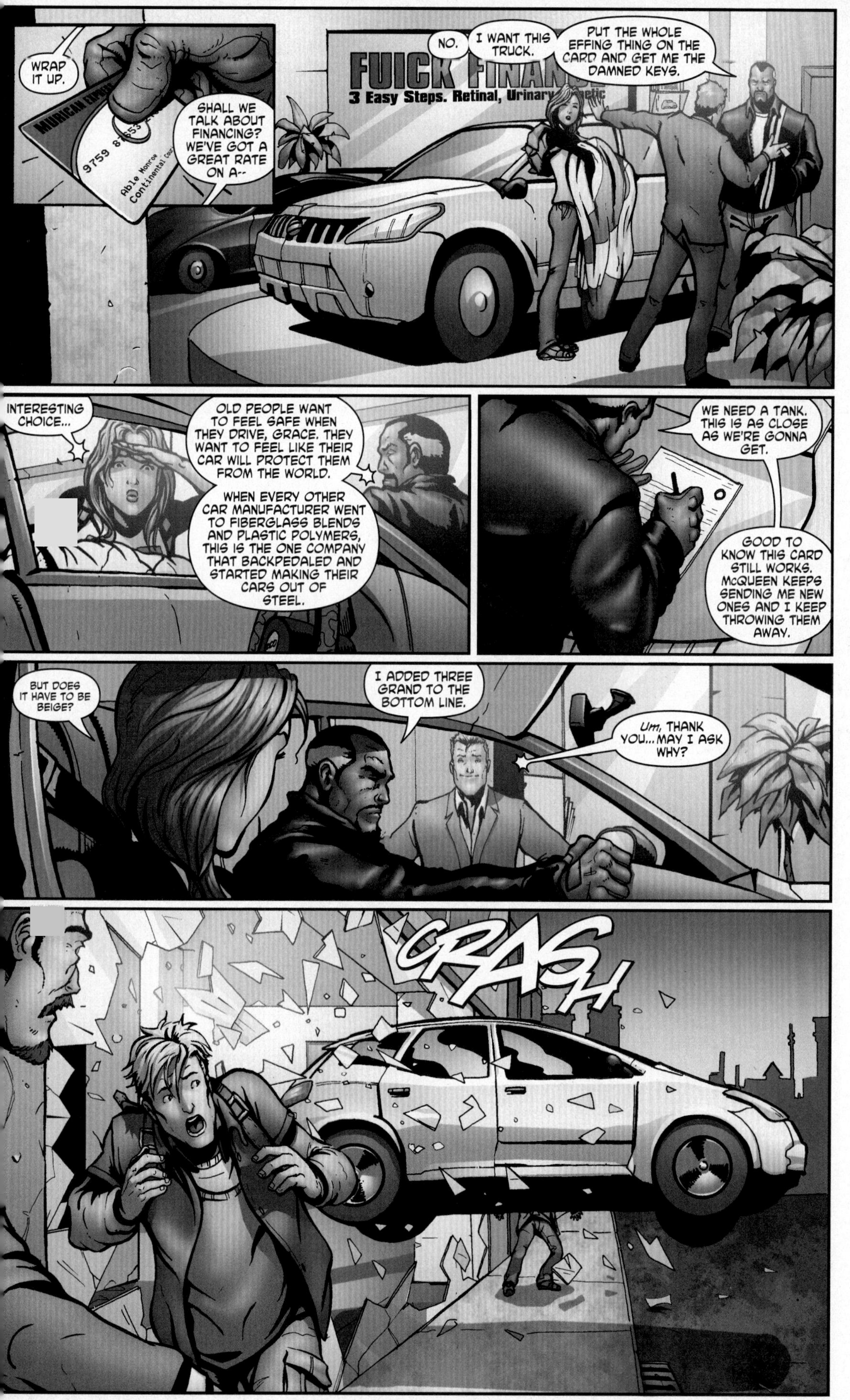
WRAP IT UP.
MURICAN EXPRESS
9759 87653
Able Monroe
Continental Couri
SHALL WE TALK ABOUT FINANCING? WE'VE GOT A GREAT RATE ON A--
FUICK FINANCE
3 Easy Steps. Retinal, Urinary
NO.
I WANT THIS TRUCK.
PUT THE WHOLE EFFING THING ON THE CARD AND GET ME THE DAMNED KEYS.
INTERESTING CHOICE...
OLD PEOPLE WANT TO FEEL SAFE WHEN THEY DRIVE, GRACE. THEY WANT TO FEEL LIKE THEIR CAR WILL PROTECT THEM FROM THE WORLD.
WHEN EVERY OTHER CAR MANUFACTURER WENT TO FIBERGLASS BLENDS AND PLASTIC POLYMERS, THIS IS THE ONE COMPANY THAT BACKPEDALED AND STARTED MAKING THEIR CARS OUT OF STEEL.
WE NEED A TANK. THIS IS AS CLOSE AS WE'RE GONNA GET.
GOOD TO KNOW THIS CARD STILL WORKS. McQUEEN KEEPS SENDING ME NEW ONES AND I KEEP THROWING THEM AWAY.
BUT DOES IT HAVE TO BE BEIGE?
I ADDED THREE GRAND TO THE BOTTOM LINE.
Um, THANK YOU...MAY I ASK WHY?
CRASH

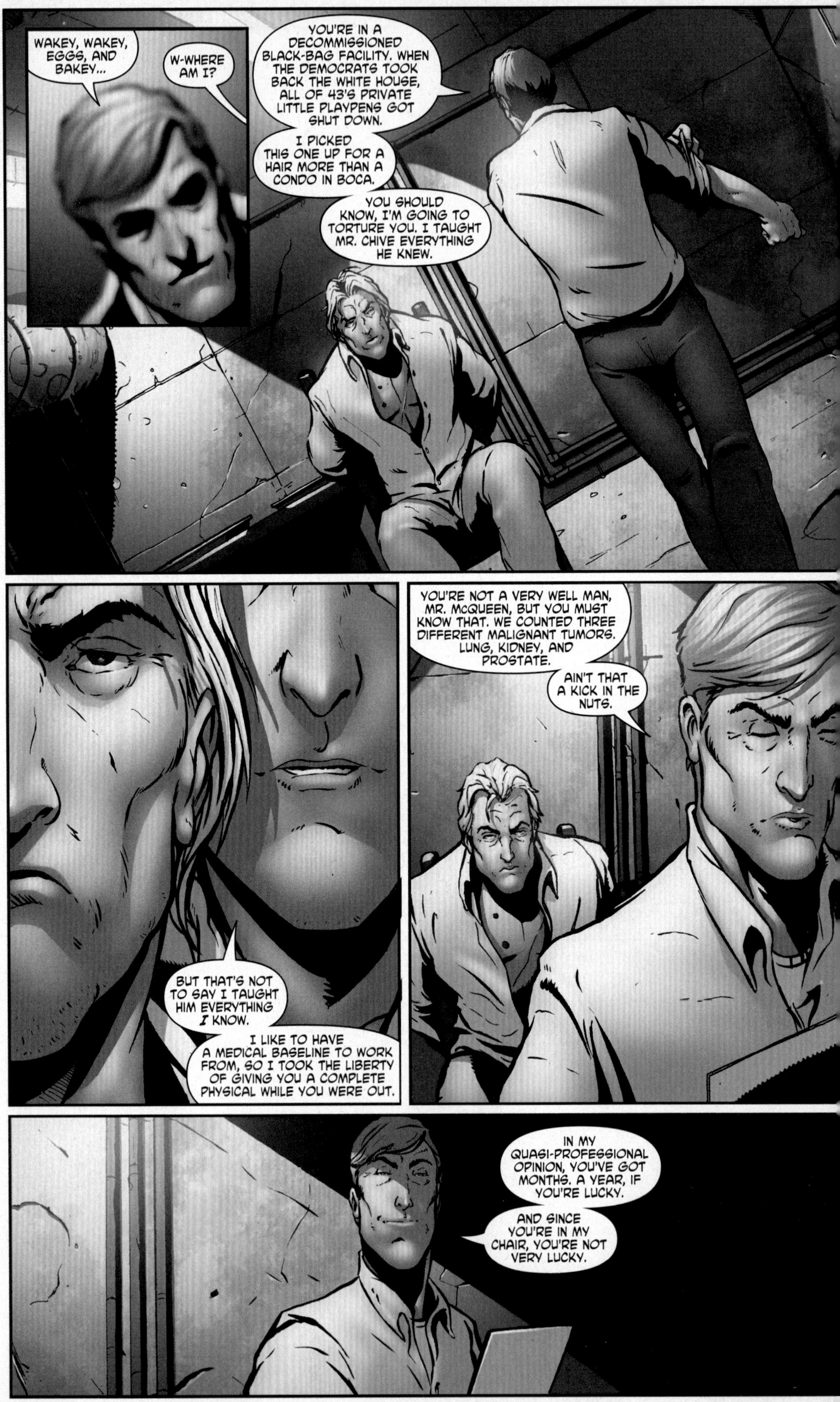
WAKEY, WAKEY, EGGS, AND BAKEY...
W-WHERE AM I?
YOU'RE IN A DECOMMISSIONED BLACK-BAG FACILITY. WHEN THE DEMOCRATS TOOK BACK THE WHITE HOUSE, ALL OF 43'S PRIVATE LITTLE PLAYPENS GOT SHUT DOWN.
I PICKED THIS ONE UP FOR A HAIR MORE THAN A CONDO IN BOCA.
YOU SHOULD KNOW, I'M GOING TO TORTURE YOU. I TAUGHT MR. CHIVE EVERYTHING HE KNEW.
BUT THAT'S NOT TO SAY I TAUGHT HIM EVERYTHING I KNOW.
I LIKE TO HAVE A MEDICAL BASELINE TO WORK FROM, SO I TOOK THE LIBERTY OF GIVING YOU A COMPLETE PHYSICAL WHILE YOU WERE OUT.
YOU'RE NOT A VERY WELL MAN, MR. McQUEEN, BUT YOU MUST KNOW THAT. WE COUNTED THREE DIFFERENT MALIGNANT TUMORS. LUNG, KIDNEY, AND PROSTATE.
AIN'T THAT A KICK IN THE NUTS.
IN MY QUASI-PROFESSIONAL OPINION, YOU'VE GOT MONTHS. A YEAR, IF YOU'RE LUCKY.
AND SINCE YOU'RE IN MY CHAIR, YOU'RE NOT VERY LUCKY.

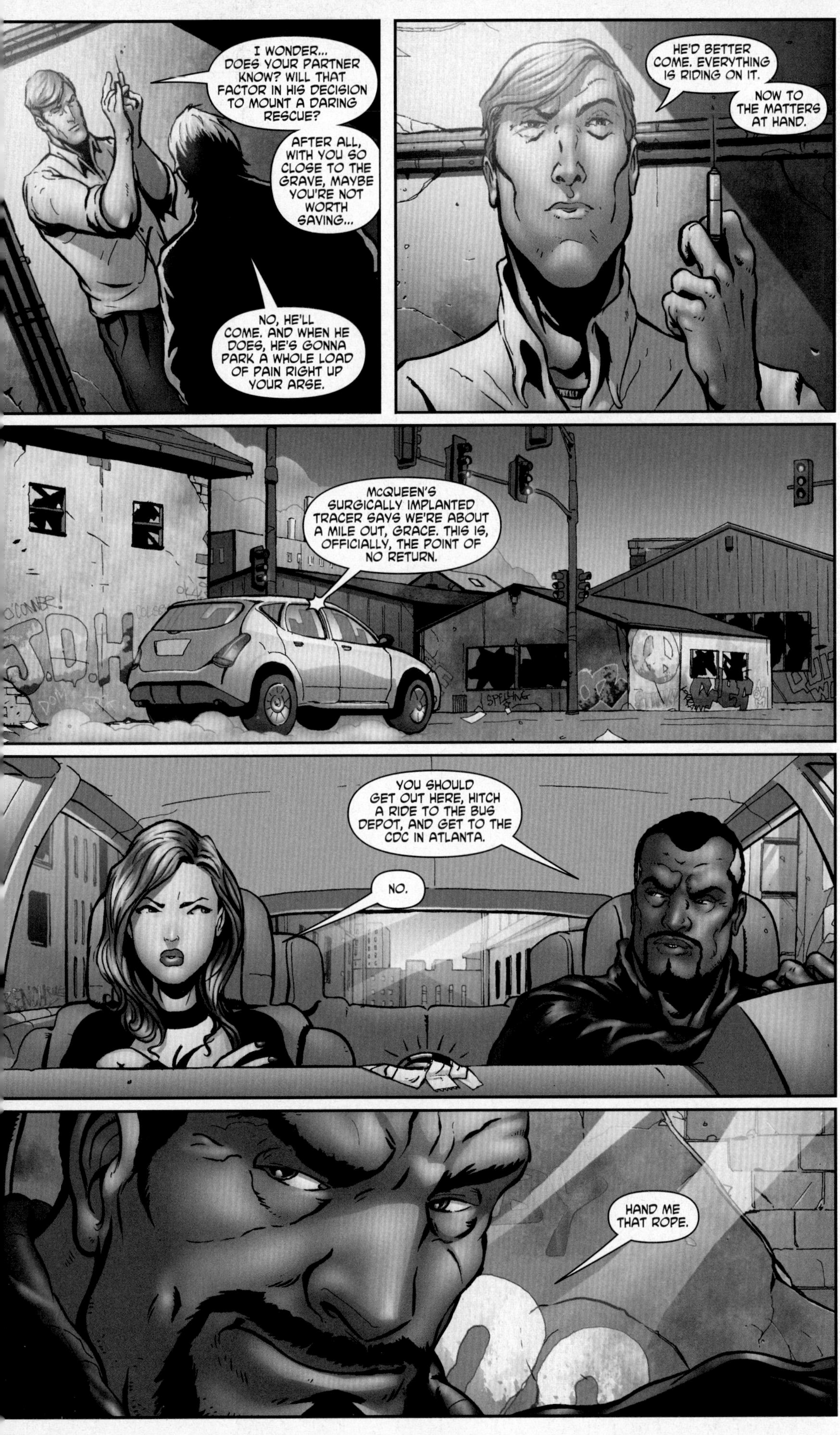
I WONDER... DOES YOUR PARTNER KNOW? WILL THAT FACTOR IN HIS DECISION TO MOUNT A DARING RESCUE?
AFTER ALL, WITH YOU SO CLOSE TO THE GRAVE, MAYBE YOU'RE NOT WORTH SAVING...
NO, HE'LL COME. AND WHEN HE DOES, HE'S GONNA PARK A WHOLE LOAD OF PAIN RIGHT UP YOUR ARSE.
HE'D BETTER COME. EVERYTHING IS RIDING ON IT.
NOW TO THE MATTERS AT HAND.
McQUEEN'S SURGICALLY IMPLANTED TRACER SAYS WE'RE ABOUT A MILE OUT, GRACE. THIS IS, OFFICIALLY, THE POINT OF NO RETURN.
YOU SHOULD GET OUT HERE, HITCH A RIDE TO THE BUS DEPOT, AND GET TO THE CDC IN ATLANTA.
NO.
HAND ME THAT ROPE.

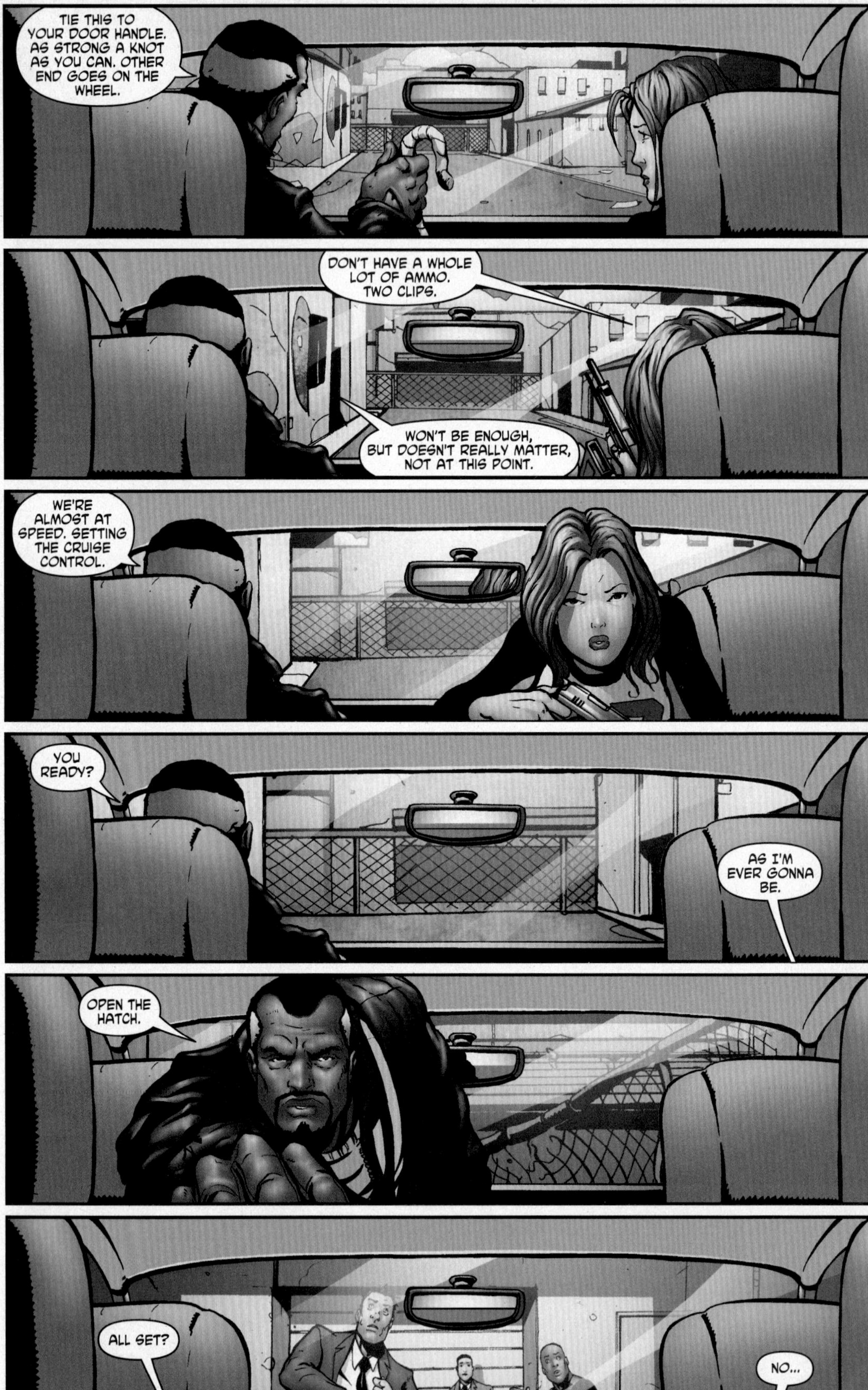
TIE THIS TO YOUR DOOR HANDLE. AS STRONG A KNOT AS YOU CAN. OTHER END GOES ON THE WHEEL.
DON'T HAVE A WHOLE LOT OF AMMO. TWO CLIPS.
WON'T BE ENOUGH, BUT DOESN'T REALLY MATTER, NOT AT THIS POINT.
WE'RE ALMOST AT SPEED. SETTING THE CRUISE CONTROL.
YOU READY?
AS I'M EVER GONNA BE.
OPEN THE HATCH.
ALL SET?
NO...

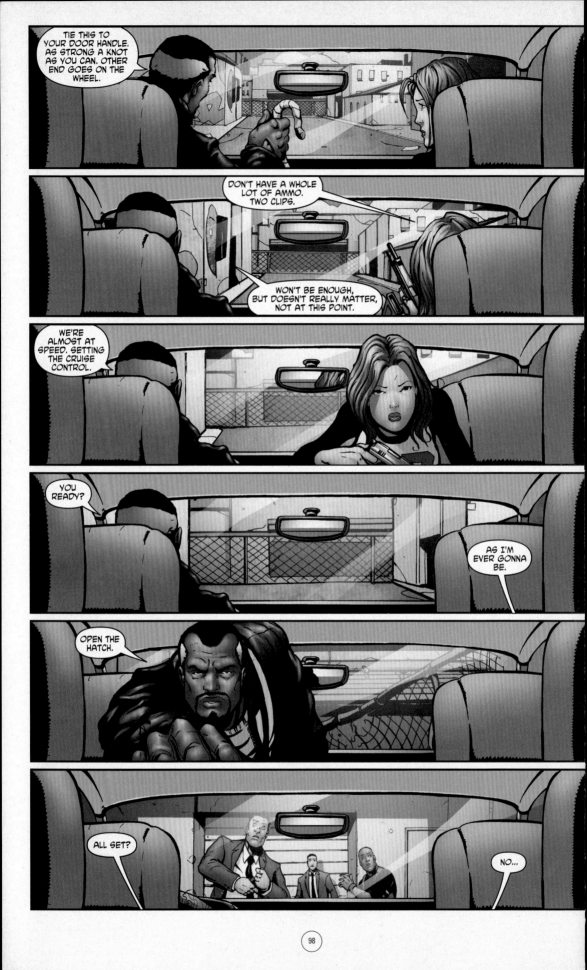

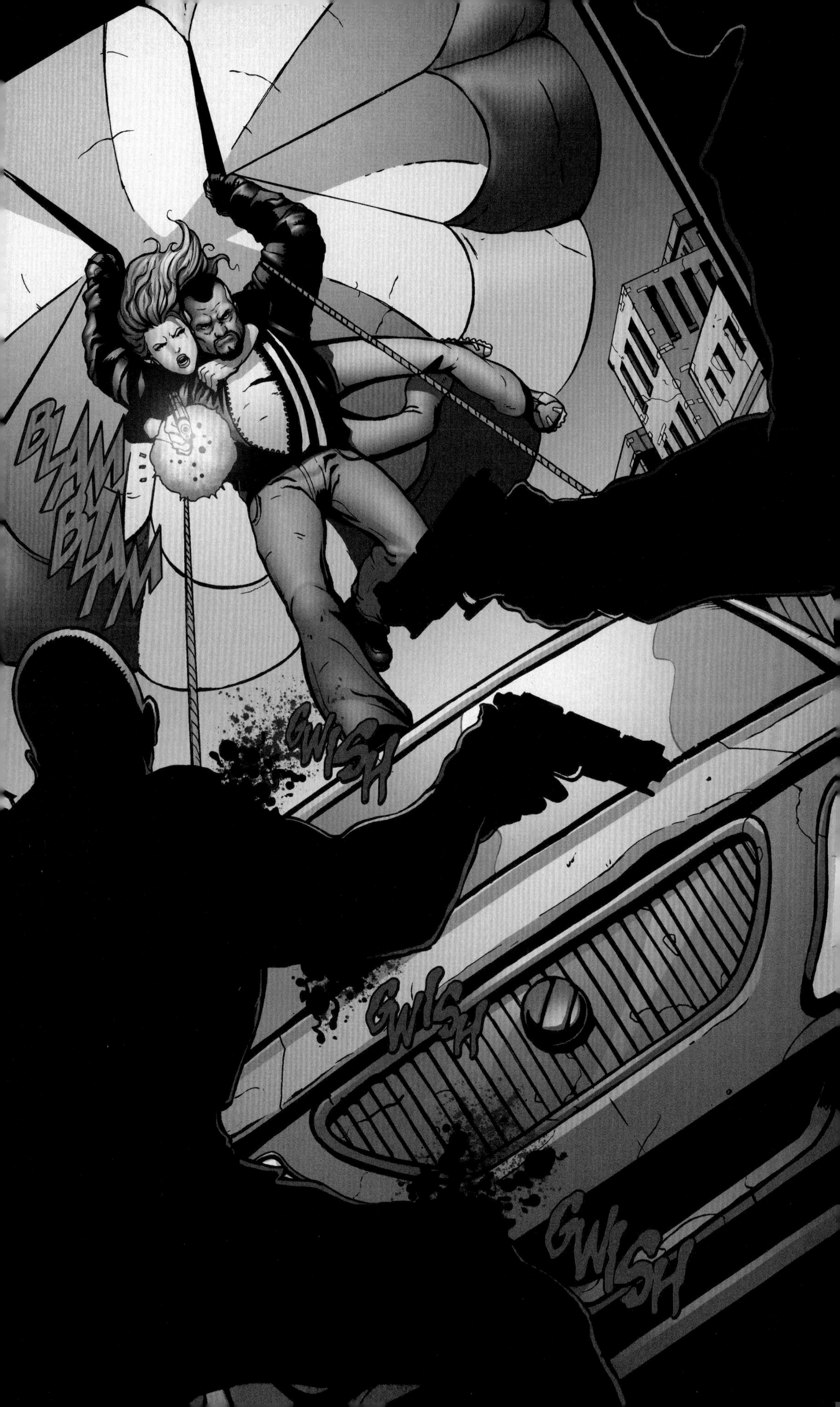
BLAM
BLAM
BLAM
BLAM
GWISH
GWISH
GWISH

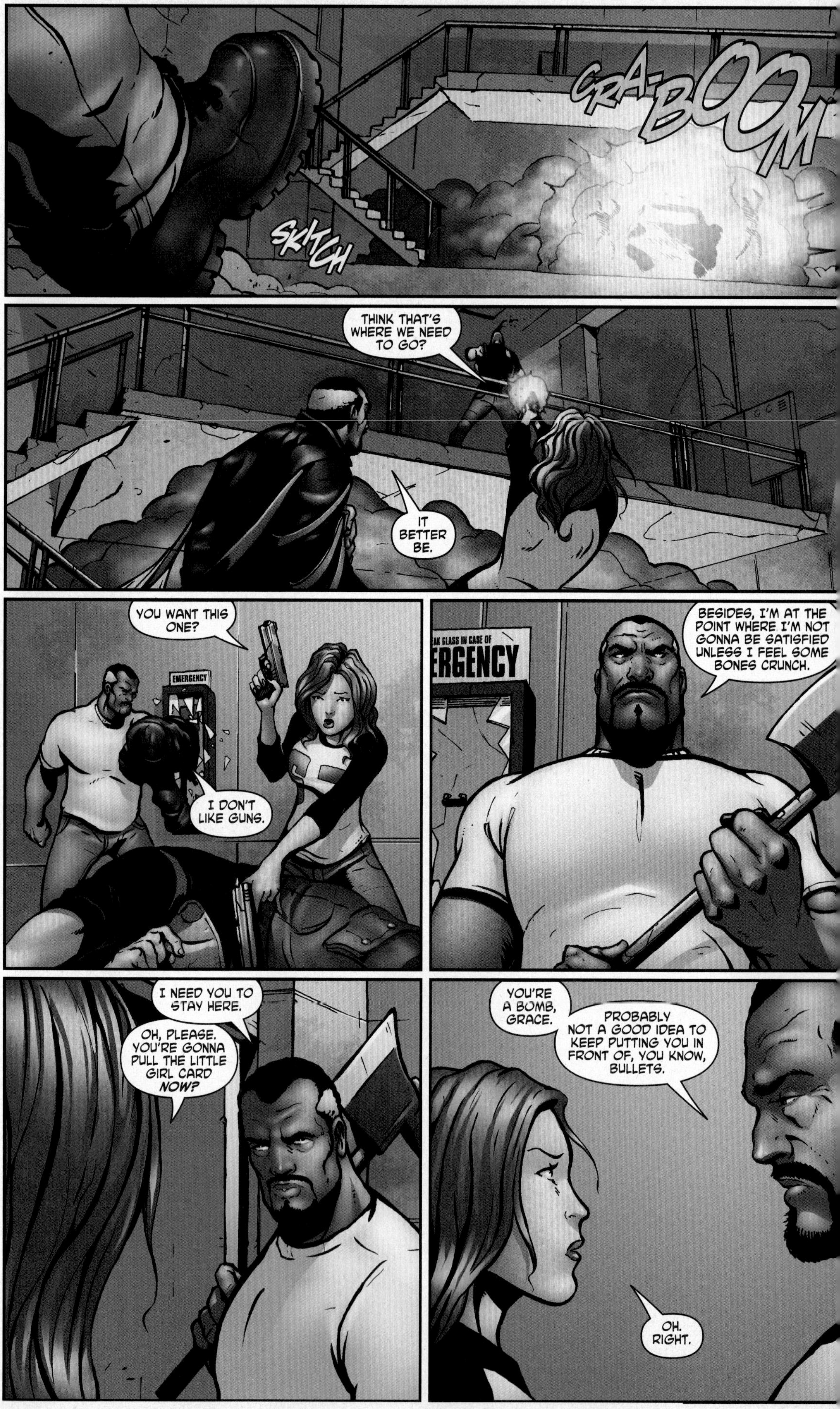
CRA-BOOM
SKITCH
THINK THAT'S WHERE WE NEED TO GO?
IT BETTER BE.
YOU WANT THIS ONE?
I DON'T LIKE GUNS.
EMERGENCY
BESIDES, I'M AT THE POINT WHERE I'M NOT GONNA BE SATISFIED UNLESS I FEEL SOME BONES CRUNCH.
I NEED YOU TO STAY HERE.
OH, PLEASE. YOU'RE GONNA PULL THE LITTLE GIRL CARD *NOW?*
YOU'RE A BOMB, GRACE.
PROBABLY NOT A GOOD IDEA TO KEEP PUTTING YOU IN FRONT OF, YOU KNOW, BULLETS.
OH. RIGHT.

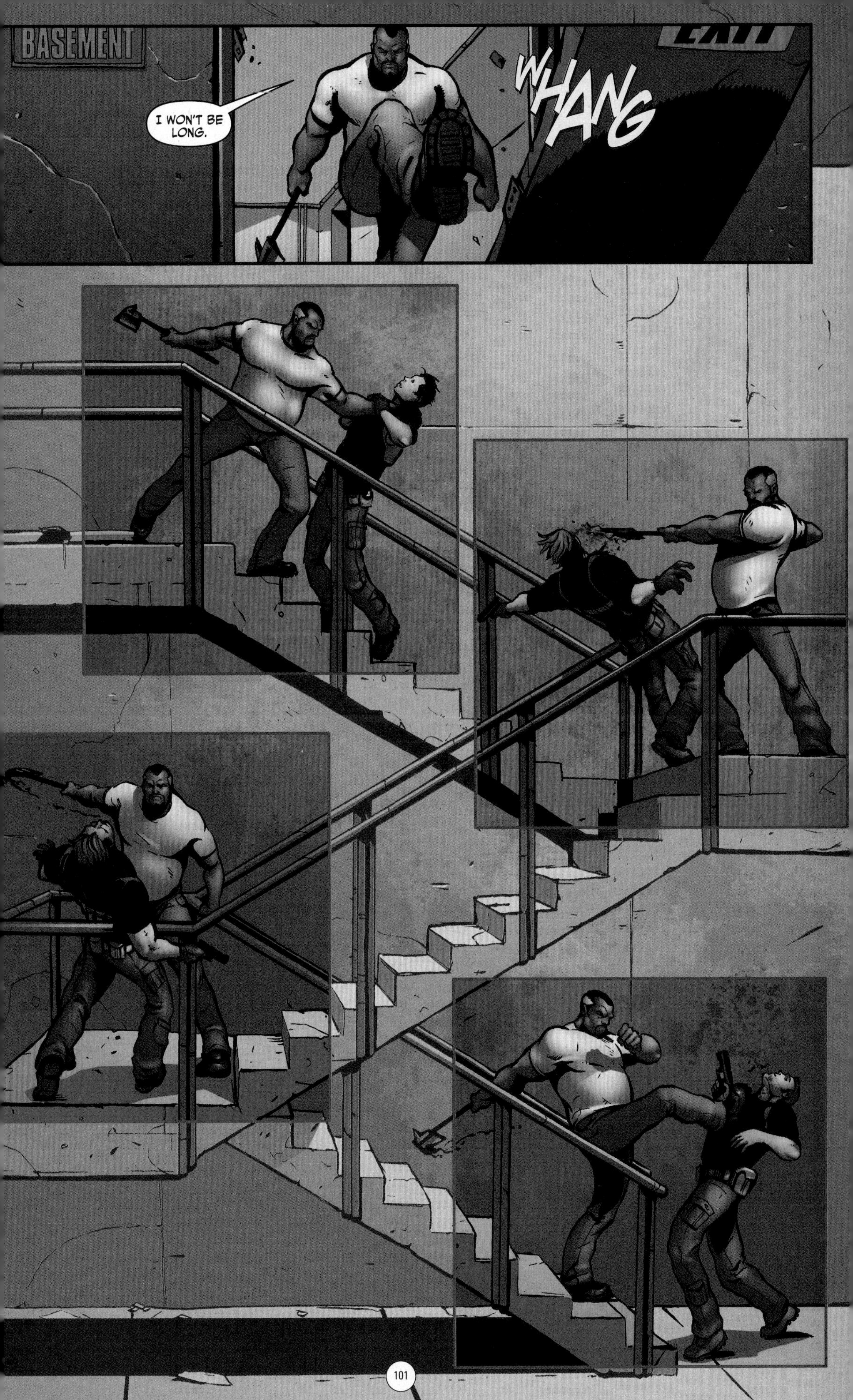
BASEMENT
I WON'T BE LONG.
WHANG

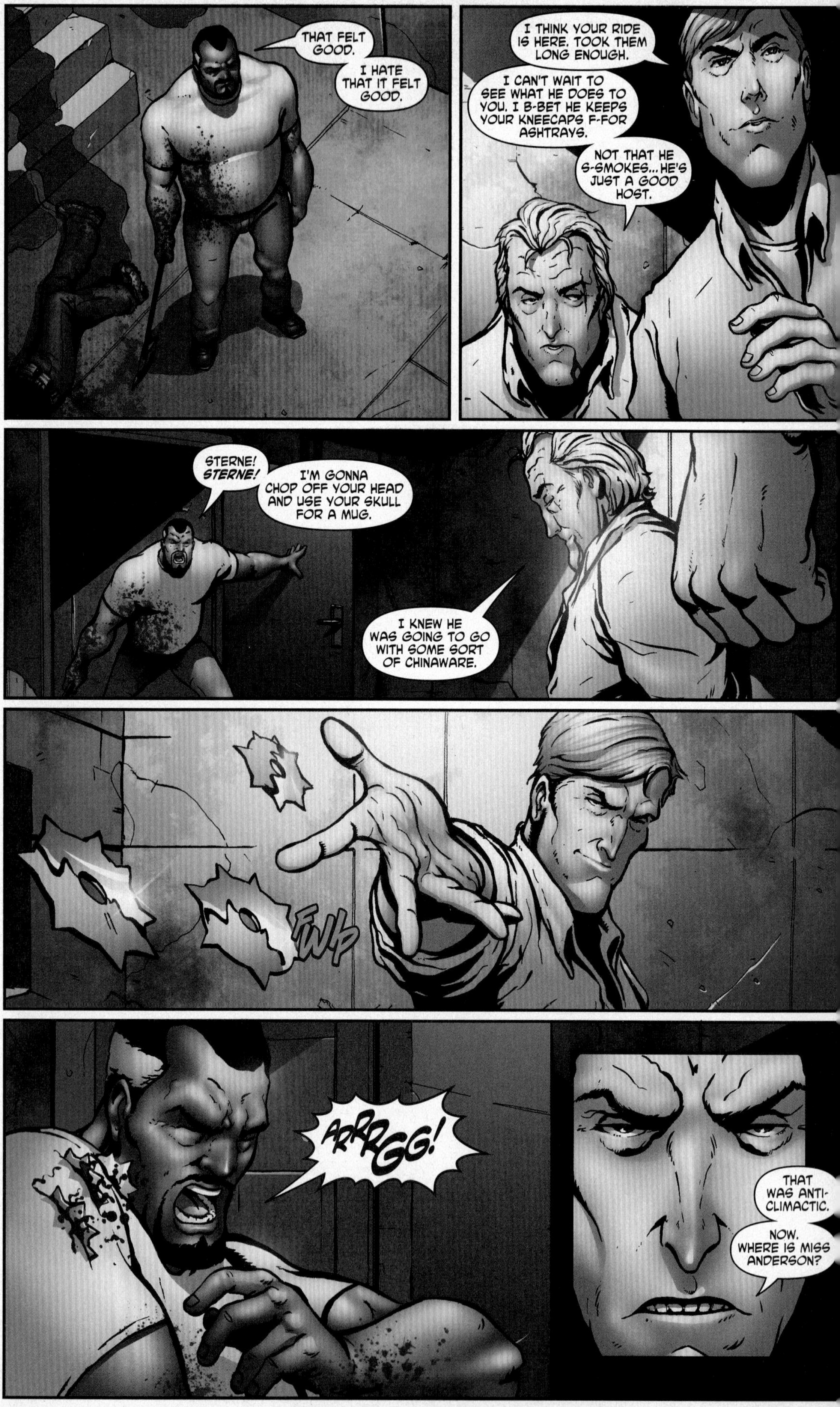
THAT FELT GOOD.
I HATE THAT IT FELT GOOD.
I THINK YOUR RIDE IS HERE. TOOK THEM LONG ENOUGH.
I CAN'T WAIT TO SEE WHAT HE DOES TO YOU. I B-BET HE KEEPS YOUR KNEECAPS F-FOR ASHTRAYS.
NOT THAT HE S-SMOKES... HE'S JUST A GOOD HOST.
STERNE! STERNE!
I'M GONNA CHOP OFF YOUR HEAD AND USE YOUR SKULL FOR A MUG.
I KNEW HE WAS GOING TO GO WITH SOME SORT OF CHINAWARE.
FWIP
ARRRGG!
THAT WAS ANTI-CLIMACTIC.
NOW. WHERE IS MISS ANDERSON?

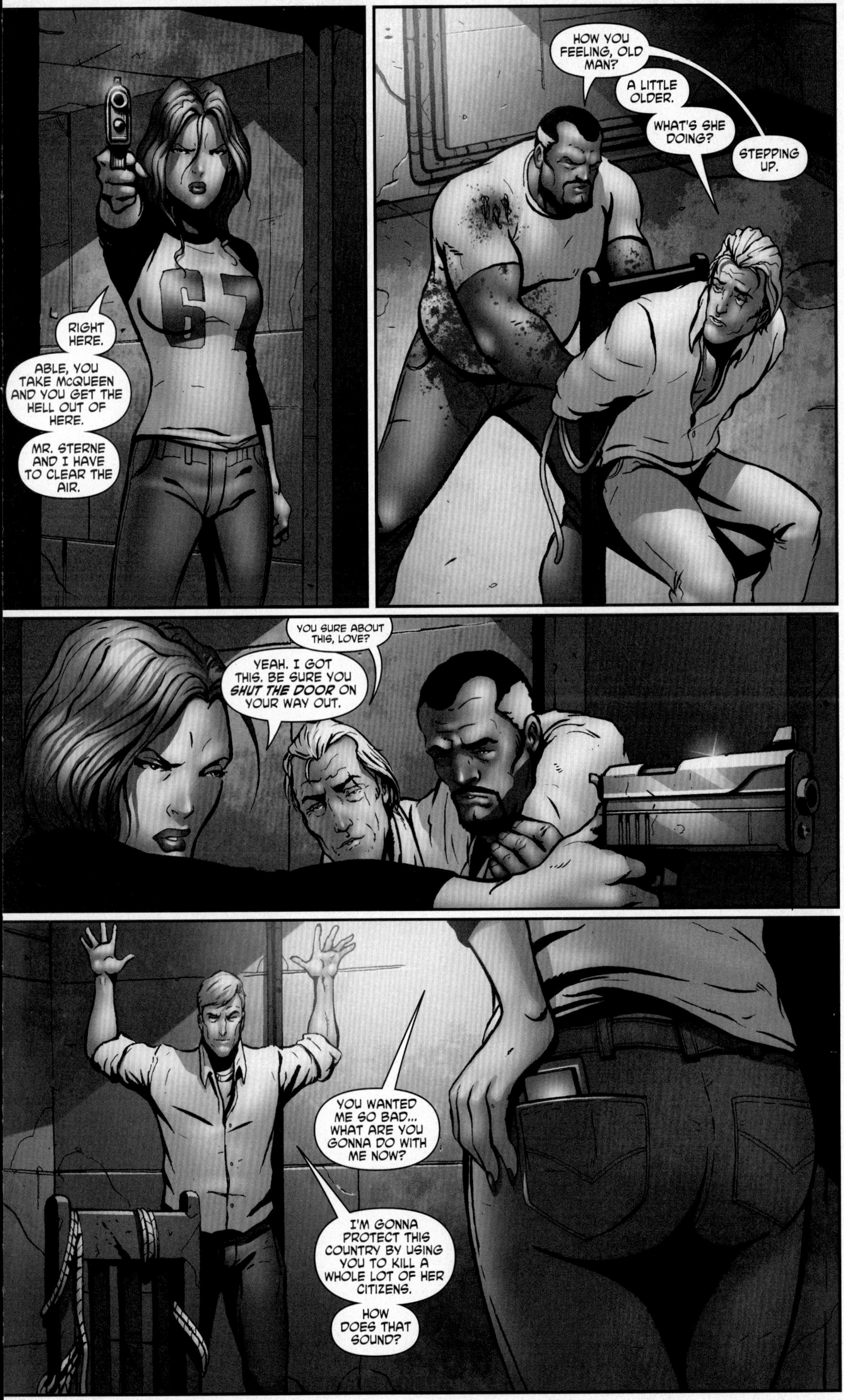
RIGHT HERE.
ABLE, YOU TAKE McQUEEN AND YOU GET THE HELL OUT OF HERE.
MR. STERNE AND I HAVE TO CLEAR THE AIR.
HOW YOU FEELING, OLD MAN?
A LITTLE OLDER.
WHAT'S SHE DOING?
STEPPING UP.
YOU SURE ABOUT THIS, LOVE?
YEAH. I GOT THIS. BE SURE YOU *SHUT THE DOOR* ON YOUR WAY OUT.
YOU WANTED ME SO BAD... WHAT ARE YOU GONNA DO WITH ME NOW?
I'M GONNA PROTECT THIS COUNTRY BY USING YOU TO KILL A WHOLE LOT OF HER CITIZENS.
HOW DOES THAT SOUND?

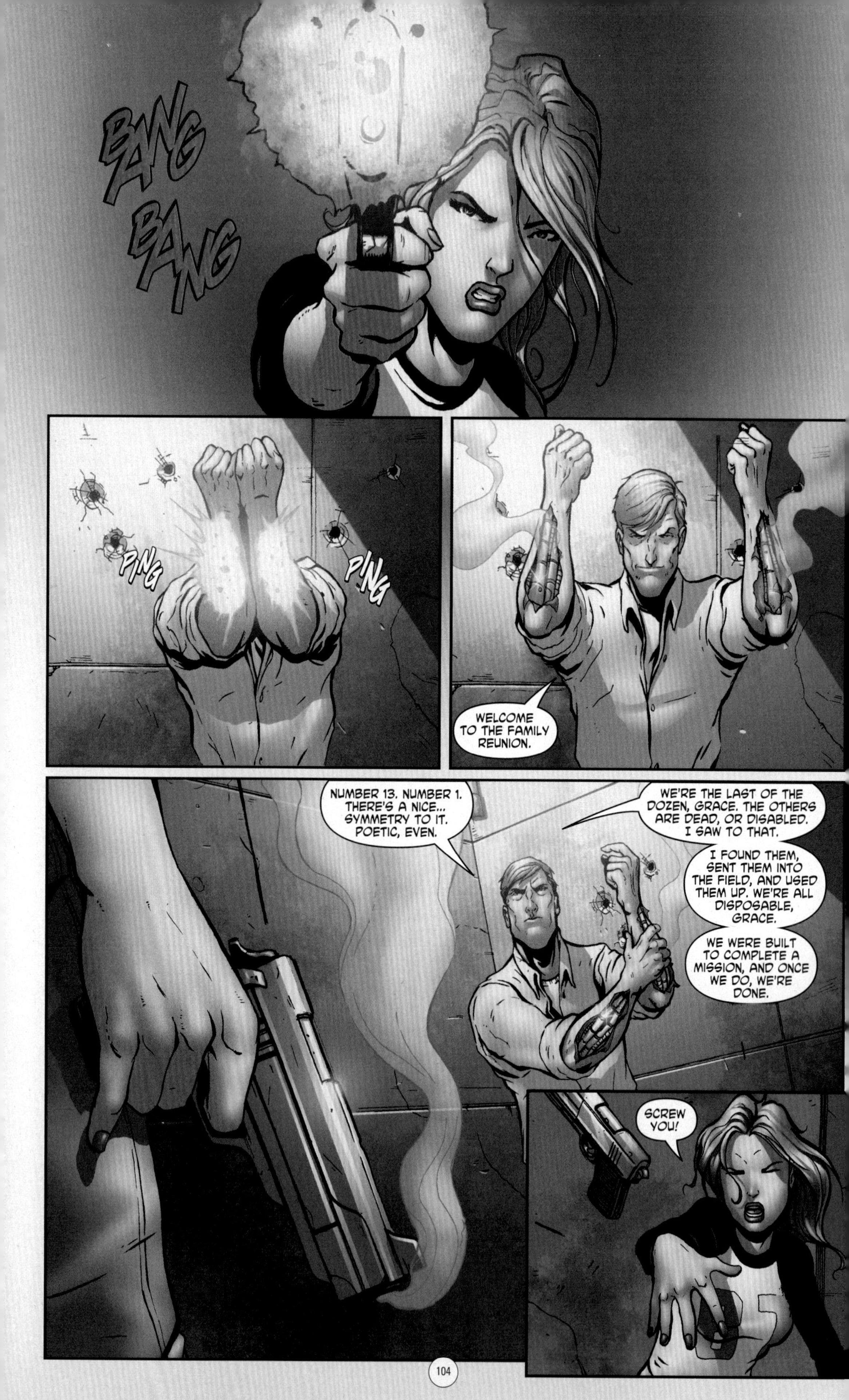
BANG
BANG
PING
PING
WELCOME TO THE FAMILY REUNION.
NUMBER 13. NUMBER 1. THERE'S A NICE... SYMMETRY TO IT. POETIC, EVEN.
WE'RE THE LAST OF THE DOZEN, GRACE. THE OTHERS ARE DEAD, OR DISABLED. I SAW TO THAT.
I FOUND THEM, SENT THEM INTO THE FIELD, AND USED THEM UP. WE'RE ALL DISPOSABLE, GRACE.
WE WERE BUILT TO COMPLETE A MISSION, AND ONCE WE DO, WE'RE DONE.
SCREW YOU!

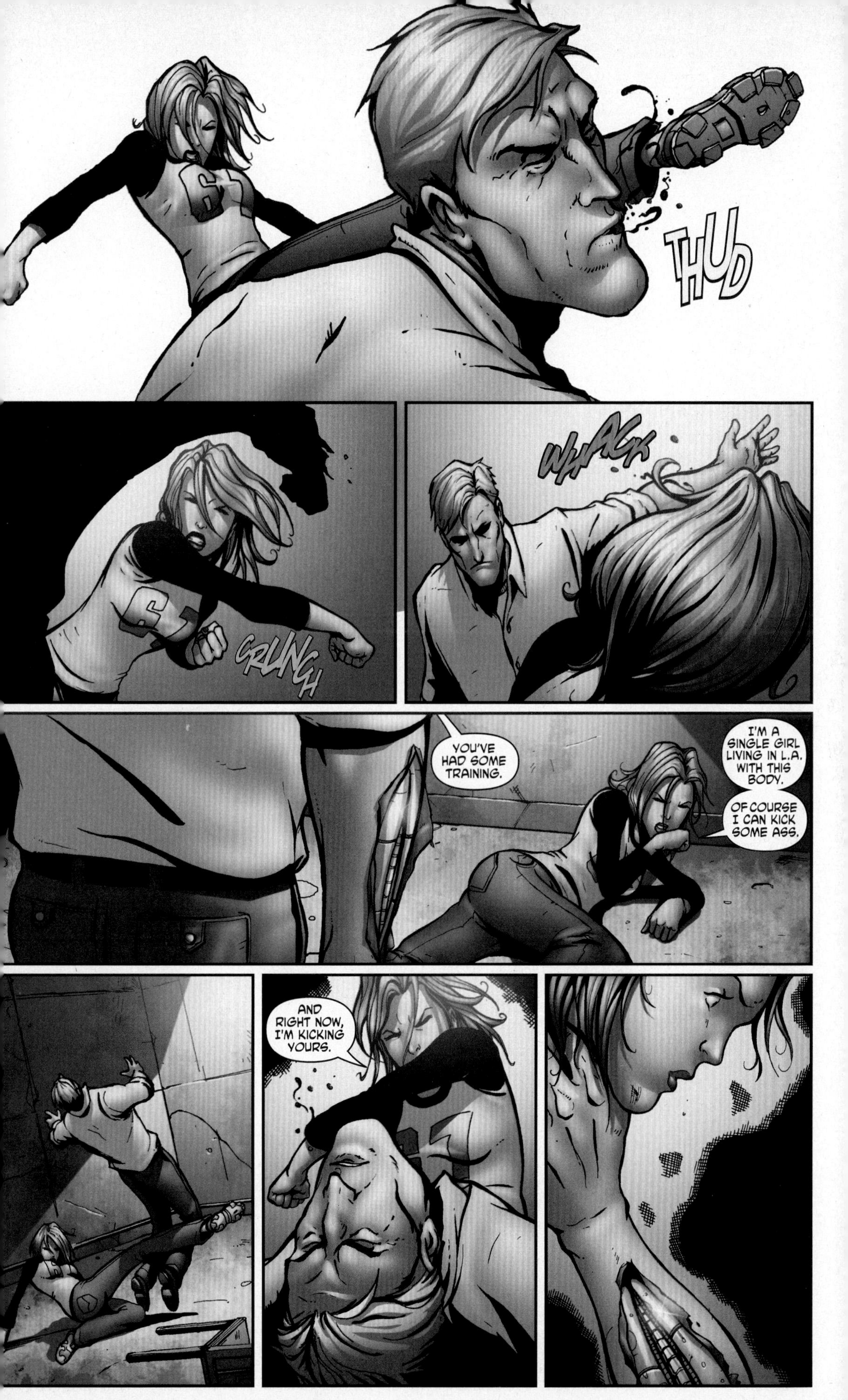
THUD
CRUNCH
WHACK
YOU'VE HAD SOME TRAINING.
I'M A SINGLE GIRL LIVING IN L.A. WITH THIS BODY.
OF COURSE I CAN KICK SOME ASS.
AND RIGHT NOW, I'M KICKING YOURS.

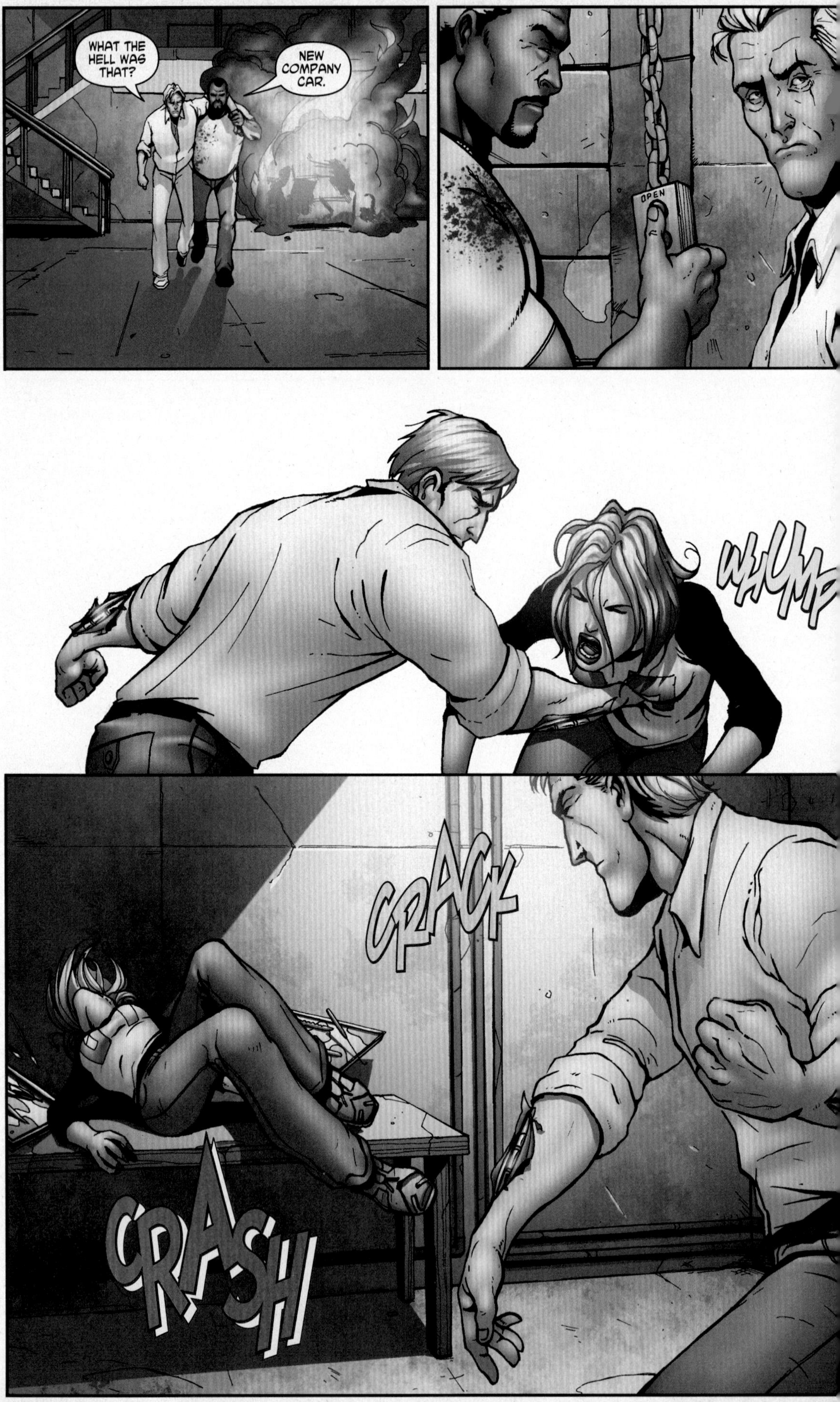
WHAT THE HELL WAS THAT?
NEW COMPANY CAR.
OPEN
WHUMP
CRACK
CRASH

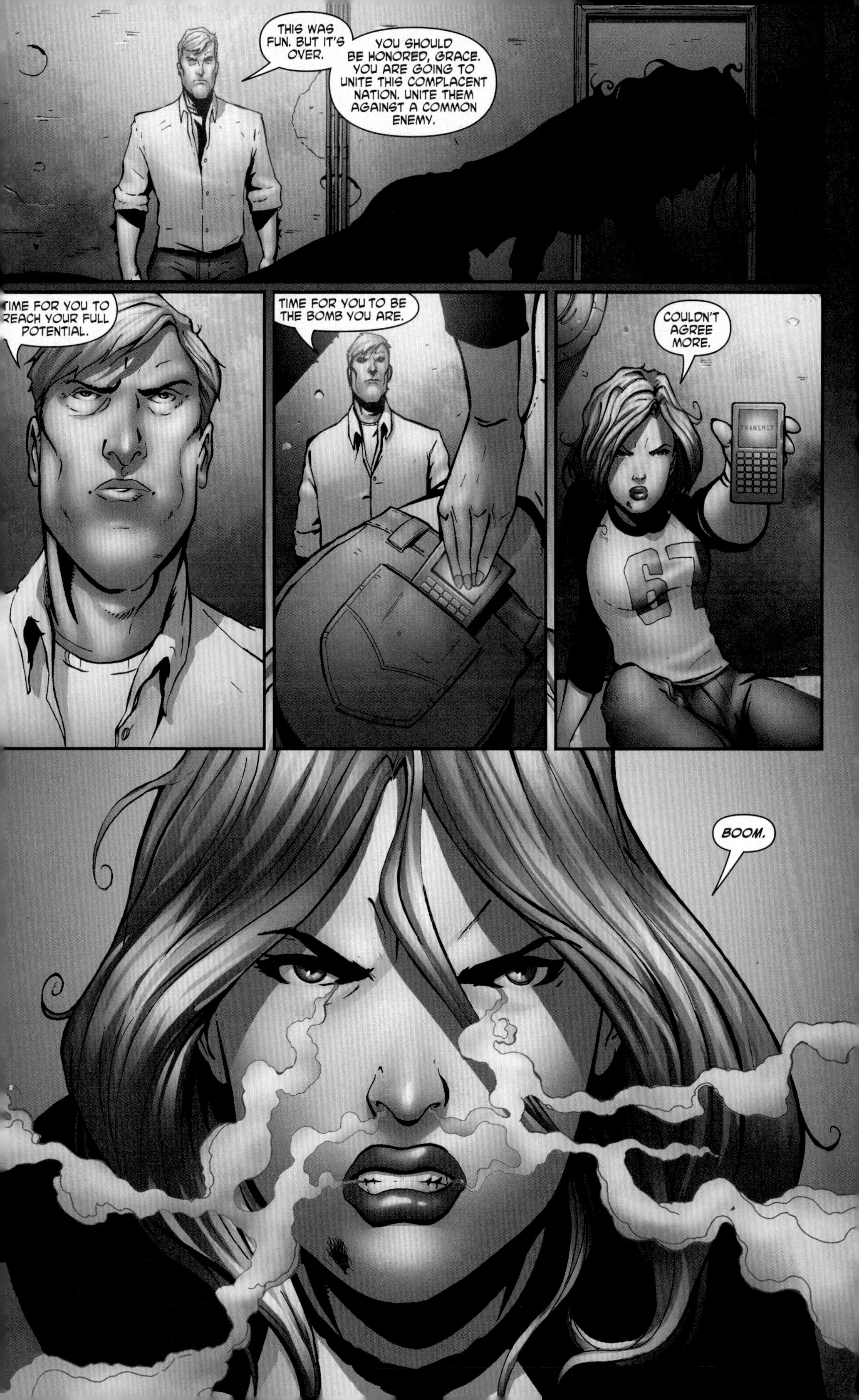
THIS WAS FUN. BUT IT'S OVER.
YOU SHOULD BE HONORED, GRACE. YOU ARE GOING TO UNITE THIS COMPLACENT NATION. UNITE THEM AGAINST A COMMON ENEMY.
TIME FOR YOU TO REACH YOUR FULL POTENTIAL.
TIME FOR YOU TO BE THE BOMB YOU ARE.
COULDN'T AGREE MORE.
TRANSMIT
BOOM.

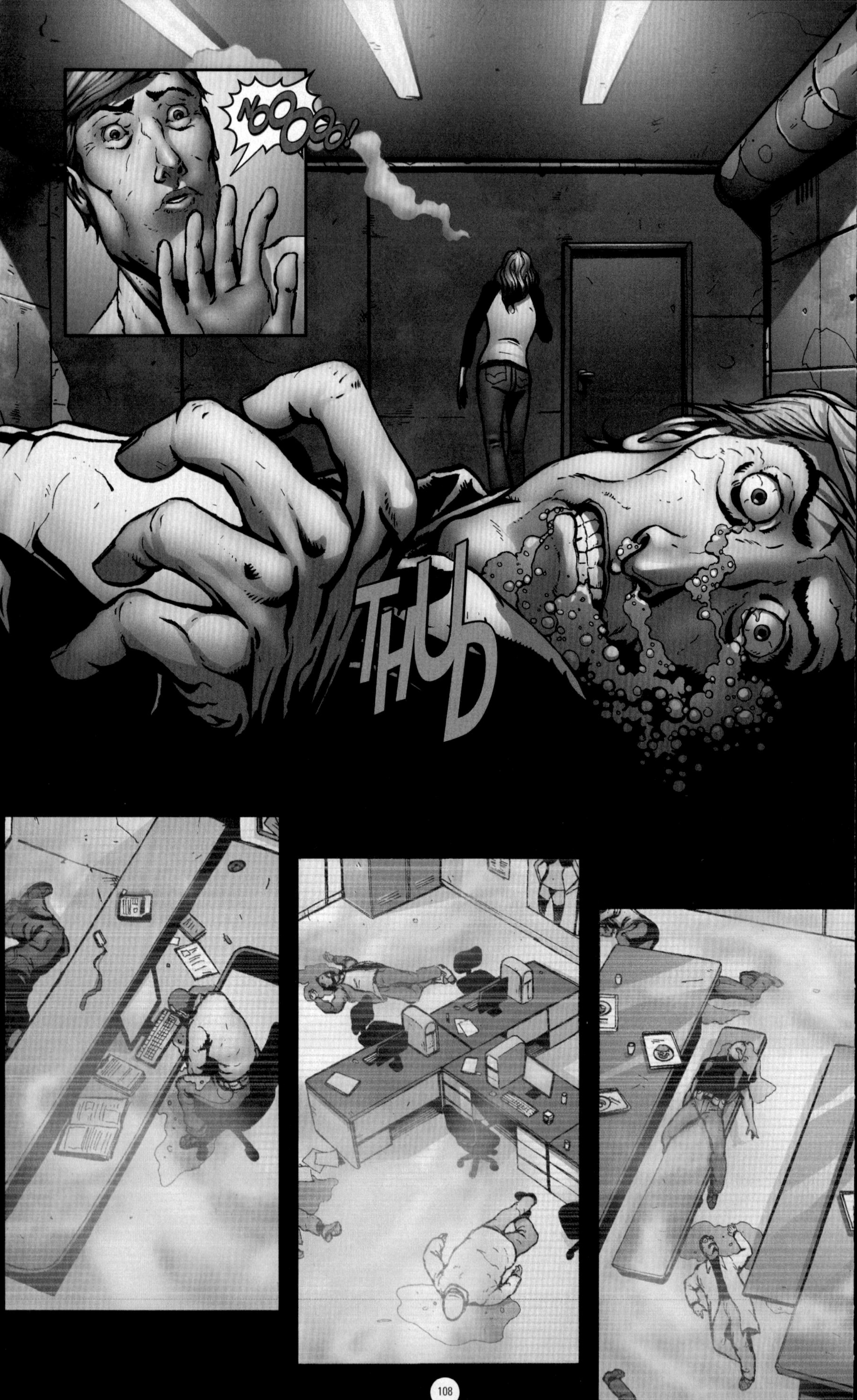
NOOOOO!
THUD

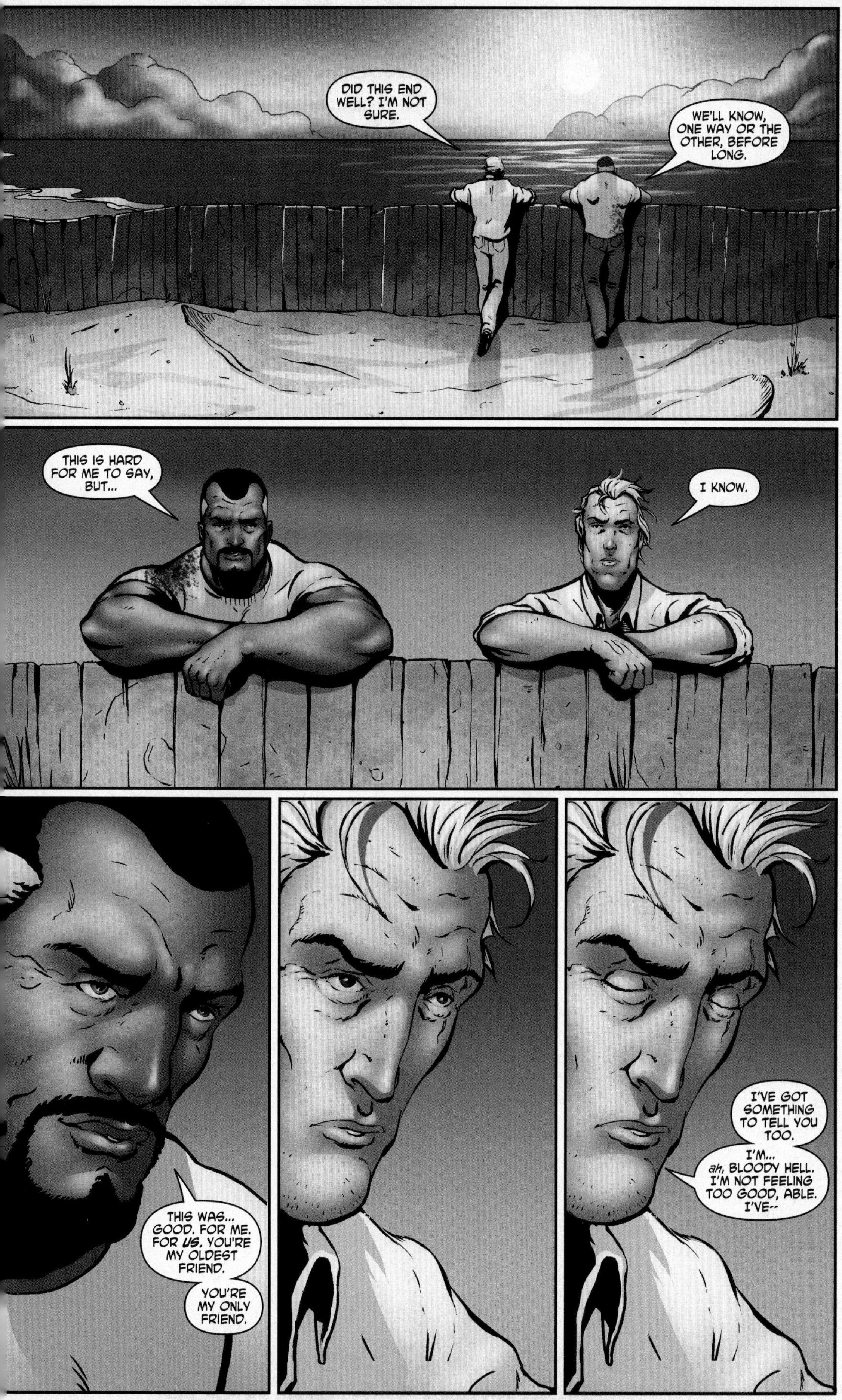
DID THIS END WELL? I'M NOT SURE.
WE'LL KNOW, ONE WAY OR THE OTHER, BEFORE LONG.
THIS IS HARD FOR ME TO SAY, BUT...
I KNOW.
THIS WAS... GOOD. FOR ME. FOR *US*. YOU'RE MY OLDEST FRIEND.
YOU'RE MY ONLY FRIEND.
I'VE GOT SOMETHING TO TELL YOU TOO.
I'M... *ah*, BLOODY HELL. I'M NOT FEELING TOO GOOD, ABLE. I'VE--

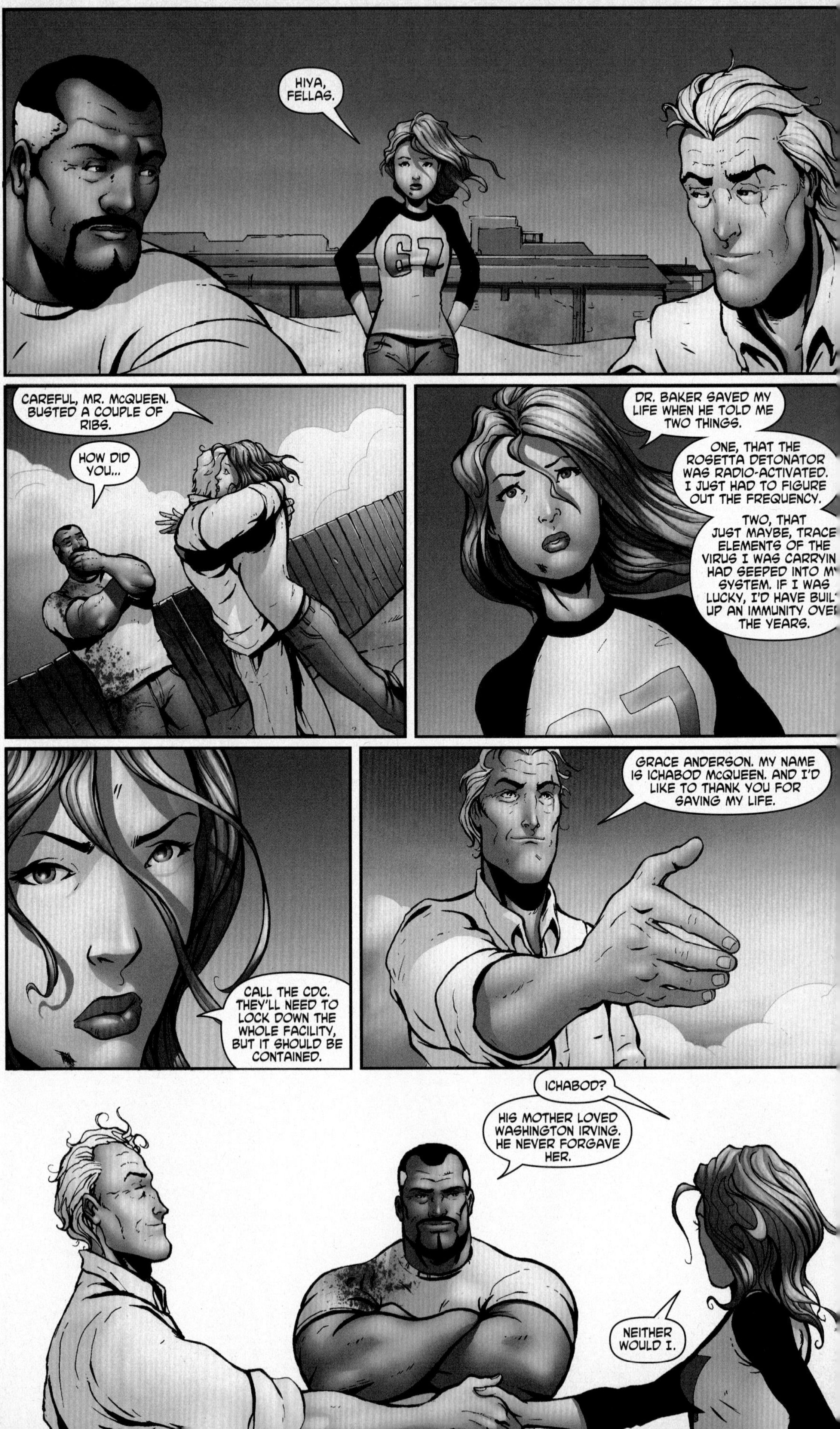
HIYA, FELLAS.
CAREFUL, MR. McQUEEN. BUSTED A COUPLE OF RIBS.
HOW DID YOU...
DR. BAKER SAVED MY LIFE WHEN HE TOLD ME TWO THINGS.
ONE, THAT THE ROSETTA DETONATOR WAS RADIO-ACTIVATED. I JUST HAD TO FIGURE OUT THE FREQUENCY.
TWO, THAT JUST MAYBE, TRACE ELEMENTS OF THE VIRUS I WAS CARRYIN HAD SEEPED INTO M SYSTEM. IF I WAS LUCKY, I'D HAVE BUIL UP AN IMMUNITY OVE THE YEARS.
CALL THE CDC. THEY'LL NEED TO LOCK DOWN THE WHOLE FACILITY, BUT IT SHOULD BE CONTAINED.
GRACE ANDERSON. MY NAME IS ICHABOD McQUEEN. AND I'D LIKE TO THANK YOU FOR SAVING MY LIFE.
ICHABOD?
HIS MOTHER LOVED WASHINGTON IRVING. HE NEVER FORGAVE HER.
NEITHER WOULD I.

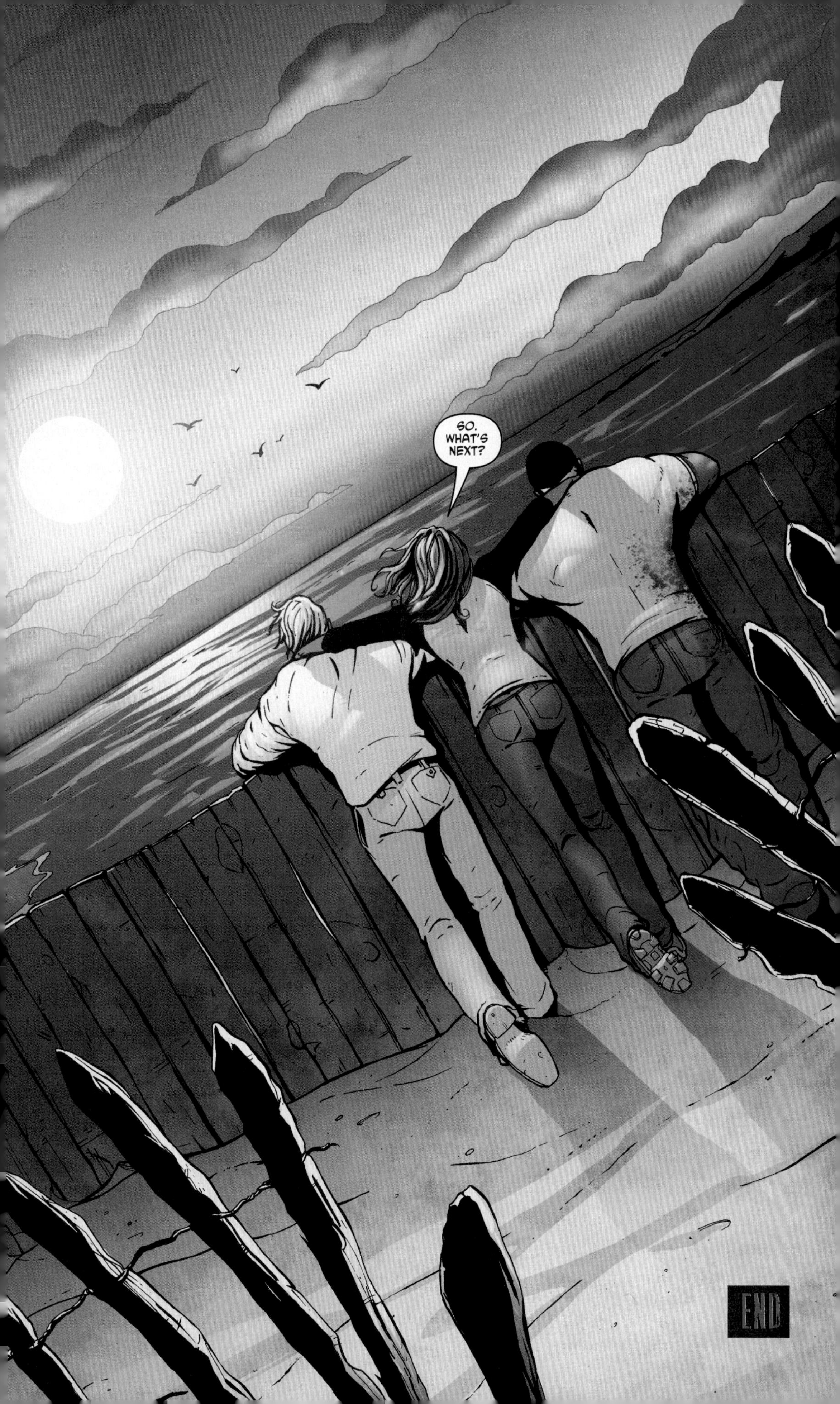
SO, WHAT'S NEXT?
END

BECAUSE IT'S THE

The American Way

Ridley • Jeanty • Story
The American Way
WILDSTORM

Twenty years after the United States government created the Civil Defense Corps to combat alien invasions, evil super-powered-beings and communism, they hire Public Relations Executive Wesley Catham to "fix" the program. His first duty? Hide the fact that the CDC has been lying to the American public since its inception—most of their highly publicized victories have been staged! Will the introduction of the first Black hero revive the public's faith...or set the world on fire?

Written by acclaimed novelist and screenwriter John Ridley, with art by Georges Jeanty, in THE AMERICAN WAY, the 1960s are about to become a little more black and white!

STORIES FROM THE PAST...AND THE FUTURE:

CITY OF TOMORROW

Howard Chaykin
City of TOMORROW!

CHAYKIN

GLOBAL FREQUENCY BOOKS 1 & 2

WARREN ELLIS
GARRY LEACH
GLENN FABRY
STEVE DILLON
ROY MARTINEZ
JON J MUTH
DAVID LLOYD
DAVID BARON
GLOBAL FREQUENCY
PLANET ABLAZE

ELLIS•VARIOUS

RED MENACE

BILSON • DeMEO • BRODY • ORDWAY • VEY
Red Menace
EAGLE TESTIFIES BEFORE HUAC

BILSON•DEMEO•BRODY ORDWAY•VEY

TO FIND MORE COLLECTED EDITIONS AND MONTHLY COMIC BOOKS FROM WILDSTORM AND DC COMICS

CALL 1-888-COMIC BOOK

FOR THE NEAREST COMICS SHOP OR GO TO YOUR LOCAL BOOK STORE

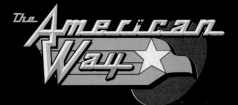

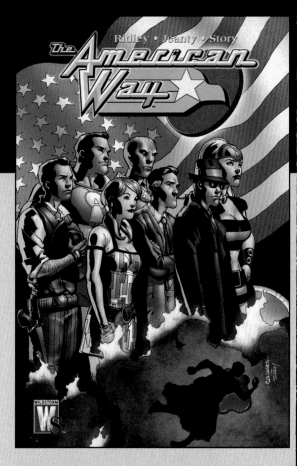

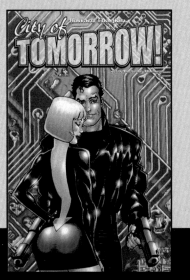

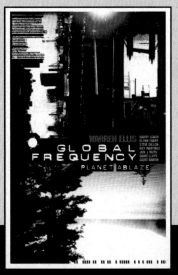

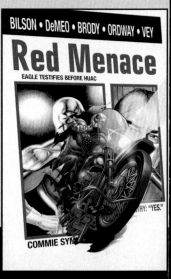

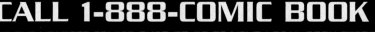